Music History and Cosmopolitanism

This collection of essays is the first book-length study of music history and cosmopolitanism, and is informed by arguments that culture and identity do not have to be viewed as primarily located in the context of nationalist narratives. Rather than trying to distinguish between a true cosmopolitanism and a false cosmopolitanism, the book presents studies that deepen understanding of the heritage of this concept – the various ways in which the term has been used to describe a wide range of activity and social outlooks. It ranges over a two-hundred-year period, and more than a dozen countries, revealing how musicians and audiences have responded to a common humanity by embracing culture beyond regional or national boundaries. Among the various topics investigated are: musical cosmopolitanism among composers in Latin America, the Ottoman Empire and the Austro-Hungarian Empire; cosmopolitan popular music historiography; cosmopolitan musical entrepreneurs; and musical cosmopolitanism in the metropolis of Shanghai.

Anastasia Belina is a Senior Research Fellow at the University of Leeds, UK.

Kaarina Kilpiö (Doctor of Social Sciences) works as a university lecturer at Sibelius Academy, University of the Arts, Helsinki, Finland.

Derek B. Scott is Professor of Critical Musicology at the University of Leeds, UK.

Music History and Cosmopolitanism

Edited by
Anastasia Belina, Kaarina Kilpiö
and Derek B. Scott

LONDON AND NEW YORK

First published 2019 by Routledge

2 Park Square, Milton Park, Abingdon, Oxon, OX14 4RN
605 Third Avenue, New York, NY 10017

Routledge is an imprint of the Taylor & Francis Group, an informa business

First issued in paperback 2020

Copyright © 2019 selection and editorial matter, Anastasia Belina, Kaarina Kilpiö and Derek B. Scott; individual chapters, the contributors

The right of Anastasia Belina, Kaarina Kilpiö and Derek B. Scott to be identified as the authors of the editorial material, and of the authors for their individual chapters, has been asserted in accordance with sections 77 and 78 of the Copyright, Designs and Patents Act 1988.

All rights reserved. No part of this book may be reprinted or reproduced or utilised in any form or by any electronic, mechanical, or other means, now known or hereafter invented, including photocopying and recording, or in any information storage or retrieval system, without permission in writing from the publishers.

Notice:
Product or corporate names may be trademarks or registered trademarks, and are used only for identification and explanation without intent to infringe.

British Library Cataloguing-in-Publication Data
A catalogue record for this book is available from the British Library

Library of Congress Cataloging-in-Publication Data
A catalog record has been requested for this book

ISBN: 978-1-138-48113-8 (hbk)
ISBN: 978-0-367-78595-6 (pbk)

Typeset in Times
by Deanta Global Publishing Services, Chennai, India

Contents

List of figures vii
List of maps viii
List of tables ix
List of contributors x

Introduction 1
ANASTASIA BELINA, KAARINA KILPIÖ AND DEREK B. SCOTT

PART 1
Music and cosmopolitanism in the nineteenth century 11

1 Cosmopolitanism and music for the theatre: Europe and beyond, 1800–1870 13
  MARK EVERIST

2 Cosmopolitanism in nineteenth-century opera management 33
  INGEBORG ZECHNER

3 Carl Goldmark and cosmopolitan patriotism 47
  DAVID BRODBECK

4 The cosmopolitan muse: Searching for a musical style in early nineteenth-century Latin America 59
  JOSÉ MANUEL IZQUIERDO KÖNIG

PART 2
Music and cosmopolitanism in the twentieth century   75

5 An 'intricate fabric of influences and coincidences in the history of popular music': Reflections on the challenging work of popular music historians   77
FRANCO FABBRI

6 Mapping musical modernism   90
BJÖRN HEILE

7 André Tchaikowsky (1935–1982): A cosmopolitan in a closet   106
ANASTASIA BELINA

8 The elision of difference, newness and participation: Edward J. Dent's cosmopolitan ethics of opera performance   117
SARAH COLLINS

PART 3
Music and urban cosmopolitanism   131

9 Tip, *Trinkgeld, bakšiš:* Cosmopolitan and other strategies of touring music groups before the Great War in Sarajevo   133
RISTO PEKKA PENNANEN

10 Musicians as cosmopolitan entrepreneurs: Orchestras in Finnish cities before the modern city orchestra institution   147
OLLI HEIKKINEN AND SAIJALEENA RANTANEN

11 'A foreign cosmopolitanism': Treaty port Shanghai, ad hoc municipal ensembles, and an epistemic modality   162
YVONNE LIAO

Index   175

Figures

2.1	Overview of the singers and the works during Lumley's combined management of the Théâtre Italien in Paris and Her Majesty's Theatre in London	39
3.1	Map of nationalities within Austria-Hungary	48
4.1	Front page of MI37 (Sinfonia by Pleyel), score surviving in the private collection of Andrés Orías Blüchner	68
4.2	Front page of MI47 (Ximénez's 7th Symphony), score surviving in the private collection of Andrés Orías Blüchner	68
5.1	Digraph summarizing some of the relations between genres and individuals	85
9.1	Postcard of Wiener Damenorchester Portugal with bandleader Maria Portugal in the centre	136

Maps

6.1 ISCM members: darker shading indicates earlier entry dates; hachures stand for former members, dots for non-members 95
6.2 Diffusion of dodecaphonic composition: darker shading indicates earlier dates; dots – no data 96

Tables

1.1	Music in the Theatre: Batavia/Jakarta, 1836–1866	17
1.2	Repertory of Copenhagen Kongelige Teater, 1847	20
1.3	Repertory of Copenhagen Kongelige Teater, 1847: Analysis by Genre	23
1.4	Music in the Khedival Theatre, Cairo, 1869–1877	25
1.5	Repertory of Kaiserlich-königliches Hofoperntheater im neuen Hause, Vienna, 1869	26
9.1	Some epithets which Biro himself and the venues used for describing Graničar	140

Contributors

The editors

Anastasia Belina is Senior Research Fellow at the University of Leeds, UK, where she worked with Derek B. Scott on the project *German Operetta in London, New York, and Warsaw 1906–38: Cultural Transfer and Transformation* (funded by the ERC). She is author and editor of *A Musician Divided: André Tchaikowsky in His Own Words* (2013), *Die tägliche Mühe ein Mensch zu sein* (2013), *Wagner in Russia, Poland and the Czech Lands: Musical, Literary, and Cultural Perspectives* (2013, co-edited edition), and *The Business of Opera* (2015, co-edited with D. B. Scott). She is also an opera director and librettist, has appeared on BBC3, and appeared in a feature-length documentary film *Rebel of the Keys* (2016) about the life and music of André Tchaikowsky. She was instrumental in bringing André Tchaikowsky's opera *The Merchant of Venice* to international stages in Austria (Bregenz), Poland (Warsaw), and the UK (Cardiff, Birmingham and London).

Kaarina Kilpiö (Doctor of Social Sciences) currently works as a university lecturer at Sibelius Academy, University of the Arts, Helsinki, Finland. Her research interests include the study of different (mainly historical) uses of music and sound technologies. In addition to numerous articles about music in advertising and propaganda, background music and Finns as music listeners, she published a dissertation in 2005, *Kulutuksen sävel. Suomalaisen mainoselokuvan musiikki 1950-luvulta 1970-luvulle* (with an English summary 'Consumer Tunes. Music in Finnish advertising films from 1950s to 1970s') and a book on cassette culture in Finland, *Koko kansan kasetti* (2015). She has also co-edited several volumes, including *Kuultava menneisyys*, an anthology of Finnish soundscape history.

Derek B. Scott is Professor of Critical Musicology at the University of Leeds, UK. His research field is music, cultural history and ideology, and his books include *Sounds of the Metropolis: The 19th-Century Popular Music Revolution in London, New York, Paris, and Vienna* (2008) and *Musical Style and Social Meaning* (2010). He was the general editor of Ashgate's Popular and Folk Music Series for 15 years, overseeing the publication of more than 100 books between 2000 and 2015. His recent research was funded by a European Research Council advanced grant, and focused on the reception in London and New York of operettas from the German stage, 1907–1938.

Other contributors

David Brodbeck is Professor of Music at the University of California, Irvine, CA, USA. He has published widely on topics in Central European musical culture during the long nineteenth century. Among his more recent publications are '*Heimat* is Where the Heart Is; or, What Kind of Hungarian was Goldmark?', *Austrian History Yearbook* (2017); 'A Tale of Two Brothers: Behind the Scenes of Goldmark's First Opera', *Musical Quarterly* (2015), 'Music and the Marketplace: On the Backstory of Carlos Chávez's Violin Concerto', *Carlos Chávez and His World* (2015); and the monograph *Defining Deutschtum: Political Ideology, German Identity, and Music-Critical Discourse in Liberal Vienna* (2014), a political and cultural history that won the ASCAP Foundation's Virgil Thomson Award for Music Criticism for 2015.

Sarah Collins is currently Marie Curie Research Fellow at Durham University, UK, and in 2018 she will take up an ongoing lectureship in musicology at the University of Western Australia. Her work focuses on the intersection between political, aesthetic and ethical concerns in music literature of the late nineteenth and early twentieth centuries (including in music historiography, music criticism and aesthetics). She is the author of *The Aesthetic Life of Cyril Scott* (2013) and has had articles published in the *Journal of the Royal Musical Association, Twentieth-Century Music, Music & Letters* and elsewhere. She is a co-editor, with Paul Watt and Michael Allis, of the *Oxford Handbook of Music and Intellectual Culture in the Nineteenth Century* (forthcoming), and is currently the review editor of the *Journal of the Royal Musical Association* and the *RMA Research Chronicle*.

Mark Everist is Professor of Music at the University of Southampton, UK. His research focuses on the music of western Europe in the period 1150–1330, French nineteenth-century stage music between the Restoration and the Commune, Mozart, reception theory and historiography. He is the author of *Polyphonic Music in Thirteenth-Century France* (1989), *French Motets in the Thirteenth Century* (1994), *Music Drama at the Paris Odéon, 1824–1828* (2002), *Giacomo Meyerbeer and Music Drama in Nineteenth-Century Paris* (2005) and *Mozart's Ghosts: Haunting the Halls of Musical Culture* (2012), as well as editor of three volumes of the *Magnus Liber Organi* for Editions de l'Oiseau-Lyre (2001–2003) and six collections of essays. He has published in numerous scholarly journals and was the editor of the Royal Musical Association's monographs series from 1995 to 2011.

Franco Fabbri teaches popular music history, analysis and economy at the Conservatory of Parma and the University of Milan, Italy. His main interests are in the fields of genre theories and music typologies, the impact of media and

xii *Contributors*

technology across genres and musical cultures and the history of popular music. He has served twice as chairman of the International Association for the Study of Popular Music (IASPM). His most read book (*Il suono in cui viviamo*, three editions) contains articles on diverse subjects including genres, analysis of popular music and aesthetics of sound. He is co-editor, with Goffredo Plastino (Newcastle University, UK), of the Routledge *Global Popular Music* series.

Olli Heikkinen is a postdoctoral researcher at the Sibelius Academy, University of the Arts, Helsinki, Finland. Currently he is working on distinction in cultural politics and music classification systems. He has published articles on sound recording aesthetics, folk song collecting, musical genres, the birth of 'Finnish' musical language, the history of brass bands in Finland and on Jean Sibelius. Previously he has worked as a professional musician in a rock band and as a remembrance from that period he has four gold records and one platinum. Nowadays he composes mainly for the theatre.

Björn Heile is Reader in Music since 1900 and Head of Music at the University of Glasgow, UK. He is author of *The Music of Mauricio Kagel* (2006), editor of *The Modernist Legacy: Essays on New Music* (2009), co-editor (with Martin Iddon) of *Mauricio Kagel bei den Darmstädter Ferienkursen für Neue Musik: Eine Dokumentation* (2009) and co-editor (with Peter Elsdon and Jenny Doctor) of *Watching Jazz: Encountering Jazz Performance on Screen* (2016) and other publications on new music, experimental music theatre and jazz. Among other projects, he is writing a book on cosmopolitanism and musical modernism.

José Manuel Izquierdo is currently Gates Cambridge Scholar in his last year as a PhD in Music at the University of Cambridge, UK. He studies nineteenth-century music in Latin America, being particularly interested in the appropriation of European styles and ideas by local composers and transatlantic connections between both regions. He has been involved in the creation and organization of several music archives in the Andean region, discovering important new sources of music in Peru, Bolivia and Chile. For his recent published work, he was awarded both the Ruspoli prize for Euro-Latin American musicology (2014) and the Otto Mayer Serra prize for Ibero-American musicology (2015).

Yvonne Liao obtained a doctorate in Musicology at King's College London, UK. During her doctoral research, she was also Scholar-in-Residence at the David C. Lam Institute for East-West Studies, Hong Kong Baptist University. She read music as an undergraduate at Christ Church, Oxford, UK, and worked at Naxos and Universal Music before returning to academia. Her current research centres on Western music, venues and politics of sound in China's treaty ports from the late nineteenth century through to the first half of the twentieth century. This research covers sources in Chinese, English, French, German and Japanese. Her publications include an article in *The Musical Quarterly* on European-Jewish refugee cafés, *Unterhaltungsmusik* and 'Little Vienna' in Japanese-occupied Shanghai; and an essay in the forthcoming volume *Operatic Geographies* (edited by Suzanne Aspden) on Western opera and political geography in 1930s and 1940s Shanghai. She has presented at such conferences as the American Musicological Society, Royal Musical Association and the Society for Ethnomusicology; and co-organized a symposium on British music, empire and politics of the archive that was supported by the Royal Musical Association and the Faculty of Arts & Humanities at King's College London, UK.

Risto Pekka Pennanen is an ethnomusicologist and historian of ideas specializing in the Balkans. He is Adjunct Professor of Ethnomusicology at University of Tampere, Finland. He received his PhD from the University of Tampere and has been Alexander von Humboldt Research Fellow at the Department of Musicology at Georg-August-University in Göttingen, Germany; research associate at the School of Oriental and African Studies (SOAS), University of London, UK; and research fellow at Helsinki Collegium for Advanced Studies, Finland. He has published articles on various Balkan musical styles, especially those of Greece, Bulgaria and Bosnia-Herzegovina, and on discography, the recording industry, soundscape and the canons of music theory and music history in the peninsula. His current research project is *Music, Musicians, Soundscape and Colonial Policies in Habsburg Bosnia-Herzegovina, 1878–1918*.

Saijaleena Rantanen works as postdoctoral research fellow at the Sibelius Academy, University of the Arts, Helsinki, Finland. She is a music historian, and her research interests are in social, political and cultural history of music. She defended her doctoral thesis in 2013 about the relationship between music and popular education in Finland in the late nineteenth century. After that she joined the research project *Rethinking 'Finnish' Music History – Transnational Construction of Musical Life in Finland from the 1870s until the 1920s* focusing on the emergence of music festivals in Finland from the first festival in 1884 until 1910, when the labour movement was separated into its own political group and began to organize their own festivals. Her current research project examines the music culture of Finnish emigrants in the USA and Canada from the 1890s to the 1930s.

Ingeborg Zechner is a Postdoctoral Researcher at the Department of Musicology and Dance Studies, University of Salzburg, Austria. She is currently editing the ballet music of Christoph Willibald Gluck from the early 1760s for the composer's complete edition. Her research interest in the social history of music in a transnational context is reflected in recent publications such as an article in *Die Musikforschung* (2016) about piano adaptations of Gluck's music by Camille Saint-Saëns and Hans von Bülow and the monograph *Das englische Geschäft mit der Nachtigall: Die italienische Oper im London des 19. Jahrhunderts//The English Dealings with the Nightingale: Italian Opera in Nineteenth-Century London* (2017). The monograph deals with London's Italian opera stages and focuses on the role of the singers therein. Publications about orientalism in Ambroise Thomas's opera comique *Le caïd*, and about singers in Gluck operas in the nineteenth century are in preparation.

Introduction

Anastasia Belina, Kaarina Kilpiö and Derek B. Scott

This is the first book-length study of music history and cosmopolitanism, and it is informed by arguments that culture and identity do not have to be viewed as primarily located in the context of nationalist narratives. The term 'cosmopolitan' has been used to describe a wide range of activity and social outlooks, and it was not the wish of the editors to impose a particular meaning on the contributors to this book. The aim was to understand different ways in which the term might be applied, rather than to attempt a distinction between a true and false cosmopolitanism. The editors have striven to give the book a cohesive character. We decided that the best way of achieving this was to highlight three topics under the overarching theme of cosmopolitanism. In their chapters, however, authors had the flexibility to demonstrate how cosmopolitanism might cast new light on historical processes in music, or to concentrate on illustrating cosmopolitanism in action or to debate cosmopolitan values in relation to the music itself. The chapters range over a two-hundred-year period, and more than a dozen countries, revealing how musicians and audiences have responded to a common humanity by embracing culture beyond regional or national boundaries.

Contributors were asked not to devote too much time discussing challenges to cosmopolitanism in national cultures, or anti-cosmopolitanism in national narratives. The reason for this, in brief, is that we are keen to avoid yet another book focusing on national identity. Instead, we have encouraged our authors to focus on what unites, rather than divides, nations and cultures, and to find something upbeat and positive to say about cosmopolitanism – especially after a referendum in the UK in June 2016 revealed that a small majority of voters in England and Wales (but not Scotland or Northern Ireland) were in favour of leaving the European Union. Those in favour of what became known as Brexit often stressed the importance of sovereignty and taking back control. Fears of loss of sovereignty may be related to Europe's inclination to misconstrue itself as a nation-state. Cosmopolitan sociologists Ulrich Beck and Edgar Grande argue that this tendency means it is often viewed as an incomplete nation or federal state, when what is needed, instead, is 'a new, post-national model of democracy for Europe' (2007, p. 67).

Cosmopolitanism vs. nationalist populism

Another blow to cosmopolitan aspirations in recent years has been the rise of nationalist populism. In 2016, the same year as the UK's Brexit vote, came the surprise victory of Donald Trump in the US presidential election. In contemporary right-wing populist discourse, cosmopolitanism is usually dismissed as unpatriotic. What it means to proclaim oneself a 'citizen of the world' is being debated heatedly again in the face of the new nationalism that has surged to the forefront of the political agenda. In her speech at the Conservative Conference, Birmingham, in October 2016, British Prime Minister Theresa May declared that those who believed themselves to be citizens of the world were, in fact, 'citizens of nowhere'. It was an unfortunate and alarming echo of former attacks on the 'rootless cosmopolitans' (often meaning Jews) in Soviet Russia.

Cosmopolitan ideas have been garnering more and more interest at the same time as nationalist populism has been growing in its appeal. This may seem contradictory, but both may be viewed as opposite means of reacting to feelings of threatened values, a sense of crisis, and disillusionment with existing social and political policies. The UK's Brexit vote and the presidential election in the USA seemed to suggest a new world was emerging. These events prompted the Barry S. Brook Center in New York to organize an international conference for 2018 on the topic 'Musicology in the Age of (Post)Globalization'. Brook was a founder of *RILM* (*Répertoire International de Littérature Musicale*) and, till his death in 1997, had remained committed to his vision of a global music research community. The conference aimed to nourish a dialogue that would examine global music research in the context of the political and cultural shifts that had taken place in the twenty-first century.

Champions of nationalist populism not only have a distaste for cosmopolitanism, but also attack social democracy as obsolete, on the grounds that it has given too much priority to economic matters and has failed to recognize the attachments people have to ideas of national culture and identity. It is clear that identity issues have risen with much force in recent years, and cultural sociologists recognize that concerns about identity have created rifts between nations and ethnic groups. It is significant and illuminating, however, that the support for populist politics is often considered to be at its strongest among those who have lost jobs or seen their wages fall. If this experience has led to xenophobia, then it surely has to be explicable not only in terms of culture and identity, but also in economic terms – the fear of immigrant workers taking jobs at cut-price wages.

The cosmopolitan argues that culture and identity do not have to be viewed as exclusively located in the context of nationalist narratives. There is a cosmopolitan story to be told, and it is one with a long history. In ancient Greece, Diogenes of Sinope may have been the first to declare himself a citizen of the world, but some years before he made that personal statement, the Athenian politician Pericles had boasted that Athens was open to all, and foreigners were never prevented from seeing or learning something.[1] Since then, the theorizing of cosmopolitanism has undergone two significant phases of development. The first was during the Enlightenment, and was sparked by the appearance of Immanuel Kant's 'Idea for a Universal History with a Cosmopolitan Purpose' (1784), and 'Perpetual Peace' (1795), an influential essay in which he argued for a 'cosmopolitan law' (*ius cosmopoliticum*), which would ensure an end to wars between nations.[2] Kant's arguments in 'Perpetual Peace' failed to curb the growth of later nineteenth-century nationalism, or prevent the global war of nation against nation during 1914–18. Yet cosmopolitan arguments did not entirely disappear even at the height of the nineteenth century's nationalistic fervour, and ideas of *Weltbürgertum* (world citizenship) were generally viewed positively in Europe. Today, international law is a familiar concept (if a little tarnished), as well as the concept of crimes against humanity.

There is also evidence of city differences being able to override ethnic differences. A spoken accent can often prompt the hearer to associate a person with a city, as, say, a 'Brummie' (from Birmingham) or a Mancunian (from Manchester), rather than as a member of an ethnic group. Moreover, urban dwellers can feel an affection for their cities that binds them with others, of whatever ethnicity, who live there. The error of viewing the city as an 'ethnic signifier' was made clear in the UK a year or two ago, when a piece of right-wing nationalist propaganda depicted two cities and asked: 'Which is Britain?' It contained a photograph of a high street in a small English town full of people in Muslim dress and another of a street in the Pakistani metropolis of Karachi full of people in Western-style clothing. It may be wondered how the propagandist could be sure that the viewer would interpret the message as 'Asians are taking over the UK', rather than 'Westerners are taking over Pakistan'. It all depends on the subject position of the viewer, of course, and, in this case, it was intended for the eyes of an insecure and xenophobic Briton. A city today is likely to have an area marked by the tastes of an ethnic minority (a Chinatown, for example), but will also have areas that are not strongly characterized by the preferences (in food, fashions or leisure pursuits) of a single ethnic group.

Cosmopolitanism and globalization

Cosmopolitanism returned to the philosophical and sociological agenda in the 1990s, in the context of debates about globalization, migration, and new communications media. Among the scholars leading the new cosmopolitan debate were Kwame A. Appiah, Ulrich Beck, Homi Bhabha, Martha C. Nussbaum and Steven Vertovec. Many writers (for example, Beck and Grande 2007; Collins and Gooley 2016) have called for an ethical response that links to theorizations born of the Enlightenment, such as Martin Wieland's *Das Geheimnis des Kosmopolitenordens* (1788) and those of Kant. Following the growing disillusionment with multiculturalism, which has often produced social divisions rather than enriching a larger culture (Žižek 1997), transculturalism has been gaining more attention, and with it the notion of cosmopolitan citizenship (Cuccioletta 2001/2002). Cosmopolitanism has also been making itself felt in musicology (Stokes 2007; Feld 2012; Regev 2013; Cohen 2014; Collins and Gooley 2016; Scott 2018), and the present book illustrates the current interest shown by music scholars around the world. Cosmopolitanism puts human agency back into view, whereas the term 'globalization' immediately suggests rigid top-down manipulation.

This second stage in re-theorizing cosmopolitanism, which is, of course, the one most relevant to the present book, laid the foundation for the flourishing scholarly work on cosmopolitanism in the twenty-first century. The emphasis often falls on shared norms, and Jürgen Habermas's efforts to establish a means of achieving consensus on such norms in his *Theory of Communicative Action* (1981) prove a valuable reference point, since he attempted to understand how validity claims might be accepted across different cultures. Habermas also looked to an expansion of politics beyond the nation-state, believing that globalization and its political and economic consequences necessitated that politics should globalize in response.

The term 'aesthetic cosmopolitanism' has been advocated by Motti Regev, in particular, in his book *Pop-Rock Music: Aesthetic Cosmopolitanism in Late Modernity* (2013). He uses the term to describe the process in which cultural practices that once signified particular identities can become part of a complexly interconnected entity (2013, p. 3). David Hesmondhalgh, an acute critic of matters related to music's social meanings, observes that Regev's formulation of aesthetic cosmopolitanism is detached from the ethical demands made in the classic cosmopolitan texts by Kant and others, and comes closer to the vernacular understanding of cosmopolitanism as a cultural mix of features from different countries. Hesmondhalgh goes on to argue that Regev fails to show, for the most part, how 'the integration of foreign styles and tastes into the local hybrid styles involves any engagement with the otherness of foreign styles in a way that would meaningfully establish commonality and equal moral standing across peoples' (2013, p. 154). However, it is debatable how often this kind of engagement happens anywhere. Perhaps the Clash were attempting something like this in their version of the reggae song 'Police and Thieves' (1976), but a whole host of others were often simply doing their best to imitate a 'foreign' style and make it their own: the early effort by the Beatles to turn themselves into a convincing rhythm and blues band springs to mind.

It is also not clear what 'hybrid' means in the phrase 'local hybrid styles'. Are these styles the consequence of an integration of foreign styles into a previously 'pure' local style? The exclusive and individual local style is a rarity, indeed. The term 'hybrid', as a replacement for 'syncretic', was originally used by postcolonial theorists to indicate that a mix of local and foreign remained detectable and often created a clash or mismatch in the culture of colonized peoples. Cosmopolitanism may help in addressing the intersection between the global and the local, which, in the twenty-first century, has come to seem more of a to-and-fro affair than an oppositional clash (Roudometof 2005).

Some accounts of hybridity have served to essentialize racial difference, while other accounts have flattened out difference, and, where music is concerned, it is up for debate whether 'hybridity' now possesses anything but a vague meaning. Instant and often free access via wi-fi networks has allowed more people than ever before to acquaint themselves with the music of other cultures, and the mixing of cultural elements has become commonplace, especially in electronic dance music. The words for describing such mixing have multiplied. A conference in Turkey in 2017, as part of a European Research Council funded project 'Beyond East and West', listed the following: 'synthetic, syncretic, trans-traditional, trans-cultural, intercultural, cross-cultural, borrowed, or globalized', and there are more that could be added. The conference was held in Istanbul, a city long recognized as having a cosmopolitan character. The theme was 'Creating Music across Cultures in the 21st Century' and papers were invited on topics related to the mixing of musics from different musical traditions.

In the twenty-first century, it is often difficult, if not impossible, to read any political content into music variously described as 'world beat' or 'global fusion'. Sampling technology has led to DJs from around the world picking on anything that catches their fancy and including it in electronic dance music. Perhaps it is time to consider the arguments that might be made in support of efforts to erode a sense of otherness or foreignness, rather than emphasizing difference. Hesmondhalgh observes that musicians from various countries struggle to differentiate themselves when it comes to the global marketing of the popular music industry (2013, p. 153). However, this does not mean that they need to differentiate themselves in *national* terms. Was Louis Armstrong creating national music for America, or Bob Marley singing the national music of Jamaica? This is not to deny that a musical style carries markers of place, but only to assert that some musical styles can move with ease to other places and become jointly 'owned' in those other places (one has only to think of the Finnish tango). That is where cosmopolitan consumption differs strongly from the consumption of other cultures as exotic entities that are far removed from one's own sense of self. The typical Self vs. Other opposition that is found in Orientalism can lead to stereotyping and fabrication of the foreign culture supposedly being represented (for a range of Orientalist musical devices, see Scott 2003, pp. 155–78).

There are, of course, problems with regarding globalization or post-globalization as a process that leads unproblematically to a cosmopolitan future. It was a mistake of which Jeremy Gilbert accused Tony Blair's Labour government in 1997, with its vision of a 'third way', neither left nor right, adopting a liberal attitude to sexual and multicultural matters, but also a commitment to privatization and competition in the jobs market.

> Accepting globalization as a fact of life, New Labour made no effort to bring back industrial jobs. When migrants came from Eastern Europe, looking for work, many citizens of the post-industrial towns experienced this as a threat to their already precarious livelihoods.
> (Gilbert 2017, p. 22)

Gilbert asks if this has led to a political situation in which support for internationalism, cosmopolitanism and social liberalism now inhibits a party from achieving power. The answer is not simple, because what may be resisted in regions of industrial decay may be desirable in multicultural cities and university towns. Gilbert sees a rejection of cosmopolitan culture as a reaction to its having become associated with de-industrialization and argues that a break with stagnation and decline could turn this perception around.

Cosmopolitanism now

Cosmopolitanism as a term is difficult to pin down, and, as Martin Stokes concedes, it is a term that sometimes becomes 'messy' (2007, p. 7). However, there are a number of messy concepts – liberty being another – that play an important role in building a humane and tolerant society. The classic accounts of cosmopolitanism have an ethical dimension, and that has resurfaced in the new cosmopolitanism. Nevertheless, Steven Vertovec argues that cosmopolitanism can be viewed or invoked in at least six different ways:

> a) a socio-cultural condition; b) a kind of philosophy or worldview; c) a political project towards building transnational institutions; d) a political project for recognizing multiple identities; e) an attitudinal or dispositional orientation; and/or f) a mode of practice of competence.
> (Vertovec and Cohen 2002, p. 9)

It must be conceded that not every objection to cosmopolitanism is born of nationalist prejudice. To some, it is still tainted by elitist forms of cosmopolitanism that had roots in imperialism, and those forms can still undoubtedly be found. It is also necessary to remain aware that cultural sharing and borrowing is wrapped up in power relations that are seldom equal. This accounts for the confusion that sometimes exists between what represents the cosmopolitan disposition and what constitutes that of the global industrial capitalist. There are certain ethnomusicologists who have never liked commercial popular forms of music, who prefer to clamber up mountains to seek out isolated villages with music unsullied by the capitalist world, or who journey to faraway islands hoping to capture some 'pure' local culture before it is watered down and degraded by capitalist traders. On the other hand, there are ethnomusicologists who have engaged with the popular and learned to live with 'compromised' terminology such as 'world music'. The important point to recognize is that meaning is made in the way objects are used and consumed, rather than something that exists as an essence in the objects themselves. Another thorny issue is multiculturalism. Cosmopolitanism requires an engagement with another culture, but multiculturalism, as a social-political project for the co-existence of separate ethnic and religious identities, does not demand anything beyond tolerance and respecting rights – although this is usually combined with the hope that mutual appreciation of cultural diversity will develop. For this reason, cosmopolitanism, in its desire to embrace culture beyond regional or national boundaries, relates more readily to transculturalism (a cross-fertilization of cultures) or interculturalism (a dialogue and interaction between cultures) than to multiculturalism.

In the twenty-first century, cosmopolitanism has become attractive to sociologists who have long been clinging to national frameworks in order to understand societies and communities but suddenly found that they are experiencing increasing difficulties caused by the rapid developments in social media networks. A phrase such as 'the Internet community' offers a simple illustration of the kind of conceptual difficulties they currently face. Does the word 'community' here relate to previous sociological ideas of community (as a group bound by an element of affective loyalty), or does it mean no more than 'people who use the Internet'?

Cosmopolitanism has also become a hot topic in musicology. It is a term that, in Martin Stokes's words, 'invites us to think about how people in specific places and at specific times have embraced the music of others' (2007, p. 6). The present publication offers examples of the various directions such thoughts can take. Part 1 of this book examines music and cosmopolitanism in the nineteenth century. Mark Everist argues that the cosmopolitan musical culture of the theatre in the first two-thirds of the nineteenth century was more influenced by Parisian *grand opéra* and *opéra comique* than Italian opera. He shows how operatic repertories reveal that the centres promoting music in the theatre could inflect their Franco-Italian choices according both to local circumstances and to wider trends. Moreover, as local practices began to enjoy a wider distribution they formed patterns of reception that correspond to the 'macro-regions', identified by cultural geographers such as Michael Mann (2012), and that these macro-regions underpinned a move to later twentieth-century global activity.

Ingeborg Zechner's chapter reveals the unexpected importance of London to the cosmopolitan and transnational networks of the business of opera. London theatre managers used diverse means to maintain these networks, opting for cooperation or, less successfully, attempting to establish a more direct control by combining operations (as Benjamin Lumley did with his London and Paris ventures). Because of differing national legal demands, Zechner argues that business relations were best delivered through cosmopolitan networks.

David Brodbeck focuses on Carl Goldmark, whose opera *Die Königin von Saba* (1875) was once so popular in Europe. Brodbeck presents the once celebrated Central European composer Carl Goldmark as an embodiment of the cosmopolitan patriotism theorized by Kwame Anthony Appiah (1996/97). Goldmark was born in Hungary, the son of a Polish father, Jewish by heritage, and German by language and culture. Brodbeck sees him as a model of 'the late Habsburg Jewish cosmopolitan, loyal to the dynasty, devoted to liberal politics and 'universal' German high culture, and nationally indifferent'.

José Manuel Izquierdo König reveals that entire periods of music creation in Latin America are devoid of much interest in defining the continent as 'different' to Europe. This is particularly obvious for early nineteenth-century composers in Latin America, who seem to be interested in using European models not in terms of their 'Europeanness', but, rather, as exemplars of a contemporary cosmopolitan style, a sign of modernity as well as independence from previous colonial models. For Izquierdo König, the writings of early nineteenth-century Mexican composer and pianist Mariano Elízaga are interesting, because he occupies a position at the crossroads between the national and the local, the global and the national. He praised Mexican composers but looked to Europe for models of higher achievement (Haydn, Mozart and Beethoven). This is partly, Izquiedo argues, because opposition to recent Spanish rule was 'attached to the hope of new cultural, social and economic contacts with the wider world'. This chapter illustrates how and why those countries that emerged from the collapse of the Spanish Empire, and possessed loosely defined borders, remained open to European culture. Rather than constructing an opposition between postcolonial Self and colonialist Other, they sought, instead, to participate in a shared global style of music.

Part II moves the book into the twentieth century. Franco Fabbri reflects on the challenging work of the popular music historian who, when examining the period 1880–1920, often encounters 'surprises' that should not be considered as such, or, better, whose surprising nature is based on wrong assumptions: the chapter presents examples, whose relations with cosmopolitanism are apparent. Björn Heile's chapter makes use of mapping to offer a cosmopolitan perspective on the spread of musical modernism. His maps aim to model the global diffusion of modernist music, the migration routes of migrant composers and musicians, and the resulting network of interactions. Anastasia Belina is the second author to offer a case study of a cosmopolitan composer. André Tchaikowsky was born in Poland but refused to be identified with any particular culture. He spoke several languages, loved world literature, theatre and music and travelled extensively around the world throughout his performing career. Her chapter examines how cosmopolitanism and cosmopolitan values manifested themselves in his life and creative output. Sarah Collins's chapter engages with Edward Dent's advocacy of opera in English, positioning his ideas about the democratization of culture in opposition to a commodifying market, but also in relation to an 'everybody' that extends beyond the version of community defined by the operation of the nation-state. She reads Dent's work on topics such as libretto translation, amateur opera productions and the history and aesthetics of opera performance alongside the radical and highly influential writings on friendship, affective bonds and alternative communities of his Cambridge colleagues.

The third and final part of the book examines music and cosmopolitanism in cities. Risto Pekka Pennanen studies the different business strategies that were adopted by three touring ensembles to maximize their audiences and earnings in Sarajevo. A ladies' salon orchestra concentrated on Viennese popular music and Western classical music. The Serbian all-Roma band of Vaso Stanković-Andolija, in contrast, had a large multilingual folk and popular music repertoire. The other touring ensemble is the *tamburica* band Graničar, which consisted of female and male musicians and dancers, usually from Croatia-Slavonia. Saijaleena Rantanen and Olli Heikkinen turn their sights on Finnish city-sponsored orchestras, which they view as a continuation of the cosmopolitan city musician (*stadtmusikanten*) system in the Baltic Sea area. The role of conductors in 'domesticating' cosmopolitan institutions and musical ideas in local environments is also discussed. Yvonne Liao reconsiders Shanghai's reputation during 1930–50 as an apparent model of a cosmopolitan society. This chapter shows the necessity of understanding both the cosmopolitan and colonial setting of Shanghai as a 'treaty port'.

She structures her discussion around the ad hoc ensembles of the Shanghai Municipal Orchestra and the senior municipal council officers who sometimes found themselves acting as (unwitting) cosmopolitan subjects.

The chapters have been written by an international array of scholars who have developed a research interest in the criticism and analysis of music from a cosmopolitan perspective. Between them, they cover a wide range of music-making around the world over the past two centuries, and their arguments often stand in sharp contrast to those found in the national narratives that have dominated this period of music history. The chapters provide a collection of examples of how cosmopolitan musicology may be put into practice. In concluding this introduction, five broad guidelines are offered here:

1 Focus on a common humanity rather than difference. This distinguishes cosmopolitanism from Orientalism.
2 Look for cultural transfer that is desired rather than endured and examine translations and revisions that take place in processes of adaptation to differing cultural environments.
3 Explore cosmopolitan spaces and their importance as venues as well as for the stimulation of artistic work, especially those spaces in large cities (theatres, dance halls, restaurants, hotels, train stations and department stores).
4 Investigate cultural mobility, cultural exchange and transcultural networks.
5 Expose concepts of nation and race as fictions. Certainly, cosmopolitans, like nationalists, are persons who imagine they share a quality with people they have never met; but there is an important difference. The cosmopolitan holds to a belief in a shared common humanity rather than in a national homogeneity – and the former is a belief that one might claim is underpinned by biology, rather than ideology. Let nature reunite what culture divides.

It is easy to feel despondent about the impact of cosmopolitan ideas in the present political climate, but many of the improvements that have occurred in the wider world of humanity can be related to cosmopolitan values and are a cause for optimism, if not complacency. Among recent improvements have been a growth in conservation activity, an improvement in health around the globe, increasing seriousness with which climate change is taken, higher global spending on aid, a decrease of crime, violence and world hunger and a wider (if still insufficient) respect being shown for human rights. The editors hope that the reader will find chapters of this book appealing, and a counterbalance to the many books narrating national histories of music.

Notes

1 τήν τε γὰρ πόλιν κοινὴν παρέχομεν καὶ οὐκ ἔστιν ὅτε ξενηλασίαις ἀπείργομέν τινα ἢ μαθήματος ἢ θεάματος. Pericles's Funeral Oration, in Thucydides, Ἱστορίαι (*History of the Peloponnesian War*), 2.34–2.46.
2 'Idee zu einer allgemeinen Geschichte in weltbürgerlicher Absicht' and 'Zum ewigen Frieden'.

Bibliography

Appiah, Kwame Anthony, 1996/97. 'Cosmopolitan Patriots'. *Critical Inquiry*, 23: 617–39.

Beck, Ulrich and Edgar Grande, 2007. 'Cosmopolitanism: Europe's Way Out of Crisis'. *European Journal of Social Theory*, 10(1): 67–85.

Cohen, Brigid, 2014. 'Limits of National History: Yoko Ono, Stefan Wolpe, and Dilemmas of Cosmopolitanism'. *The Musical Quarterly*, 97(2): 181–237.

Collins, Sarah and Dana Gooley, 2016. 'Music and the New Cosmopolitanism: Problems and Possibilities'. *The Musical Quarterly*, 99(2): 139–65.

Cuccioletta, Donald, 2001/2002. 'Multiculturalism or Transculturalism: Towards a Cosmopolitan Citizenship'. *London Journal of Canadian Studies*, 17: 1–11.

Feld, Steven, 2012. *Jazz Cosmopolitanism in Accra: Five Musical Years in Ghana*. Durham, NC: Duke University Press.

Gilbert, Jeremy, 2017. 'Can Labour Win Back Its Heartlands?'. *The Guardian*. 26 May 2017. 22.

Hesmondhalgh, David, 2013. *Why Music Matters*. Oxford: Wiley Blackwell.

Mann, Michael, [1993] 2012. *The Sources of Social Power: Volume 2, The Rise of Classes and Nation-States, 1760–1914*. 2nd ed. Cambridge: Cambridge University Press.

Regev, Motti, 2013. *Pop-Rock Music: Aesthetic Cosmopolitanism in Late Modernity*. Cambridge: Polity Press.

Roudometof, Victor, 2005. 'Transnationalism, Cosmopolitanism, and Glocalization'. *Current Sociology*, 53(1): 113–35.

Scott, Derek B., 2003. 'Orientalism and Musical Style'. In *From the Erotic to the Demonic: On Critical Musicology*, edited by Derek B. Scott. New York: Oxford University Press, pp. 155–78.

Scott, Derek B., 2018. 'Cosmopolitan Musicology'. In *Confronting the National in the Musical Past*, edited with Elaine Kelly and Markus Mantere. London: Routledge, pp. 17–30.

Stokes, Martin, 2007. 'On Musical Cosmopolitanism'. *The Macalester International Roundtable 2007*, paper 3. <http://digitalcommons.macalester.edu/intlrdtable/3>.

Vertovec, Steve and Robin Cohen, eds., 2002. *Conceiving Cosmopolitanism – Theory, Context and Practice*. Oxford: Oxford University Press.

Žižek, Slavoj, 1997. 'Multiculturalism or the Cultural Logic of Multinational Capitalism'. *New Left Review*, I(225): 28–51.

Part 1
Music and cosmopolitanism in the nineteenth century

1 Cosmopolitanism and music for the theatre
Europe and beyond, 1800–1870

Mark Everist

Teutonic Universalism and the Franco-Italian

Benedict Anderson's *Imagined Communities* – despite its age – and derivative texts have bequeathed more than just a suspicion of the concept of nationalism to the early twenty-first century. The study of music has been perhaps all the more receptive to its contribution because of the nature of music historiography itself (Anderson, 1983),[1] and of its dominant trope, which has been called 'Teutonic Universalism'. Observation of Teutonic Universalism suggests that claims made about music in general are often predicated on evidence and values germane exclusively to the 'Bach to Schönberg' Austro-German canon: in other words, Austro-German – or 'Teutonic' – values masquerade as universal ones. Music of other cultures – Czech, Russian, Italian, Hungarian, Iberian, French – is somehow viewed as the product of some sort of 'national tradition', with the consequent historiographical and axiological consequences that are all too easy to imagine.[2]

The most cursory studies of nineteenth-century musical cultures betray an enormous mismatch between this view of 'Teutonic Universalism' and the reality of the cosmopolitan basis for almost everything that underpinned quotidian musical life. This disparity is most revealing in the study of music in the theatre. 'National opera', as it is called, is frequently characterised as creative response, political criticism or linguistic rebellion: some sort of counterweight to a pre-existent – usually foreign – culture that is supposed to mark a decisive break with the repertorial status quo. The disadvantage is that such a historiography downplays, deplores or even ignores the largely cosmopolitan musical cultures in the theatre against which 'national opera' apparently sets itself. As William Weber puts it, speaking of a slightly earlier period, 'Little has been done to analyse what nationalistic movements *opposed* within musical culture' (Weber, 2011, 209). When this question has been asked, the answers have tended to be couched in terms either of a response to the 'invasion' of or 'craze' for Italian opera, most often Rossini, or of the tacit assumption of 'Teutonic Universalism', without ever trying to reconstruct what the underlying musical culture might in fact have been.[3] The preoccupations in recent work by Christophe Charle and Philippe Ther with such larger questions of repertorial architecture are striking in that neither of these scholars would self-identify as a musicologist; it might well be thought that this makes them just slightly more immune to the 'Teutonic Universalism' that risks paralysing not only the study of cosmopolitanism in music but the examination of musical cultures *tout court* (Charle, 2008; Ther, 2014). The challenge, then, is to recover the underpinning cosmopolitan culture of music in the theatre against which 'national opera' might be thought to be a creative response.

What is this quotidian cosmopolitanism against which 'national opera' is supposed to be struggling? Teutonic music in the theatre has little role beyond German-speaking environments – and even there, much less of a position than has always been assumed. More importantly, the idea of a mix of the local with the Italian needs to be reoriented to encompass a mix of the local with the Franco-Italian. The exclusion of the French dimension to the analysis of this underpinning culture in favour of an Italian one may well be a consequence of the imperatives of 'Teutonic Universalism'. A dispassionate appraisal of the daily musical repertories in the theatre reveals that both French and Italian musical traditions in the theatre underpinned practice across Europe and well beyond. These traditions are complex, multifaceted and interwoven, and their analysis involves understanding the lives and actions of a large number and wide variety of agents and actors.[4] Sitting behind this analysis then is the question: how extensive was the international circulation of Italian and French music for the theatre? Questions of reception are central: what was the significance of, say, Boieldieu's *opéra comique* or Donizetti's serious opera in locations as familiar as Hamburg or Hanover or as remote as Shanghai or Sydney, and what sort of company did they keep? In other words, what was the balance between French, Italian and other music in Europe's theatres and in institutions further afield? Such questions entail others: what can be known about the institutions, personnel, audiences and civic and commercial structures that supported these cultures? These questions, their methodological implications and their answers might be less than congenial to those who trade in the currency of major composers and canonic works from the beginning of the twenty-first century; the issues are, however, central to a reimagining of the history of music in nineteenth-century European theatre.

Cosmopolitanism, 'globalism' and the macro-region

'Cosmopolitanism' has been a term at the centre of much thought in the social sciences for a quarter of a century, and has recently taken on the same mystique in music as a number of concepts and authors that have characterised the subject during the last half-century: sources, Schenker, interdisciplinarity, gender, Adorno, the post-colonial and so on. Recent colloquies on cosmopolitanism are found in the *Journal of the American Musicological Society* and in a special issue of the *Musical Quarterly*; and collections of essays and individual studies abound (Gooley et al. 2013, 523–50; Gooley and Collins, 2016, 139–279).[5] Theorising the subject is contingent on questions of territoriality, globalism, macro-regionalism, cultural transfer, cultural exchange, transnationalism and other ways of explaining the world. Making sense of music in this theoretical context has revealed views stretching from fatigue to impatience, and such weariness may well be engendered by the relatively slender range of material with which the discussion functions (Liszt and Meyerbeer seem to be endless points of reference for the study of cosmopolitanism in the music of the nineteenth century). This understanding of instances of the Franco-Italian in macro-regional contexts acts as a foil to emerging exhaustion with the subject.

A further barrier to responding to questions of cosmopolitanism has been the casual use of the terms 'global', 'globalism', 'globalisation' and cognates to describe the diffusion of music in the theatre – usually designated in this context by the shorthand 'opera'. Jürgen Osterhammel's well-known claim that 'Opera globalised early', for example, has been quoted with approval in attempts to highlight the Italian nature of 'global opera' (Walton, 2012, 462).[6] Osterhammel's quotation was, however, as follows: 'Opera globalized early on. In the mid-1800s *it had a clear radial point: Paris* [emphasis added].'[7] Furthermore, Osterhammel's evidence depends on a doubtful correspondence between the emergence of music for the European stage *c.*1600 and 'the rise of an urban music theater in southern China', which seems to result – Osterhammel's argument is unclear here – in the zenith of both *jingju* (京剧 [Beijing Opera]) and Gluck and Mozart after 1790.[8] It is undoubtedly true, for example, that vocal artists travelled long distances to further their careers, whether they were well known such as Lind or Melba or more modest such as Anna Thillon. Thillon was English, but born in Calcutta (Kolkata now), and made her first career moves in Paris in 1838 at the Théâtre de la Renaissance, then the Opéra Comique, which she left in 1844 for London's Drury Lane theatre. She ended her career in San Francisco during the early years of the troupe there.[9] Similar stories could be told about the circulation of singers not only between *France métropolitaine* and its *départements* and *territoires d'outre-mer* but also with French colonies recently ceded elsewhere as a result of the Louisiana Purchase of 1803 (see Jones Wilson, 2015; 2016, 361–82). Such travels do not, however, constitute the existence of a 'global operatic culture' in which the repertories, conventions, audiences and literate discourses on the subject would be shared across the planet in a globally integrated way, as they were later.[10] What are found, however, are the beginnings of regional clusters – South America, Central Europe, what is today thought of as the 'Middle East', the Dutch East Indies, the Sinosphere – the analysis of which better represents the realities of transnational music in the theatre in the nineteenth century. Bringing the concept of an undifferentiated 'globalism' much earlier than 1900 seriously impoverishes the understanding of how music functioned in nineteenth-century theatre, while its substitution by a series of interlocking macro-regions constitutes a significantly more productive alternative.

This general distinction between the macro-regional and the global has been developed in two texts by Michael Mann. One of the difficulties of theorising nineteenth-century cosmopolitanism is that so much work in sociology and cultural geography has so little of a historical dimension, and this in part explains the attraction of Mann's work. The historical elements of his multi-volume *Sources*

16 *Mark Everist*

of Social Power, a massive study that treats the subject from 'The Beginnings' up to 2011, could not be clearer (Mann, 1986–2013, 2: 254–98, 2: 723–39). Mann's 2006 attempt to categorise socio-spatial networks identifies five types: local, national, international, transnational and global. He engages directly with Ulrich Beck's *What Is Globalization* (1997) to posit an opposition between globalisation and what he terms 'macro-regions' (Beck, 1997/2000). Mann's fundamental argument is that there was no genuinely global activity before the end of the nineteenth century. He writes:

> There was no global or world system until the 20th century, only macro regional ones, with loose, attenuated relations between them. In the 18th century, for example there was the sphere of influence of the Chinese Empire, a dispersed South-East Asian diaspora trading network, an expanding European imperialism, plus other smaller macro-regions.... In the 20th century this expanding economy truly became global.
>
> (Mann, 2006, 28)

Such a distinction between the macro-regional and the global provides a context for early- to mid-nineteenth-century touring opera troupes, whether they be French companies touring from New Orleans up the east coast of the United States, Italian troupes in South America or other French companies exploring the Malaysian archipelago. Mann's specific mention of the 'dispersed South-East Asian diaspora trading network' gives a clear indication as to how the last of these examples might be investigated, and this is, furthermore, a macro-region where it is possible to put some musical flesh on theatrical bones.

Touring opera in the Dutch East Indies

There is a world of difference between the ways in which a state enterprise like the Vienna Opera, say, and a home for a touring opera in such a city as Batavia (known as Jakarta after 1949) might be analysed. Furthermore, this single location, among several in the Malaysian archipelago, also invites other types of investigation – the nature of the touring troupe, the other centres in which it was active (Singapore, Saigon, Macao, Hong Kong and Shanghai) and the relationship between touring and trade routes.[11] That is clearly work for the future, and although there are some studies that already fill gaps in our knowledge, the study of Batavia in 1850 is not one of them.

The simplest way to understand the cosmopolitan nature of the musical cultures of the Batavian theatre is to recover as much of the repertory that was heard there before 1870. It will reveal a good deal about the type of work that was deemed suitable for taking on this particular tour. Table 1.1 presents an outline of the repertory.[12]

Of the twelve works that were performed in Batavia between 1836 and 1866, three are French *opéra comique* – effectively four since the version of Gounod's *Faust* was probably the original 1859 one with spoken dialogue, and

Table 1.1 Music in the Theatre: Batavia/Jakarta, 1836–1866

Batavia premiere	Title (composer)	Genre (date); translation
1836	*La dame blanche* (Boieldieu)	*opéra comique* (1825)
1836	*La muette de Portici* (Auber)	*grand opéra* (1828)
1842	*Lucie de Lammermoor* (Donizetti)	*dramma tragico* (1835); French translation Paris 1839
1850	*Robert le diable* (Meyerbeer)	*grand opéra* (1831)
1851	*Les Huguenots* (Meyerbeer)	*grand opéra* (1836)
1863	*Le barbier de Séville* (Rossini)	*Commedia* (1816); French translation Lyon 1819; Paris 1824
1864	*Martha* (Flotow)	*romantische-komische Oper* (1847); French translation Brussels 1858
1864	*Le Caïd* (Thomas)	*opéra comique* (1849)
1866	*Charles VI* (Halévy)	*grand opéra* (1843)
1866	*Les mousquetaires de la reine* (Halévy)	*opéra comique* (1846)
1866	*Le trouvère* (Verdi)	*dramma* (1853); French translation Paris 1857
1866	*Faust* (Gounod)	*opéra* (1859)

so, effectively, an *opéra comique*. Four are French *grands opéras*: Auber's *La muette de Portici*, Meyerbeer's *Robert le diable* and *Les Huguenots* and Halévy's *Charles VI*. It is highly likely that, whatever their origins, the following *grands opéras* would have had their recitatives replaced with spoken dialogue, bringing them closer to the style of the *opéras comiques* listed in Table 1.1: Boieldieu's *La dame blanche*, Thomas's *Le Caïd* and Halévy's *Les mousquetaires de la reine*. That leaves three Italian works and a single German one. This in itself is significant – when touring companies chose their repertory for Batavia, they were twice as likely to choose French works as opposed to Italian ones.

Even the Italian and German pieces may have been filtered through French theatrical culture. All the performances in Batavia were in French, and all the Italian originals seem to have been based on French versions known in Europe. *Lucia di Lammermoor* was heard in French at Paris's Théâtre de la Renaissance in 1839, and it seems that Batavia heard the piece in French before it reached the Paris Opéra, which it did only in 1846. Rossini's *Il barbiere di Siviglia* was widely performed across France in Castil-Blaze's 1819 translation, and it was probably this that was heard. Similarly, it was the Paris Opéra's 1857 translation of Verdi's *Il trovatore* as *Le trouvère* that was heard there, and Flotow's *Martha* was known in an 1858 French translation from Brussels.

There is much that requires careful commentary here. Table 1.1 gives the end product of these performances, not the means by which they were achieved. This repertory is the result of perhaps five different visits to Batavia by quite possibly different opera troupes in 1836, 1842, 1850–1851, 1863–1864 and 1866. Although it is dangerous to generalise about the currency of one particular type, it seems clear that the immediate background to these repertories is clearly French –

and not Italian or German. As a piece of evidence plucked, far from randomly, between the Indian Ocean and the Java Sea, it provides a perspective on music in a macro-regional theatre that is separate from, for example, the Indian subcontinent or South America.[13]

Two questions that arise from this tiny fragment of the history of touring opera in South-East Asia are the question of audience and language, and the question of the macro-regional and the global. The question of audience is key here. Batavia was the capital of the Dutch East Indies, effectively a nationalisation of the Dutch East India Company that had taken place in 1800. The city's population was divided – along rigid caste lines – between the indigenous and the Dutch, who had already built a permanent theatre by 1821. It goes almost without saying that the audiences in Batavia who heard their Meyerbeer, Rossini and contemporaries were Dutch or other Western diplomats. And this largely explains the predominance of the French language and of French works. In the ears of the grandees of the Dutch East Indies, most music that was heard in the theatre was either French or translated into French.[14] While late-eighteenth-century enthusiasms for Flemish and Dutch lay largely dormant until the second half of the nineteenth century, those Italian works in French translation that were heard in Batavia – *Il barbiere di Siviglia*, *Lucia di Lammermoor* and *Il trovatore* – had already been familiar in the same French translations to their expatriate audiences before they had left Europe.

By the second quarter of the nineteenth century, then, Batavia was on a touring route for theatrical companies that plied their trade from one Western-dominated trading centre to another: Singapore, Saigon, Macao, Hong Kong and Shanghai. These centres represented a very clear and circumscribed regional centre of activity in South-ast Asia that neatly complemented – with almost no overlap – the Italian troupes active in South America. Unlike these Italian troupes, whose wares were exclusively Italian – Rossini and Bellini in the early years – the Batavia troupe was French, and their repertory of French origin was filtered through the francophone culture of the Netherlands.

The cosmopolitan: Copenhagen 1847 and the 'melee'

Unlike the incomplete and ambiguous data for the Batavia opera troupe, there are some institutions where it is possible to give more than the superficial, impressionistic accounts of the repertory of a single opera house.[15] The Kongelige Teater in Copenhagen was founded in 1748, and the details of its performances – all in Danish translation, whatever their national origins – have been documented on a day-by-day basis up to 1975. An investigation can be made by taking the date 1847 – approximately in the middle of the span of dates found for the Batavia company – as a sample. The results of the investigation are presented in Table 1.2, which gives the summary title of the work as it appears in Danish in the left-hand column, and information about the origins of the work in the right-hand one. Indications of genre are based on the original title pages of the libretti to ensure that the descriptor is consistent. The generic range here is enormous, and the only omissions in Table 1.2 – for reasons of space – are the ballets produced by the local choreographer, Auguste Bournonville, an artist so successful and so highly renowned that the quantities of imported ballet were negligible.

If the repertory is summarised by genre (Table 1.3), it becomes clear that, in addition to Bournonville's ballets, there are theatrical classics from as early as Shakespeare and Molière to works as recent as d'Ennery and Dumanoir's *Don César de Bazan* from 1844 or Bulwer-Lytton's *The Lady of Lyons* from 1838. This concentration on theatrical classics and recent works – mostly French, as Table 1.3 shows – is nearly equalled by the preponderance of *vaudeville* – exclusively French – all of which were originally premiered at a handful of Parisian theatres dedicated to this genre. In musical terms, the ground is unevenly shared between Danish translations of Italian and French works: there are two Mozart–Da Ponte collaborations (*Le nozze di Figaro* and *Don Giovanni*) and two recent Italian *tragedie liriche* by Bellini (*Norma* and *I Capuleti e i Montecchi*), as well as Rossini's *Il barbiere di Siviglia*. The single other work is Lortzing's *Zar und Zimmermann*. French *opéra comique* and *grand opéra* predominate, however. Three *grands opéras* from three consecutive years – *La muette de Portici*, *Guillaume Tell* and *Le dieu et la bayadère* – are central to the year's programming.[16] The five *opéras comiques* range from two Méhul classics, through Restoration works by Boieldieu and Auber to the latter's *Le domino noir*, which was premiered in Paris only a decade earlier than its Copenhagen premiere. Again, choosing a single year is misleading since Copenhagen consumed *opéra comique* voraciously: three of Auber's *opéras comiques* from the 1840s were mounted in Copenhagen within months of their Paris premieres: *Zanetta*, *Les diamants de la couronne*, *La part du diable*, and also Halévy's *Les mousquetaires de la reine*, were all produced there between 1841 and 1848. There can be no real doubt here about the essentially Franco-Italian culture underpinning the repertory of the Kongelige Teater, nor about the preponderance within the mix of French elements.

This analysis of Copenhagen's Kongelige Teater reveals the wide range of genres and points of origin of the works presented there: from *comédie-vaudeville* to Mozartian *dramma giocoso*, and from indigenous ballet to imported *grand opéra*, with works premiered in London, Paris, Rome, Prague and Vienna. The self-evident observation of cultural transfer at work perhaps does not do justice to the complexity of the different cultural emphases in play. The concept of the 'melee' serves as a more dynamic metaphor than cultural transfer or exchange. The term depends on work in philosophy and cultural geography by Jean-Louis Nancy and Angharad Closs Stephens that sees the city as a melee. The former suggests:

> A city doesn't need to be identified by anything other than a name, which marks a locus, the locus of a melee, of crossing and halt, of entanglement and commerce, competition, release, circulation ....
>
> (Nancy, 2003, p. 27)

The concept of 'cultural transfer', enormously valuable in certain respects, might be thought to lack the sense of contest and confrontation invoked by the

Table 1.2 Repertory of Copenhagen Kongelige Teater, 1847

Copenhagen title (1847)	Original work (excluding local ballets and plays)
Bagtalelsens Skole (Sheridan)	*The School for Scandal*, A Comedy, Richard Brinsley Sheridan (The Drury Lane Theatre, London, 8 May 1777)
Barberen i Sevilla (Rossini og Beaumarchais) *(Syngestykke)*	*Il barbiere di Siviglia*, commedia in 2 acts, Cesare Sterbini / Gioacchino Rossini (Rome, Teatro Argentina, 20 February 1816)
Blodhævnen (Pinel og Siraudin)	*La vendetta*, vaudeville en un acte, Dumanoir [Philippe-Francois Pinel] and Paul Siraudin (Théâtre des Variétés, 23 October 1842)
Brama og Bayaderen (Auber og Scribe) *(Syngestykke)*	*Le Dieu et la bayadère*, opéra en deux actes, Eugène Scribe / Daniel-François-Esprit Auber (Académie Royale de Musique, 13 October 1830)
Czaren og Tømmermanden (Lortzing) *(Syngestykke)*	*Czaar und Zimmermann*, komische Oper, Gustav Albert Lortzing (Leipzig, Stadttheater, 22 December 1837)
Den første Kjærlighed (Scribe)	*Les premières amours ou Les souvenirs d'enfance*, comédie-vaudeville en un acte, Eugène Scribe (Théâtre de S.A.R. Madame, 12 November 1825)
Den hvide Dame (Boieldieu og Scribe) *(Syngestykke)*	*La dame blanche*, opéra comique, Eugène Scribe-François / Adrien Boïeldieu (Théâtre de l'Opéra-Comique, Paris, 10 December 1825)
Den Stumme i Portici (Auber m.fl.) *(Syngestykke)*	*La muette de Portici*, opéra en 5 actes, Eugène Scribe and Germain Delavigne (Académie Royale de Musique, 29 February 1828)
Den unge Formynderske (Scribe og Duport)	*La tutrice, ou L'emploi des richesses*, comédie en 3 actes, Eugène Scribe / Paul Duport (Théâtre Français, 29 November 1843)
Doctor Robin (Premaray)	*Le docteur Robin*, comédie-vaudeville en un acte, Jules de Premary (Théâtre du Gymnase Dramatique, 21 October 1821)
Doctoren imod sin Villie (Molière)	*Le médecin malgré lui*, comédie en 3 actes, Molière (Théâtre du Palais Royal, 6 April 1666)
Don Cæsar de Bazan (Pinel og Dennery)	*Don César de Bazan*, drame en 5 actes, mêlé de chant, Adolphe d'Ennery and Dumanoir [Philippe-François Pinel] (Théâtre de la Porte-Saint-Martin, Paris, 30 July 1844)
Don Juan (Molière)	*Don Juan ou Le festin de pierre*, comédie en 5 actes (Théâtre du Palais Royal, Paris, 15 February 1665)
Don Juan (Mozart og Ponte) *(Syngestykke)*	*Il dissoluto punito, ossia Il Don Giovanni*, dramma giocoso in 2 acts, Lorenzo da Ponte / Wolfagang Amadeus Mozart (Prague National Theatre, 29 October 1787)
En Bedstemoder (Scribe)	*La grand'mère*, comédie en 3 actes, Eugène Scribe (Théâtre du Gymnase-Dramatique, Paris, 14 March 1840)
En Comedie i det Grønne (Dorvigny og Kotzebue)	*Der Schauspieler wider Willen*, August von Kotzebue's arrangement of *L'intendant comédien malgré lui*, Dorvigny [Louis-François Archambault] (Variétés-Amusantes, 1 January 1784)

(Continued)

Table 1.2 (Continued)

Copenhagen title (1847)	Original work (excluding local ballets and plays)
En Kone, der springer ud af Vinduet (Scribe og Lemoine)	*Une femme qui se jette par la fenêtre*, vaudeville en un acte, Gustave Lemoine (Théâtre du Gymnase Dramatique, 19 April 1847)
En Pariserinde (Souvestre og Dubois-Davesne)	*La parisienne*, comédie-vaudeville en deux actes, Emile Souvestre and Charles-Hippolyte Dubois-Davesne (Gymnase-Dramatique, 28 September 1844)
Eventyret paa Maskeraden (Auber og Scribe) *(Syngestykke)*	*Le domino noir*, Eugène Scribe / Daniel-François-Esprit Auber (Théâtre de l'Opéra-Comique, Paris, 2 December 1837)
Familien Riquebourg (Scribe)	*La famille Riquebourg, ou Le mariage mal assorti*, vaudeville, Eugène Scribe (Théâtre du Gymnase-Dramatique, Paris, 4 January 1831)
Familierne Montecchi og Capuleti (Vaccai m.fl.) *(Syngestykke)*	*I Capuleti e i Montecchi*, tragedia lirica 2 acts, Felice Romani / Vincenzo Bellini and Niccola Vaccai (Venice, La Fenice, 11 March 1830)
Figaros Bryllup (Mozart m.fl.) *(Syngestykke)*	*Le nozze di Figaro*, opera buffa in 4 acts, Lorenzo Da Ponte / Wolfgang Amadeus Mozart (Vienna, Burgtheater, 1 May 1786)
Formynder og Myndling (Scribe og Courcy)	*Simple histoire*, comédie-vaudeville en un acte, Frédéric de Courcy and Eugène Scribe (Théâtre de S.A.R. Madame, 26 May 1826)
Fruentimmerskolen (Molière)	*L'école des femmes*, comédie en 5 actes, Molière (Théâtre du Palais Royal, 26 December 1662)
Hun er afsindig (Duveyrier)	*Elle est folle*, vaudeville en 2 actes, Mélesville [Anne-Honoré-Joseph Duveyrier] (Théâtre du Vaudeville, 20 January 1835)
Joseph og hans Brødre i Ægypten (Méhul og Pineux) *(Syngestykke)*	*Joseph*, drame mêlee de chants en 3 actes, Alexandre Duval / Etienne Nicolas Méhul (Théâtre de l'Opéra-Comique, Paris, 17 February 1807)
Kean (Dumas m.fl.)	*Kean, ou Désordre et génie*, comédie en 5 actes, Alexandre Dumas (Théâtre des Variétés, 31 August 1836)
Kunsten at skaffe sig Tilbedere (Duveyrier og Duveyrier)	*La marquise de Senneterre*, comédie en trois actes, Mélesville [Anne-Honoré-Joseph Duveyrier] (Théâtre-Français, 24 October 1837)
Liden Kirsten (Hartmann og Andersen) *(Syngestykke)*	*Liden Kirsten*, romantisk Syngestykke i 1 Akt, Johan Peter Hartmann and Hans Christan Andersen (Det kongelige Teater, 12 May 1846)
Macbeth (Shakespeare)	*The Tragedy of Macbeth*, tragedy 5 acts, William Shakespeare (in Schiller's arrangement) (1599–1606)
Møllen i Marly (Duveyrier og Duveyrier)	*La meunière de Marly*, vaudeville en 1 acte, Mélesville [Anne-Honoré-Joseph Duveyrier] (Théâtre des Variétés, 21 April 1840)
Muurmesteren (Auber m.fl.) *(Syngestykke)*	*Le maçon*, opéra comique en 3 actes, Eugène Scribe and Germain Delavigne / Daniel-François-Esprit Auber (Opéra Comique, 3 May 1825)
Norma (Bellini og Romani) *(Syngestykke)*	*Norma*, tragedia lirica 2 acts, Felice Romani / Vincenzo Bellini (Milan, La Scala, 26 December 1831)

(*Continued*)

22 *Mark Everist*

Table 1.2 (Continued)

Copenhagen title (1847)	Original work (excluding local ballets and plays)
Overraskelser (Scribe)	*Les surprises*, comédie-vaudeville en un acte, Eugène Scribe (Théâtre du Gymnase Dramatique, 31 July 1844)
Pigen i Lyon (Bulwer-Lytton)	*The Lady of Lyons, or Love and Pride*, play in 5 acts, Edward George Bulwer-Lytton (Covent Garden Theatre, 15 February 1838)
Qvækeren og Dandserinden (Scribe og Duport)	*Le quaker et la danseuse*, comédie-vaudeville en un acte, Eugène Scribe / Paul Duport (Théâtre du Gymnase Dramatique, Paris, 28 March 1831)
Romeo og Julie (Shakespeare)	*Romeo and Juliet*, tragedy, William Shakespeare (?1591)
Røverborgen (Kuhlau og Oehlenschläger) (*Syngestykke*)	*Røverborgen*, Syngestykke i 3 Akter, Adam Oehlenschläger and Friedrich Kuhlau (Det kongelige Teater, 26 May 1814)
Scapins Skalkestykker (Molière)	*Les fourberies de Scapin*, comédie, Molière (Théâtre du Palais Royal, Paris, 24 May 1671)
Søvngængersken (Aumer m.fl.) *(Ballet)*	*La somnambule*, ballet-pantomime en 3 actes, Eugène Scribe and Jean Aumer / Hérold (Académie Royale de Musique, 19 September 1827)
Statsmand og Borger (Scribe)	*Bertrand et Raton, ou L'art de conspirer*, comédie en 5 actes, Eugène Scribe (Théâtre français, 14 November 1833)
Ude og hjemme (Bayard og Wailly)	*Le mari à la campagne, ou Le Tartuffe moderne*, comédie en 4 actes, Jean-François-Alfred Bayard and Jules de Wailly (Comédie-Française, 3 June 1844)
Uthal (Méhul og Victor) (*Syngestykke*)	*Uthal*, opéra en un acte, Benjamin de Saint-Victor / Etienne Nicolas Méhul (Opéra Comique, 17 May 1806)
Viola (Shakespeare)	*Twelfth-Night or What You Will*, comedy in 3 acts, William Shakespeare (1600–1601)
Wilhelm Tell (Rossini m.fl.) *(Syngestykke)*	*Guillaume Tell*, opéra en 4 actes, Victor-Joseph Etienne de Jouy and Hippolyte-Louis-Florent Bis / Giaocchino Rossini (Académie Royale de Musique, 3 August 1829)

semi-military image of the melee with its entanglement, commerce and competition.[17] Stephens develops this sense of contest into a productive concept that holds great attraction for those who seek to understand the various ways in which cultural contests might occur in a single place. She compresses her thoughts into two ideas:

- The idea of the melee points towards the possibility of another way of imagining communities and, indeed, to imagine community *as* encounters.
- A notion of urban encounter that defies a group based ontology and instead advocates that encounters are *productive* of … identities which are both contingent and multiple [Stephens's emphasis].

(Closs Stephens, 2013, 120)

Table 1.3 Repertory of Copenhagen Kongelige Teater, 1847: Analysis by Genre

Genre	Works (Copenhagen, 1847)
Opéra	Le dieu et la bayadère; La muette de Portici; Guillaume Tell (3)
Opéra comique	La dame blanche; Le domino noir; Joseph; Uthal; Le maçon (5)
Italian opera	Don Giovanni; Il barbiere di Siviglia; Le nozze di Figaro; I Capuleti e i Montecchi; Norma (5)
German opera	Czaar und Zimmermann (1)
Danish opera	Liden Kristen; Røverborgen (2)
Stage play	School for Scandal; Don César de Blazon; Les fourberies de Scapin; Bertrand et Raton; Romeo and Juliet; La grand'mère; Don Juan; L'école des femmes; The Lady of Lyons; La tutrice; La marquise de Senneterre; Le mari à la campagne; Twelfth Night; Kean; Le médecin malgré lui; Macbeth (16 [11 French and 5 English])
Vaudeville	Elle est folle; La famille Riquebourg; La meunière de Marly; [Der Schauspieler wider Willen]; Le quaker et la danseuse; La vendetta; La parisienne; Simple histoire; Les premiers amours; Le docteur Robin; Les surprises; Une femme qui se jette par la fenêtre (12)
Ballet	La somnambule (1)

The image of the city as a melee permits an analysis of the contest between various components of a cosmopolitan culture and between that culture and emergent nationalism, for example, and, at a more local level, it allows for a deeper investigation of the interaction of the various agents whose cosmopolitan backgrounds constitute further grounds for aesthetic contest. In other words, the identification of a quotidian Franco-Italian substratum of musical engagement in the theatre is only the first step in a critique of a culture that not only places Mozart alongside Shakespeare and Molière but also pits locally produced ballet against such imported genres and *comédie-vaudeville*.

Empire and vassal state, 1869: opening the lyric theatre

If Batavian touring companies reveal an exclusively French culture and Copenhagen's Kongelige Teater a complex mix of the French and Italian, further unfolding of the Franco-Italian underpinning of European and wider macro-regional cultures may be seen in the inaugural seasons of two lyric theatres that opened in 1869: Vienna and Cairo. Vienna – one of the centres of what might be considered 'Teutonic Universalism' – and Cairo – a north African locus for an Italian opera troupe – offer varied perspectives on the circulation of a fundamentally Franco-Italian culture. They are all the more striking because they are centres that might be thought to be not only more receptive to the German and the Italian respectively but also perhaps more hostile to any French engagement.

Although understanding of the circumstances of the massive theatrical building projects in Azbakeyah has now advanced to the stage where the structure and function of individual institutions – the *Comédie*, Circus and Khedivial Opera

House – are now largely understood, the repertory of each is much less clear.[18] The Opera House gave a home to an exclusively Italian troupe, with every work sung in Italian whatever its origin. What is possible to reconstruct of the first decade's repertory is given in Table 1.4.[19]

The data are scattered and imprecise, but they give a context to the premiere of Verdi's *Aida* on 24 December 1871 and to the inauguration of the Khedivial Opera House on 1 November 1869 with a cantata by Prince Jozef Poniatowski (of which there is no surviving trace) and Verdi's *Rigoletto* (Mestyan, 2011, 138–9). The four French works sung in French – two by Offenbach, two by Lecocq – were almost certainly part of the repertory of the *Comédie*. The rest of the repertory still reveals a Franco-Italian background, with both the Italian (*Il barbiere di Siviglia* and *L'elisir d'amore*) and the French (*Fra diavolo* and *La muette de Portici*) repertories reaching back to the beginning of the century and promoting the relatively new. This is a Franco-Italian culture in which the Italian outweighs the French by about three to two. Delays in new works reaching Cairo vary, but the most recent was Marchetti's *Ruy Blas*, arriving in 1873 after an 1869 premiere in Milan. Predictably, perhaps, the greatest novelties were the two 1869 Offenbach productions three and two years respectively after their Paris premieres. The presence of a French *Comédie* may also play into the precise configuration of the Franco-Italian balance during the first decade of the Khedivial Opera House's activity; a second house dedicated to French theatre in the same city could well have given a different complexion to the complementary theatre.

By contrast, the opening season of the new Vienna opera house, which was in the same year as that of the Cairo institution, gave preference to French traditions over the Italian. The *Kaiserlich-königliches Hofoperntheater im neuen Hause* opened its doors on 25 May 1869. Vienna's new opera house promoted works sung only in German but a repertory that – in the seven months up to the end of the calendar year – mounted 28 productions: ballet, works of Viennese origin and French, Italian and German works, as outlined in Table 1.5.

What is again clear from Table 1.5 is that the repertory, apart from ballet, is Franco-Italian, translated into German, this time with an emphasis on the French. The overall figures give the following: ballet: 47 per cent; French: 41 per cent; Italian: 7 per cent; Viennese: 4 per cent; German: 3 per cent. Those productions based on 'Viennese' originals (*Don Giovanni*, *Le nozze di Figaro*, *Fidelio* and *Die Zauberflöte*) could be further divided and placed into 'Italian' and 'German' categories, which would inflect the figures slightly to bring the Italian and German percentage up into the mid-teens.[20] However, the 1869 Vienna productions suggest that at a time and place where one might expect the Austro-Hungarian Empire (which it had been since 1867) to be promoting its own works – and which, to judge from the amount of space given to the relative genres in modern histories of music, might be expected – the repertory is Franco-Italian.[21] Performances of middle-period Verdi, *Il trovatore* and *Rigoletto*, are flanked by earlier and later works (*Ernani* and *Un ballo in maschera*) but only in small numbers, in the same way as non-Viennese German works – *Der Freischütz* and *Martha*.

Table 1.4 Music in the Khedival Theatre, Cairo, 1869–1877

Year	Italian opera	Opérette (in French)	French opera (in Italian)
1869	*Ernani* (Verdi)		
1869	*Il barbiere di Siviglia* (Rossini)		
1869	*L'elisir d'amore* (Donizetti)		
1869		*La belle Hélène* (Offenbach)	
1869		*La grande-duchesse de Gérolstein* (Offenbach)	
1869	*La traviata* (Verdi)		
1869	*Rigoletto* (Verdi)		
1870	*Crispino e la Comare ossia Il Medico e la Morte* (Ricci bros)		
1870	*Don Checco* (de Giosa)		
1870	*Don Giovanni* (Mozart)		
1870			*Faust* (Gounod)
1870			*Fra diavolo* (Auber)
1870	*Il trovatore* (Verdi)		
1870			*La favorite* (Donizetti)
1870			*La fille du regiment* (Donizetti)
1870			*La juive* (Halévy)
1870			*La muette de Portici* (Auber)
1870			*Les Huguenots* (Meyerbeer)
1870	*Lucia di Lammermoor* (Donizetti)		
1870	*Semiramide* (Rossini)		
1870	*Un ballo in maschera* (Verdi)		
1871	*Aida* (Verdi)		
1872	*Martha* (Flotow)		
1873	*La forza del destino* (Verdi)		
1873	*Ruy Blas* (Marchetti)		
1875		*Giroflé-Girofla* (Lecocq)	
1875			*Le pardon de Ploërmel* (Meyerbeer)
1875			*Le prophète* (Meyerbeer)
1876			*L'africaine* (Meyerbeer)
1876		*La petite mariée* (Lecocq)	
1876	*Otello* (Rossini)		
1877	*Der Freischütz* (in Italian)		
1877	*Jone* (Petrella)		
	17	4	10

Table 1.5 Repertory of Kaiserlich-königliches Hofoperntheater im neuen Hause, Vienna, 1869

Category	German title	Original work	Performances
Ballet	Flick und Flock	Flick und Flock	25
Ballet	Sprühfeuer	Fiamma d'amore	24
Ballet	Sardanapal	Sardanapal	21
Ballet	Saltarello	Saltarello	11
French	Der Prophet	Le prophète (Meyerbeer)	10
French	Armida	Armide Gluck)	9
French	Die Hugenotten	Les Huguenots (Meyerbeer)	8
French	Der Postillon von Lonjumeau	Le postillon de Lonjumeau (Adam)	7
French	Romeo und Julie	Roméo et Juliette (Gounod)	7
French	Wilhelm Tell	Guillaume Tell (Rossini)	6
French	Fra Diavolo oder Das Gasthaus zu Terracina	Fra Diavolo (Auber)	6
French	Die Stumme von Portici	La muette de Portici (Auber)	5
French	Margarethe	Faust (Gounod)	4
French	Mignon	Mignon (Thomas)	4
French	Die Favoritin	La favorite (Donizetti)	3
French	Robert der Teufel	Robert le diable (Meyerbeer)	3
German	Martha	Martha (Flotow)	3
German	Der Freischütz	Der Freischütz (Weber)	2
Italian	Der Troubadour	Il trovatore (Verdi)	2
Italian	Rigoletto	Rigoletto (Verdi)	2
Italian	Lucia von Lammermoor	Lucia di Lammermoor (Donizetti)	2
Italian	Hernani	Ernani (Verdi)	2
Italian	Ein Maskenball	Un ballo in maschera (Verdi)	1
Italian	Lucrezia Borgia	Lucrezia Borgia (Donizetti)	1
Viennese	Die Zauberflöte	Die Zauberflöte (Mozart)	1
Viennese	Die Hochzeit des Figaro	Le nozze di Figaro (Mozart)	1
Viennese	Fidelio	Fidelio (Beethoven)	1
Viennese	Don Juan	Don Giovanni (Mozart)	1

As in the case of Copenhagen, ballet is paramount. Enthusiasm for the four works given in Table 1.5 might have been a result of Viennese premieres or new productions: *Flick und Flock* and *Sardanapal*, both by the Berlin collaboration of Paul Taglioni and Peter Ludwig Hertel, had received their premieres in Berlin in 1858 and 1865 respectively. While *Fiamma d'amore* (by Artur de St-Léon and Ludwig Minkus) had been premiered in Moscow in 1863, only *Saltarello* seems to have been an entirely new work (the music was by Louis Frappert and the choreography was anonymous).

Almost exactly the same number of performances was given to *opéra* and *opéra comique* as to ballet. Of the eleven works involved, six originated at the Opéra, three at the Opéra Comique and both Gounod works at the Théâtre-Lyrique. The French repertory reads like an inventory of the most widely distributed works of the period, stretching back to the trilogy of *La muette de Portici*,

Guillaume Tell and *Robert le diable* that had experimented early with the genre of *grand opéra*, and forward to such *opéras comiques* as *Mignon* (1866) and *Roméo et Juliette* (1867), which were still enjoying or had just completed triumphant first runs in Paris.

Both Cairo and Vienna were developing – in radically different institutional, geographic and cultural environments – a similar Franco-Italian repertory, presented in Italian and German respectively, whatever the original language of the work. In the former, the Franco-Italian balance marginally favours the Italian; in the latter, the reverse is the case. The two repertories problematise the issue – which could equally well be raised apropos Batavia or Copenhagen – as to how the producers and consumers of this music and drama viewed these works: whether they paid attention to the types of sensitivity outlined here (a Danish translation of *I Capuleti e i Montecchi* as the *Syngestykke: Familierne Montecchi og Capuleti*, for example) or whether everything sung in Italian in Cairo was considered Italian in the same way that, even in the early twenty-first century, there is some dissonance around the origins of Rossini's *Guglielmo Tell* or Verdi's *Don Carlo*.

Conclusion: the Franco-Italian, 'globalisation' and the macro-region

This chapter has examined a number of instances where the Italian and French contributions to European and global musical culture may be examined and evaluated; it has also indicated a number of problems that require resolution before the question of cultural transfer or exchange can be invoked. Replacing the idea of nation with one of centre or city as the basis for trying to examine the melee, which characterises the culture of music in the theatre across the planet, leads to the concept of the macro-region as a productive concept in place of 'global' sloganising. And even in this chapter, there have been examples of melees developed out of contrasting national backgrounds (largely French and Italian), contests over language and translation, and differences between original and copy, local and imported, resident and touring. With more examples and greater detail the list could go on ad infinitum.

There are four principal conclusions:

1 The moment that a musical work in the theatre is transferred from its native environment, its national origin and language or performance become a site of contest and exchange.
2 German theatre music plays a much smaller role on the European stage than might be thought, to judge from modern histories of music.
3 French and Italian forms of music for the theatre dominate right across the globe up to around 1870.
4 The French component of this Franco-Italian balance has been massively underestimated, although it frequently constitutes at least half of the repertory and, under certain circumstances, especially where the French language is in play, can predominate.

So the picture in many histories of music of 'operatic' cultures flooded by the implicitly degenerate Italianate and saved by German works (especially Wagner) and national opera is false. The cosmopolitan nature of musical cultures in the theatre of the first two-thirds of the nineteenth century needs to be understood much less in terms of a Rossini craze – or even a Verdi one for that matter – but in terms of a culture that is much more influenced by Parisian *grand opéra* and *opéra comique* than current understandings might suggest. The cosmopolitan framework of opera in the various macro-regions of the world up to 1870 is Franco-Italian, one in which French and Italian works, at various levels of transformation, intermingle and interbreed, and one where the two could occasionally divide up on macro-regional lines. Moreover, such a framework points to the importance of recovering the vast network of cosmopolitan music in the theatre – in all its complexity – all over the globe.

Notes

1 Anderson's fundamental concept, old as it is, has underpinned work in music from the 1980s to the present, in fields as wide apart as Chinese classical music and heavy metal. See Touhy (1988) and Hill (2014, pp. 173–87).
2 For the concept and critique of the term 'Teutonic Universalism', see Taruskin (2005, pp. 185–207). Taruskin had been preoccupied with the subject for at least a decade (see 1996, pp. 12–14). For the continuing relevance of Taruskin's claims, see Deathridge (2003/2004, pp. 128–9) and McClary (2016, pp. 25–35).
3 Manifestations of the 'Rossini craze' are legion: Beethoven was apparently damaged by it; Schubert could not resist it. Carl Dahlhaus could describe one of his key witnesses, 'Raphael Georg Kiesewetter, [as] a connoisseur of early music whom one could scarcely accuse of being brainlessly susceptible to the "Rossini craze"' (Dahlhaus, 1980/1989, p. 8 of English translation).
4 The use of the terms is designed to invoke the 'arts worlds' envisaged by Howard Becker and Bruno Latour's actor-network theory (ANT) (see Becker, 1982/2008; Latour, 2005). For a useful introduction to the ways in which ANT might play a role in the history of music, see Piekut (2014, pp. 191–215).
5 I am grateful to Professor Gooley for a productive exchange on the subject (personal communications, 3–4 May 2016) and to both authors for a pre-publication draft of their introduction.
6 Osterhammel's German is 'Die Oper globalisierte sich früh' (Osterhammel, 2009, p. 28).
7 'In der Mitte des 19. Jahrhunderts besaß sie einen weltweit ausstrahlenden Mittelpunkt: Paris' (ibid.). This translation, and all that follow, are taken from Camillier (2014, p. 5).
8 Ibid. This appears to be Osterhammel's only invocation of 'opera', despite his claim in the introduction to the 2014 translation that *The Transformation of the World* 'does not disguise personal idiosyncrasies such as a special interest in animals, the opera, and … international relations' (ibid., xiii).
9 The fullest account of Thillons's career remains Fétis (1860–1865, Suppl. 2: pp. 571–2), which may be complemented by Kutsch and Riemens (1987–1994/2003, 5, pp. 3464–5). See the summary of both in Chitty and Rosenthal (2001).
10 For Sebastian Conrad, this is exactly what global history entails: it 'presumes, and explicitly reflects on, some form of *global integration*. At its core are patterns of exchange that were *regular and sustained*, and thus able to shape societies in profound ways' (2016, p. 9 [emphasis added]). Such an integrated global history is to be differentiated from Conrad's 'second paradigm', which focuses on 'exchange and connec-

Cosmopolitanism and music for the theatre 29

tions', which he rightly recognises as 'the most popular form that research has taken in recent years' (ibid.); Conrad's second paradigm is well known in the humanities as cultural transfer or cultural exchange, which serves well as the engine driving an understanding of music in the macro-regional theatre that is described here, and better describes activities that are currently merely tagged as 'global'.

11 The fundamental study, which covers a slightly later period, is Huang (1997). I have profited in this work from discussions with Chenyin Tang, whose dissertation ('Western Opera in Maritime East Asia [1875–1941]' [in progress]) engages with later material. Despite the title's claim, Huang's dissertation has little to say about the issue before 1870.

12 Much of the data in Table 1.1 is derived from the entries in Loewenberg (1978), and should be regarded as provisional in the extreme. The *Batavische Courant* began publication in 1819, and is an obvious source for a fuller, more systematic study of the repertory in the Dutch East Indies.

13 Vicissitudes in the weather in August 1863 meant that one of the Batavia touring companies was stranded in Singapore for several weeks, and while they waited out the weather, they gave a number of performances. The surviving press gives one of the most detailed accounts of the troupe's activities. See Everist (forthcoming).

14 For a study of French music on the Amsterdam stage, its repertory and its language, see Osmond (in progress).

15 The recording of the quotidian activities of theatres that employed music across Europe is patchy in the extreme. Full listings of the day-to-day repertory of the Paris Opéra are found in a database entitled *Chronopera*, for example. Although easy to use, it has some worrying shortcomings; see http://chronopera.free.fr/index.php?. And the current section is based on data recovered from Jensen: http://danskforfatterleksikon.dk/1850t/t1850dato.htm. There are occasional printed listings of day-by-day repertories for individual theatres for relatively restricted periods: for example, Fambach (1985), Burkhardt (1891/1977) or Cambiasi (1889). Much more common are simple listings of works performed during a single year, yielding a lesser level of control. Good examples are the four works by Albert Soubies, recently digitised (Gutsche-Miller and Everist, http://fmc.ac.uk/collections/bibliographical-resources-and-work-in-progress/; and Hadamowsky, 1966–1975).

16 The relatively early date for these three *grands opéras* should not obscure the fact that both Meyerbeer's *Les Huguenots* and Halévy's *La juive* were in the repertory of the Kongelige Teater (premiered in 1838 and 1844 respectively), but not performed in 1847.

17 Standard texts on cultural transfer are Espagne and Werner (1987, pp. 969–92) and Espagne (1999). For an attempt at considering its significance for music, see Fauser and Everist (2009, pp. 1–8).

18 For the outline of the new theatres in Azbakeyah, see Mestyan (2011, pp. 121–51).

19 As in the case of the Batavia troupe, the data in Table 1.4 are derived from Loewenberg (1978).

20 It goes without saying that, strictly speaking, *Don Giovanni* was premiered in Prague, that *Le nozze di Figaro* enjoyed its greatest success there, and that *Die Zauberflöte* was the project of the suburban (in 1791) Theater auf der Wieden. Even *Leonore/Fidelio* was premiered at the Theater an der Wien rather than the Burgtheater. Considering these works 'Viennese', even in 1869, might be thought an act of appropriation.

21 The data underpinning this paragraph are taken from Glanz et al., retrieved from www.mdw.ac.at/iatgm/operapolitics/spielplan-wiener-oper/web/.

Bibliography

Anderson, Benedict, 1983. *Imagined Communities: Reflections on the Origin and Spread of Nationalism*. London: Verso.

Beck, Ulrich, 1997. *Was ist Globalisierung?* Frankfurt am Main: Suhrkamp. Translated by Patrick Camiller, 2000. *What Is Globalization?* Cambridge: Polity Press.

Becker, Howard, 1982. *Art Worlds*. Berkeley: University of California Press. 25th anniversary edition, updated and expanded, 2008.

Burkhardt, Carl August Hugo, 1891. *Das Repertoire des Weimarischen Theaters unter Goethes Leitung, 1791–1817*. Theatergeschichtliche Forschungen, Band 1. Hamburg: Voss; repr. Nendeln: Kraus, 1977.

Cambiasi, Pompeo, 1889. *La Scala, 1778–1889: Note storiche e statistiche*, 4th edition. Milan: Ricordi.

Charle, Christophe, 2008. *Théâtres en capitales: naissance de la société du spectacle à Paris, Berlin, Londres et Vienne, 1860–1914*. Bibliothèque Albin Michel de l'histoire. Paris: Michel.

Chitty, Alexis and Harold Rosenthal, 2001. 'Thillon [née Hunt], Sophie Anne'. *Grove Music Online*. Retrieved 14 June 2018, from www.oxfordmusiconline.com/grovemusic/view/10.1093/gmo/9781561592630.001.0001/omo-9781561592630-e-0000027844.

Closs Stephens, Angharad, 2013. *The Persistence of Nationalism: From Imagined Communities to Urban Encounters*. Interventions. London and New York: Routledge.

Conrad, Sebastian, 2016. *What Is Global History*. Princeton: Princeton University Press.

Dahlhaus, Carl, 1980. *Die Musik des 19. Jahrhunderts*. Neues Handbuch der Musikwissenschaft, Band 6. Wiesbaden: Akademische Verlagsgesellschaft Athenaion. Translated by J. Bradford Robinson, 1989, as *Nineteenth-Century Music*. Berkeley and Los Angeles: University of California Press.

Deathridge, John, 2003/2004. 'The Invention of German Music *c*. 1800', paper read at conference 'Unity and Diversity in European Culture c. 1800', London, 26–27 September 2003 (summary in *Bulletin of the German Historical Institute*, 26, 2004, pp. 128–9).

Espagne, Michel, 1999. *Les Transferts Culturels Franco-Allemands*. Perspectives Germaniques. Paris: Presses Universitaires de France.

Espagne, Michel and Michael Werner, 1987. 'La construction d'une référence culturelle allemande en France: genèse et histoire (1750–1914)'. *Annales ESC*, 4 pp. 969–92.

Everist, Mark. '*Ouverture*: Power, Licence and Technology', in *Opera in Paris from the Empire to the Commune*. London: Routledge. [forthcoming]

Fambach, Oscar, 1985. *Das Repertorium des Königlichen Theaters und der italienischen Oper zu Dresden 1814–1832*. Mitteilungen zur Theatergeschichte der Goethezeit, Band 8. Bonn: Bouvier.

Fauser, Annegret and Mark Everist, 2009. 'Introduction', in *Music, Theater and Cultural Transfer: Paris, 1830–1914*, edited by Everist and Fauser, pp. 1–8. Chicago: Chicago University Press.

Fétis, François-Joseph, 1860–1865. *Biographie universelle des musiciens et bibliographie générale de la musique*, 8 vols., 2nd ed. [with supplement in two vols]. Paris: Firmin Didot.

Glanz, Christian et al., 'Spielplan der Wiener Oper: 1869 bis 1955'. Retrieved from www.mdw.ac.at/iatgm/operapolitics/spielplan-wiener-oper/web/.

Gooley, Dana and Sarah Collins, 2016. 'Cosmopolitanisms'. *Musical Quarterly*, 99, pp. 139–279.

Gooley, Dana et al., 2013. 'Cosmopolitanism in the Age of Nationalism, 1848–1914'. *Journal of the American Musicological Society*, 66, pp. 523–50.

Gutsche-Miller, Sarah and Mark Everist. 'List of Paris Music Drama Performances'. *France: Musiques, Cultures, 1789–1914*. Retrieved from http://fmc.ac.uk/collections/bibliographical-resources-and-work-in-progress/.

Hadamowsky, Franz, 1966–1975. *Die Wiener Hoftheater (Staatstheater), 1776–1966: Verzeichnis der aufgeführten Stücke mit Bestandsnachweis und Täglichem Spielplan*, 2 vols. Museion: Veröffentlichungen der Österreichischen Nationalbibliothek, vol. 4. Vienna: Prachner.

Hill, Rosemary, 2014. 'Reconceptualizing Hard Rock and Metal Fans as a Group: Imaginary Community'. *International Journal of Contemporary Music*, 7, pp. 173–87.

Huang, Chun-Zen, 1997. 'Traveling Opera Troupes in Shanghai: 1842–1949'. PhD diss., Washington, D.C.: Catholic University of America.

Jensen, Niels. 'Dansk Forfatterleksikon. Teatrenes repertoire 1722–1975'. Retrieved from http://danskforfatterleksikon.dk/1850t/t1850dato.htm.

Jones Wilson, Jennifer C. H., 2015. 'The Impact of French Opera in Nineteenth-Century New York: The New Orleans French Opera Company, 1827–1845'. PhD diss., New York: City University of New York.

Jones Wilson, Jennifer C. H., 2016. 'Meyerbeer and New Orleans French Opera Company in New York, 1845: How, Therefore, Could New York have Remained Behind', in Mark Everist (ed.) *Meyerbeer and Grand Opéra: From the July Monarchy to the Present*, pp. 361–82. Speculum musicae, vol. 28. Turnhout: Brepols.

Kutsch, Karl-Josef and Leo Riemens, 1987–1994. *Großes Sängerlexikon*, 4th ed., 7 vols. Munich: Saur, 2003. 5: 3464–5.

Latour, Bruno, 2005. *Reassembling the Social: An Introduction to Actor-Network Theory*, Clarendon Lectures in Management Studies. Oxford and New York: Oxford University Press.

Loewenberg, Alfred, 1978. *Annals of Opera: 1597–1940*, 3rd ed revised and corrected. London: Calder.

Mann, Michael, 1986–2013. *The Sources of Social Power*, 4 vols. Cambridge: Cambridge University Press.

Mann, Michael, 2006. 'Globalization, Macro-Regions and Nation-States', in Gunilla Budde, Sebastian Conrad, and Oliver Janz (eds.) *Transnationale Geschichte: Themen, Tendenzen und Theorien*. Göttingen: Vandenhoeck & Ruprecht, 21–31.

Mestyan, Adam, 2011. '"A Garden with Mellow Fruits of Refinement": Music Theatres and Cultural Politics in Cairo and Istanbul, 1867–1892'. PhD diss., Budapest: Central European University .

McClary, Susan, 2016. 'From the Universal and Timeless to the Here and Now', in Sally Macarthur, Jody Lochhead, and Jennifer Shaw (eds.) *Music's Immanent Future: The Deleuzian Turn in Music Studies*, pp. 25–35. London and New York: Routledge.

Nancy, Jean-Luc, 2003. 'In Praise of the Melee (for Sarajevo, March 1993)', in Simon Sparks (ed.) *A Finite Thinking*, Cultural Memory in the Present, pp. 277–88. Stanford: Stanford University Press.

Osmond, William, [in progress]. 'The Reception of French Opera in Amsterdam 1830–1848'. PhD diss., University of Southampton.

Osterhammel, Jürgen, 2009. *Die Verwandlung der Welt. Eine Geschichte des 19. Jahrhunderts*. Munich: Beck. Translated by Camillier, Patrick. 2014. *The Transformation of the World. A Global History of the Nineteenth Century*. Princeton: Princeton University Press.

Piekut, Benjamin, 2014. 'Actor-Networks in Music History: Clarifications and Critiques'. *Twentieth-Century Music*, 11, pp. 191–215.

Tang, Chenyin, [in progress]. 'Western Opera in Maritime East Asia (1875–1941)'. PhD diss., Southampton: University of Southampton.

Taruskin, Richard, 1996. 'Introduction'. *Nationalism and Music*, special issue of *repercussions*, 5, pp. 12–14.

Taruskin, Richard, 2005. 'Speed Bumps'. *19th-Century Music*, 29, pp. 185–207.

Ther, Philippe, 2014. *Center Stage: Operatic Culture and Nation Building in Nineteenth-Century Central Europe*. Translated by Charlotte Hughes-Kreutzmuller. West Lafayette: Purdue University Press.

Touhy, Sue Mary Clare, 1988. 'Imagining the Chinese Tradition: The Case of hua'er Songs, Festivals and Scholarship'. PhD diss., Bloomington: Indiana University.

Walton, Benjamin, 2012. 'Italian Operatic Fantasies in Latin America'. *Journal of Modern Italian Studies*, 17, pp. 460–71.

Weber, William, 2011. 'Cosmopolitanism, National and Regional Identities in Eighteenth-Century European Musical Life', in Jane Fulcher (ed.) *The Oxford Handbook of the New Cultural History of Music*, pp. 209–27. New York: Oxford University Press.

2 Cosmopolitanism in nineteenth-century opera management

Ingeborg Zechner

Transnational transfer processes can be considered as an integral part of the history of opera. These processes can occur on the level of works, which travelled transnationally in order to be performed, and on the level of the opera personnel, such as singers, musicians, managers, etc. Without question, these two levels of mobility are closely connected. Travelling opera troupes in the eighteenth century, such as Pietro and Angelo Mingotti's (to name one example), supported the distribution of a specific repertoire of works. After the first half of the nineteenth century, the processes of transfer and mobility were enhanced considerably through the massive technological innovations of the time, which considerably facilitated travelling (see among others Walter 2016, pp. 47–57). Thus the availability and the dependence on transnational operatic networks for the 'global art' of nineteenth-century opera increased. Jürgen Osterhammel, in his large-scale study about the nineteenth century, emphasizes Paris's role as a centre for the global opera market (Osterhammel 2010, p. 28), without taking notice of London, which maintained a particularly rich musical theatrical scene throughout the century (see Zechner 2017a, pp. 11–22 and Davis, Emeljanov 2001, pp. 168–225). For London's Italian opera market, which relied strongly on the import of star singers and operas, being part of the network of Italian opera can be seen as a crucial necessity. Indeed, London's opera managers needed to be all the more cosmopolitan in order to keep their international businesses running and to secure the most renowned star singers of the time.

This study thus aims to illustrate the cosmopolitan nature of London's opera market through the examples of Pierre François Laporte (1799–1841) and Benjamin Lumley (1811–1875), two figures who managed the Italian opera season at the King's/Her Majesty's Theatre consecutively in the 1830s to 1850s by holding close ties to the Italian opera of Paris, the Théâtre Italien. It will furthermore analyse and contextualize the challenges and opportunities for the international opera market that resulted from their transnational and cosmopolitan management strategies.

The Paris–London connection in the 1830s–1850s

Throughout the nineteenth century the *saison* of the Parisian Théâtre Italien – lasting usually from November until April – served as an important hub for London's opera managers. The programme, which in both cases consisted of Italian opera and ballet, as well as the aristocratic audience of both opera venues, drew London's attention towards Paris. As a centre of the musical world, Paris fostered new operatic compositions not only for the city's French stages, but also for its Italian one, among them Vincenzo Bellini's *I puritani* and Gaetano Donizetti's *Marino Faliero*, which saw their first performances in 1835. London's opera managers were interested in importing new Italian operas, often bundled together with a company of singers and dancers, in order to expand their programmes in novel ways. The music press of both London and Paris encouraged the links between the two cities by regularly reporting on the latest performances of Parisian opera houses. Successes and failures of works and singers were thus communicated on both sides of the Channel.[1] London's opera managers deliberately used reports about Parisian performances to advertise their upcoming production or singers' company.

During the 1830s, and especially through the efforts of Pierre-François Laporte, the timing of the Parisian *saison* and the consecutive Italian season in London – April to September – were ideally coordinated in order to facilitate operatic exchange. Already in the 1820s the contracts of the Théâtre Italien usually contained a clause that indicated the consecutive season in London (see Roccatagliati 2002, p. 197). In the years that followed, business relations between London's opera managers and the Parisian *directeurs* intensified.

Paris–London alliances: Pierre François Laporte and Edouard Robert/Carlo Severini

The former French actor Pierre François Laporte, who led the King's Theatre from 1828 until his sudden death in 1841, took advantage of consecutive seasons when establishing continuous management collaborations with Edouard Robert and Carlo Severini (1793–1838), the directors of the Théâtre Italien. The managerial alliance was terminated tragically in 1838 when the Théâtre Italien burnt down and Severini was killed in the fire.[2] Various letters from the period 1830 to 1838 between the Parisian management team Robert/Severini and Laporte, document the extent of this relation in full detail and shed new insight into the contemporary practice of musical contracts.[3]

For the 1832 season, Thomas Monck Mason leased the King's Theatre from Laporte, who – aiming to establish a monopoly on opera in London – became manager of the Theatre Royal Covent Garden (see Hall-Witt 2007, p. 158). Monck Mason continued to capitalize on Laporte's ties with Severini/Robert to gain access to prominent star singers, such as the baritone Antonio Tamburini. In the end, this engagement put him in severe financial difficulties, though it reveals just how much power star singers had, especially over London's opera managers (see Zechner 2017a, pp. 46–49). Tamburini, knowing his worth on the market, insisted shortly before the start of the Parisian *saison* in October, that he would not leave for Paris until the management of the King's Theatre agreed to pay him in full for the previous season.[4] It was common at the time for London's opera managers to default on payments, as the lack of public subsidies made such enterprises vulnerable to enormous financial risks. Indeed, these institutions relied solely on private funding, which complicated season planning financially, and in turn naturally brought a certain extent of mistrust against London's managers and a willingness to form managerial alliances. For this reason, Severini/Robert used Giovanni Battista Benelli, the former but discredited manager of the King's Theatre, as an informant on Laporte's current business situation (see Roccatagliati 2002, pp. 206–209).[5]

Under the pressure of his audience to engage the singer[6], Monck Mason offered Tamburini a generous salary for the 1832 season, a sum that lay far above his salary in Paris. Tamburini used the situation to leverage a salary increase from Severini and Robert to match the level of the London engagement. Under the pressure of Severini, Monck Mason was forced to fulfil Tamburini's demands and pay the demanded sum from his budget – an expense that contributed immensely to his financial ruin after the season (see Roccatagliati 2002, pp. 198–199).

The exchange of star singers remained the most important issue in the collaboration between Laporte and Robert/Severini, and it increased the need to simplify the legal framework of singers' contracts. In the first years of the management cooperation, letters between the managers, in which the main terms of an engagement were negotiated, were informal, handwritten contracts with the singers. These contracts did not regulate every detail of the engagement but were, rather, supplemented by the additional conditions of the correspondence. Combining the legal framework of the two enterprises brought the advantage of being able to block a singer from making appearances at other European opera houses all year long. An example of this can be found in the contract of the management cooperation with the bass, Luigi Lablache, from 1833 for an engagement in London (see Zechner 2017a, p. 93).[7] This contract only regulated the terms of the exchange between the singer and managers, but not the exact terms of the engagements in London and Paris. As the content of this exchange contract hints, there might have been two additional contracts (one for London, the other one for Paris), the documents of which have unfortunately not been preserved. In any case, Robert fulfilled the role of an agent for Lablache, who sold the singer to Laporte for the London season.

The contracts with Lablache may have resembled the contracts for the 1834–1835 Italian season in London with Giulia Grisi and Antonio Tamburini from the same period.[8] The shape of these contracts, which regulated the singers' engagements in London, represents the pre-eminence of the Parisian management team in the cooperation. Laporte used the standardized printed contracts of the Théâtre Italien and adapted them slightly for the use at the King's Theatre.[9] The change of the institution was accomplished through the handwritten addition of the attribute 'de Londres' after the words 'Théâtre Royal Italien'. The most extensive amendments to the contract are represented in the handwritten additions at the end, which regulated the terms of the singers' performance at benefit concerts. This implies that the contractual and legal basis of singers' contracts in London in the 1830s was only stable and binding to the extent to which engagements could easily be transferred transnationally. Also, the fluctuating nature of these contracts allowed collaborations such as the one between Laporte and Robert/Severini, which strengthened London's long-term position on the market. Nevertheless, the Théâtre Italien, as contracts bear witness, exercised considerable influence on the selection of singers and works for London.[10] During the years of management cooperation, the Parisian first performances of operas (Bellini: *I puritani*, 1835; Donizetti: *Marino Faliero*, 1835; Mercadante: *I briganti*, 1836), together with their casts, were in the course of a few months transferred from one city to the other.

It was especially Bellini's *I puritani* and its singers (Giulia Grisi, Luigi Lablache, Antonio Tamburini and Giovanni Battista Rubini) that influenced London's Italian opera consistently over the years (see Roccatagliati 2002, p. 200). These four singers became known as the 'Puritani quartet', and collectively exercised extreme power over London's opera managers through their popularity with London audiences (see Hall-Witt 2007, pp. 218–219 and Zechner 2017a, p. 110).[11]

The transfer of other successful productions, which had their world premiere in Italy, usually took much longer and in most cases involved the Théâtre Italien as a 'gatekeeper' for London's market. In the 1840s and 1850s, this trend can be observed in the English premieres of Verdi's operas.

Merging Paris's and London's Italian operas: Benjamin Lumley

Laporte's successor Benjamin Lumley tried to use Paris's function as a gatekeeper to London's opera market to his advantage (see Zechner 2015, p. 142). Lumley's career in opera management began in 1835 when Laporte engaged him at the King's Theatre as his legal assistant. After Laporte's sudden death in 1841, Lumley took over the sole management of Her Majesty's Theatre.[12] Lumley was fully aware of the powerful position of the Parisian Théâtre Italien, but decided to maintain the successful Paris–London connection until, in 1847, an unexpected development changed the mode of business at London's Italian opera considerably.

In 1847, Lumley lost his monopoly over Italian opera in the city when Theatre Royal Covent Garden, under the management of Frederick Gye, opened its doors as London's second Italian opera house. This led to the unique situation of two Italian opera houses competing with a similar repertoire, a similar audience demographic, and also for the engagement of star singers. The two theatres nevertheless tried to carve out their own distinct profile through strategic advertisements. With the help of the journalist Charles Gruneisen, Gye emphasized a work-oriented strategy for Covent Garden, while at the same time Lumley positioned Her Majesty's Theatre as adherent to the 'star system' (see Zechner 2017a, pp. 21–22).

Aided by relative financial stability that resulted from the engagement of the 'Swedish Nightingale', Jenny Lind, between 1847 and 1849 (see Lumley 1864, pp. 129–131), Lumley decided to take up the position of manager of the Théâtre Italien in addition to Her Majesty's Theatre. Combining the management advantages of two markets is, in the history of opera, nothing new: Domenico Barbaja (1778–1841) and Bartolomeo Merelli (1794–1879) were among the most famous figures in Italian opera to combine ventures in Naples/Milan and Vienna.[13] Lumley's management skills were compared by Harry Spillan in his 'Art-Memoir' to those of Domenico Barbaja, who was one of the very few managers who earned a fortune from his operatic enterprise – Lumley's management career did not end quite so well (see Spillan 1852, p. 21 and Hall-Witt 2007, p. 163).

In Lumley's case, the political, legal and institutional situations in the two cities during the period during which he led both opera houses (1 April 1850 to 31 March 1852) was more complex. Nevertheless, Lumley relied on the advantages of the London–Paris connection in large part due to Jenny Lind's departure from the operatic stage in 1849. Thus, Lumley's interest in acquiring a new rising star increased – for this plan, the Théâtre Italien and the press network presented a promising opportunity.

Lumley's advantage in the market was given an unexpected boost when the Théâtre Italien, under the management of the baritone Giorgio Ronconi (1810–1890), teetered on the brink of closure due to several financial difficulties (despite his contract with the French government until 1855).[14] As the Théâtre Italien was the meeting point of Paris's aristocracy and fashionable society (see Gerhard 1992, p. 34), Ronconi likewise lost the aristocratic support because of some of his management decisions. Lumley, by contrast, could rely on good relations with the Parisian aristocracy, because of hosting fashionable gatherings in his house in Fulham, where influential international aristocrats were regular guests (see *The Spectator* 23 (1850), p. 970 and Lumley 1864, p. 198).

Lumley had already built himself a good reputation in opera management due to his recent success in London with Jenny Lind and Henriette Sontag (whom he brought back on stage after she temporarily retired after her marriage to Count Rossi in 1827). To the Parisian press Lumley seemed to be the right choice for the management of Paris's Italian stage. This is illustrated by a comparison of the management skills of Lumley and his predecessor Ronconi in the *Revue et gazette musicale*. Being a singer, and having a wife who was also a singer, were considered Ronconi's greatest weaknesses. Lumley as an established opera manager, as it was implied, was more likely to act in the interest of the theatre – even despite the fact that he was an Englishman (see *The Revue et gazette musicale* 17 (1850), p. 331).

The opera-going public in 1840s Paris was more interested in the French productions at the Opéra than those at the Théâtre Italien. The Italian opera house in Paris therefore sought out an able *directeur*, someone who had the power to give 'à la scène italienne de Paris toute la splendeur, toute l'influence de ses plus beaux jours' (*Revue et gazette musicale* 17 (1850), p. 350).[15]

Because of the sudden end of Ronconi's management of the Théâtre Italien, the engagements between him and several singers for the upcoming *saison* had already been concluded. Lumley, to save time, was therefore interested in taking over Ronconi's existing engagements, something he had done before in London at Her Majesty's Theatre after the sudden death of Laporte.

Lumley was, in fact, able to form a respectable company during his first Parisian *saison* in 1850–1851, supported by the sensation of the reappearance of the prima donna Henriette Sontag, who had appeared in London beforehand. Lumley's combined management of the Italian opera houses of Paris and London

> [enabled] him to have a stronger company than either of them singly could afford; and the two consecutive seasons of Paris and London, forming one long season from November to August, will much increase his power in the advantageous production of novelties.
> (*The Spectator* 23 (1850), p. 970)

Such operatic novelties can be understood to have had an effect on both markets: an opera, as well as a singer established in London, could be new to Paris and vice versa. This opportunity to create novelty was used by Lumley, with the help of the press, in many respects. In 1848, Lumley celebrated an enormous success with Verdi's *Ernani* (first performance in London, 1845), the much-anticipated Sofia Cruvelli as Elvira, and Sims Reeves in the titular role (see Zicari 2016, pp. 106–107). In 1851, both Cruvelli and Reeves had their Parisian debuts in the same opera, which due to copyright reasons was performed as *Il proscritto*, and had not been given in Paris since its premiere six years previously (see *Revue et gazette musicale* 18 (1851), p. 113).

Giulio Alary's opera *Le tre nozze*, which was composed for the Théâtre Italien in 1851, was – the cast included – directly exported from Paris to London. It certainly helped Lumley's intention to market the production. The *Musical World*'s correspondent in Paris reported about the inimitable effect of Lablache's and Sontag's performance at the Théâtre Italien:

> There is an admirable scene in the second act, in which Louisa [Sontag] undertakes to give the Baron a lesson in the graces. The peculiarities of Lablache's physique are brought out in strong relief. In order to acquire the *aria di Francèse,* he is paraded about the stage, with his head erect, his toes pointed, and his hat under his arm, till he is ready to drop; and after a lesson in French, which leads to some ludicrous mistakes, he is (when utterly exhausted) obliged to commence a polka.
> (*The Musical World* 26 (1851), p. 219)

Figure 2.1 gives an overview of Lumley's years as manager in Paris and London. The repertoire listed here clearly reveals that Lumley's system relied mainly on the exchange of major operatic stars and works. Lumley used his Parisian enterprise for bringing French singers, such as Caroline Duprez, Jean-Etienne-August Massol or Placide Poultier, or highly acclaimed prima donnas, such as Marianna Barbieri-Nini, to the stage of Her Majesty's Theatre in order to create novelty for London's opera audience (see Spillan 1852, p. 22).

The season of 1851, in which London hosted the world exhibition, thus drew a comparatively large company of singers to the city's theatres. This also included

Cosmopolitanism in opera management 39

Her Majesty's Theatre: Season1850 (Apr.–Sept.)		Théâtre Italien: Saison1850/51 (Nov.–Apr.)		Her Majesty's Theatre: Season1851 (Apr.–Sept.)		Théâtre Italien: Saison1851/52 (Nov.–Apr.)		Her Majesty's Theatre: Season1852 (Apr.–Sept.)	
Singers	Operas	Singers	Operas	Singers	Operas	Singers	Operas	Singers	Operas
Carlo Baucardé	Bellini - *I puritani*	Ida Bertrand	Alary - *Le tre nozze*	Carolina Alaimo	Alary - *Le tre nozze*	Marianna Barbieri Nini	Bellini - *Norma*	Giovanni Beletti	Bellini - *I puritani*
GiovanniBeletti	Bellini - *I Capuleti e i Montecchi*	Caroline Duprez	Bellini - *La sonnambula*	Marietta Alboni	Auber - *Gustavo III.*	Giovanni Beletti	Donizetti - *Don Pasquale*	Ida Betrand	Bellini - *La sonnambula*
Ida Bertrand	Bellini - *Norma*	Enrico Calzolari	Bellini - *Norma*	Marianna Barbieri-Nini	Auber - *Masaniello*	Ida Betrand	Donizetti - *La figlia del regimento*	Enrico Calzolari	Bellini - *Norma*
Enrico Calzolari	Cimarosa - *Il matrimonio segreto*	Giancarlo Casanova	Donizetti - *La figlia del regimento*	Ida Bertrand	Auber - *Il prodigo*	Caroline Duprez	Donizetti - *Lucia di Lammermoor*	Anne Charton	Donizetti - *Don Pasquale*
Filippo Coletti	Donizetti - *Lucia di Lammermoor*	Filippo Colini	Donizetti - *Linda di Chamounix*	Blanche	Auber - Zerlina / *La Corbeille d'Oranges*	Enrico Calzolari	Donizetti - *Lucrezia Borgia*	Sofia Cruvelli	Donizetti - *Lucia di Lammermoor*
Claudina Fiorentini	Donizetti - *Don Pasquale*	Pietro Ferranti	Donizetti - *Lucia di Lammermoor*	Enrico Calzolari	Balfe - *I quattro fratelli /Les Quatre Fils Aymon*	Filippo Colini	Rossini - *Il barbiere di Siviglia*	Achille de Bassini	Donizetti - *Maria di Rohan*
Erminia Frezzolini	Donizetti - *L'elisir d'amore*	Claudina Fiorentini	Donizetti - *Lucrezia Borgia*	Filippo Coletti	Bellini - *La sonnambula*	Amalia Corbari	Rossini - *Semiramide*	Anna de la Grange	Gnecco - *La prova di un opera seria*
Italo Gardoni	Donizetti - *Lucrezia Borgia*	Italo Gardoni	Halévy - *La tempesta*	Sofia Cruvelli	Bellini - *Norma*	Sofia Cruvelli	Verdi - *Il proscritto/Ernani*	Rita Favanti	Mozart - *Don Giovanni*
Giuliani (Esther Eliza Julian van Gelder)	Donizetti - *La figlia del regimento*	Giuliani (Esther Eliza Julian van Gelder)	Rossini - *Il barbiere di Siviglia*	Caroline Duprez	Beethoven - *Fidelio*	Pietro Ferranti		Mdle. Feller	Rossini - *Il barbiere di Siviglia*
CatherineHayes	Halévy - *La Tempesta*	Nicola Ivanoff	Rossini - *Otello*	Federico Lablache	Donizetti - *Lucia di Lammermoor*	Claudina Fiorentini		Raffaele Ferlotti	Rossini - *La Cenerentola*
Luigi Lablache	Halévy - *Medea*	Luigi Lablache		Mdle. Feller	Donizetti - *Lucrezia Borgia*	Antonio Ghislanzoni		Claudina Fiorentini	Rossini - *L'Italiana in Algeri*
Lorenzo (Lorenzo Montemerli)	Mozart - *Don Giovanni*	Carmen del Montenegro		Pietro Ferranti	Donizetti - *Linda di Chamounix*	Lodovico Graziani		Italo Gardoni	Rossini - *Semiramide*
Sgr. Micheli	Verdi - *Ernani*	Sims Reeves		Claudina Fiorentini	Mozart - *Le nozze di Figaro*	Carlo Guasco		Luigi Lablache	Verdi - *Ernani*
Teresa Parodi	Verdi - *I Lombardi*	Henriette Sontag		Italo Gardoni	Rossini - *La Cenerentola*	Nicola Ivanoff		Mdle. Feller	Von Sachsen-Coburg- *Casilda*
Sims Reeves	Verdi - *Nino/Nabucco*			Giuliani (Esther Eliza Julian van Gelder)	Thalberg - *Florinda*	Luigi Lablache			
Henriette Sontag				Luigi Lablache		Giuseppe Pardini			
Federico Lablache				Lorenzo (Lorenzo Montemerli)		Stefano Scapini			
				Jean-Etienne-Auguste Massol		Henriette Sontag			
				Dolores Nau		Agostino Susini			
				Giuseppe Pardini					
				Placide Poultier					
				Sims Reeves					
				Sgr. Romagnoli					
				Stefano Scapini					
				HenrietteSontag					
				Delphine Ugalde					

Figure 2.1 Overview of the singers and the works during Lumley's combined management of the Théâtre Italien in Paris and Her Majesty's Theatre in London.

The information in this table has been compiled from Chorley (1862), Fouque (1881) and the periodicals *Revue et gazette musicale* and *The Musical World*.

two operatic novelties: Michael William Balfe's opéra comique, *Les quatre fils Aymon*, performed in Italian as *I quattro fratelli* and featuring operatic stars such as Sofia Cruvelli (see Lumley 1864, p. 320), and the piano virtuoso Sigismond Thalberg's *Florinda* (for the occasion of a state visit), both of which flopped and thus did not transfer to Paris (see Tyldesley 2003, p. 139; Lumley 1864, p. 315; Leech and Smith 1851, p. 156). The expensive and ambitious season of 1851 might have had an influence on the composition of the consecutive *saison* in Paris, which was composed entirely of operas performed before in London; Cruvelli's debut was not in fact without an element of novelty for the Parisian audience.

Lumley's network in selling singers went even beyond the Atlantic. Teresa Parodi, who built her reputation as an operatic star in London in 1850, unexpectedly cancelled an appearance in Paris during Lumley's management. Lumley had sold his contract with Parodi to Max Maretzek, a former employee at Her Majesty's Theatre, who had been an assistant of musical director Michael William Balfe. Maretzek managed a travelling opera company in America but desperately needed a prima donna to compete successfully against Jenny Lind's tour organized by P.T. Barnum (see Maretzek 1855, pp. 123–124).[16] This demonstrates that London's opera market and its globally operating managers served throughout the nineteenth century as a point of orientation for opera productions in North America, setting the ground for the transatlantic tours of Jenny Lind, Henriette Sontag, Giulia Grisi and Mario (Giovanni Matteo de Candia), among others (see Walter 2016, pp. 125–129).

Challenges of cosmopolitanism in opera management

At first glance, merging the Théâtre Italien with Her Majesty's Theatre not only saved Lumley contractual costs devised by Laporte (his scope of action was much more limited), it also gave him a significant amount of liberty to select singers and plan upcoming seasons. But as fortunate as the situation seemed to be for a cosmopolitan opera manager, the combination of two operatic ventures in two different countries also presented multifaceted problems to the management – something Laporte in his arrangement with Robert was not concerned about at all.

The opera houses of Paris were subsidized by the government, which required regular reports about the planning of the *saison*.[17] In London, as noted above, opera houses were dependent solely on private funding; reports to governmental or royal institutions were not required at all. This independence offered the manager a range of short-term possibilities. Lumley, who was very well accustomed to the habits in London, found it hard to accommodate the French regulations, which concerned every department of the operatic venture (see Lumley 1864, pp. 292–293). It was necessary, for example, to put aside large sums of money as deposits for future debts. This served as a guarantee for the government,[18] but conflicted with Lumley's management practice, which relied on short-term financing. To come up with the deposit for Paris, Lumley sold leases of Her Majesty's Theatre in London to gain financial liquidity (see *Neue Zeitschrift für Musik* 37 (1852), pp. 176–177) – a decision that substantially harmed his financial basis. It nevertheless illustrates how strongly the two opera houses were connected under Lumley's lead.

Furthermore, lists of the singers engaged and the works to be performed had to be submitted to the minister of interior prior to the *saison*, with the obvious purpose of making the planning more transparent (see Lumley 1864, p. 292). Lumley's success in London, though based on well-aimed and distinct gossip spread through the media, inadvertently created a large amount of speculation in the public about who was going to sing in the upcoming season. In September 1851, to note one example, the *Rheinische Musik-Zeitung* reported the following about a possible dispute between Lumley and Henriette Sontag:

> For the past few weeks rumors spread that massive discords, if not even a break, between Mrs. H. Sontag and Mr. Lumley has occurred. People talked about liabilities, which have not been met by the manager and about unsatisfied contractual demands of the singer – besides other more vulgar rumours. Everything has in fact been confirmed through Sontag's non-appearance on

stage. And everything was a farce! [...] Just at once the stimulating message about Mrs. Sontag's and Mr. Lumley's reconciliation was spread [...] Suddenly the demand of tickets increased, all boxes have been sold and the price of the seats costing one guinea, has been risen up to ten guineas – the smart manager brought the singer fresh laurels and his box office a fruitful shower of gold.

(translated by the author from *Rheinische Musik-Zeitung* 2 (1851/1852), pp. 501–502)[19]

Creating rumours, such as the above, had an impact on an international scale and were a speciality of Lumley's management. The Parisian public noticed such gossip as well, but the French minister of interior's policy of requiring companies to announce engagements obviated the kinds of insecurities and speculations that ran rampant among London readers.

Another major problem for Lumley's management was the demand for free tickets. The government-subsidized Théâtre Italien was obliged to produce an official list of free admissions. According to his memoirs, this list often contained a large number of people, which naturally narrowed his opportunity for making profit.

Another aggravating factor for the financial books was French copyright law, which influenced Lumley's daily affairs and financial prospects. In contrast to English law,

authors [referring to librettists] in France [had] the right to demand their share of the profits of every presentation of every opera derived from their own works, and even (at will) to prevent any representation whatsoever of such pieces.

(Lumley 1864, p. 293)

The legal definition of authorship thus not only included composers but also librettists and French text writers who had the right to get profits from every performance of the work concerned. A large number of stories, which were turned into libretti for contemporary Italian operas, were in fact by French writers. As a consequence, Lumley constantly had to deal with legal actions regarding copyright law, which often put the performance at risk.[20] One example in that matter was the 1852 case of Jean-François Bayard, Jules-Henri Vernoy de Saint-Georges and Gaetano Donizetti against Lumley concerning the performance of *La fille du régiment* in the Italian adaption as *La figlia del regimento*, which Lumley lost. Lumley produced the opera in London before without difficulties and wanted to introduce the Italian version to the audience of the Théâtre Italien. He did not intend to pay copyright fees to the librettists of the French version. Unfortunately, his plan did not quite square with French law, resulting in Lumley being sued (see Fisc and Wharton 1853, pp. 499–500).

Just how big a financial penalty there was for copyright infringement can be seen in Lumley's memoirs about his negotiations with the French poet Victor

Hugo concerning the rights of *Lucrezia Borgia* and *Ernani*. Not only did Hugo earn ten per cent of the gross receipts of each performance, but he was also able to stipulate the number and times of performances (see Lumley 1864, pp. 293–294). Because of Hugo, Verdi's *Ernani* had to change its title to *Il Proscritto* and was adapted considerably for its performance of 1851 (see *Wiener Modespiegel* 1 (1853), pp. 59–60).

Legal difficulties for Lumley's venture arose not only from copyright issues, but also from his contracts with singers, which regulated their engagement in both London and Paris. The legal action filed against Lumley by the *basso cantante* Lorenzo Montemerli was a major setback for the manager. Montemerli sued Lumley before the *Tribunal de Commerce* for compensation for his combined engagements in London and Paris in 1851. Lumley had decided to dissolve the contract for London with the singer, because Montemerli refused to sing a minor part in the Paris *saison*. Although the contract was signed in London, the *Tribunal de Commerce* judged the matter after French law (instead of English), and drew the conclusion that the contract could not be separated; Lumley was fined for compensation (see *Jurisprudence générale* 2 (1853), p. 137).

The following year was also legally inauspicious for Lumley, as he not only had to deal with the Paris settlement, but also a trial in London against Johanna Wagner and Frederick Gye (see Zechner 2017a, pp. 120–127 and Von Olenhusen 2014, pp. 458–465). After the *Süddeutsche* and the *Rheinische Musik-Zeitung* reported on Lumley's recent convictions it was also being reported about various artists, among them Henriette Sontag, that charges were supposedly being pressed against Lumley for compensatory damages for not paying their salaries (see *Süddeutsche Musik-Zeitung* 1 (1852), p. 96 and *Rheinische Musik-Zeitung* 3 (1852/1853), p. 918). There is no evidence to suggest that Sontag's claims were actually admitted to court, as she had already started her American tour in autumn 1852 by the time the reports in the paper appeared. It is highly likely Lumley's financial insolvency in both Paris and London would have made filing a lawsuit pointless.

Concluding remarks

London asserted its prominent position in the nineteenth-century opera industry mostly because it sat in the crosshairs of various overlapping cosmopolitan and transnational networks, which ranged from artistic, diplomatic, personal and political to managerial and medial networks. London's opera managers sought creative solutions to maintain this intense connection, which provided them with their artistic personnel and new operas. Together with Severini/Robert, Laporte established a management cooperation on the basis of pre-existent, informal networks, which further enhanced his business profile but at the same time increased the Théâtre Italien's influence on his management.

Lumley, on the contrary, tried to combine two operatic venues and further unify the network under his direct leadership, but was ultimately doomed for failure because of the establishment of a more binding legal system in both countries, not to mention the markedly different financial and political structures of both venues. All in all, the cumulative difficulties outweighed the advantages of a combined management venture. Although Lumley was familiar with the English law and the business of opera in general, a merger of such different systems could hardly be successful. The local specifics surrounding the business of opera – here exemplified with Paris and London – did not necessarily correspond with the operatic business models operating at the transnational level (e.g. Vienna/Naples). The movements of singers worked in this transnational and cosmopolitan context virtually without any limitations – business relations and their legal framework were limited and best delivered through cosmopolitan networks.

The expanding legal basis of national judicial systems, as witnessed in Benjamin Lumley's case, complicated transnational monopolies exponentially. For this reason, relations between managerial 'insiders' on all sides of the network were of crucial importance for the functionality of the cosmopolitan opera business as a whole. Hardly taking a proactive stance on matters, the opera industry as a whole was only able to react and respond passively to the fast-changing legal and political circumstances of individual nation-states in the early nineteenth century. It was the transnational networks that kept the international opera system working.

London's unique position as a cosmopolitan crossroads of the Italian opera industry furthermore supported the transfer of singers and works to the American continent. Italian opera venues and travelling operatic troupes in North America oriented itself through a common tongue to London's operatic fashions (see Preston 2001, 99–148). It is thus no coincidence that the biographies of managers who shaped the American opera business considerably, such as Max Maretzek, James Henry Mapleson and the conductor Luigi Arditi, were closely connected to London's operatic scene. It is also remarkable that Lumley's management contacts reached as far as America. This makes the international dimension of nineteenth-century opera management even more visible. It can thus be stated that cosmopolitanism formed an integral part in Lumley's management strategy; or as Octave Fouque described it in the *Histoire du Théâtre Ventadour*: 'Rien de plus cosmopolite, on le voit, que le Théâtre Italien sous la direction de Lumley' (Fouque 1881, p. 113).[21] Obviously his cosmopolitan ambitions were brought to an end by political and legal conditions of the local opera markets.

Notes

1 Among London's many journals and newspapers reporting about opera productions in Paris were *The Athenæum*, *The Times* and *The Musical World*. For the musical press in Paris see Ellis (1995). Reports about London's opera appeared in newspapers all over Europe (see Zechner 2017b, p. 62). *The Athenæum*'s long-term critic Henry Chorley had a strong orientation towards Paris (see Bledsoe 1998, pp. 50–56).
2 Gioachino Rossini supported Robert/Severini in the selection of productions and singers. For an overview of the managers of the Théâtre Italien see Levin (2009).
3 Roccatagliati (2002) presents transcriptions of some of the letters, which were originally held at the Bibliothèque national de France.

4 Apparently, he got that advice from the Italian impresario Domenico Barbaja (see Roccatagliati 2002, p. 199).
5 In 1824 Benelli fled from London in severe debt, was not able to pay the salary of the prima donna Giuditta Pasta (see Zechner 2017a, pp. 72, 79).
6 Tamburini's London debut had been long expected as his reputation of being an extraordinary singer had already been spread through the press (see, for instance, *The Athenæum* 240 (1832), p. 356; *The Harmonicon* 10 (1832), p. 127; or Cox 1872, pp. 235–236).
7 A transcription of the document is given in Roccatagliati (2002, p. 200).
8 Grisi's contract is held at the Bibliotéca Forlì, Tamburini's at the Houghton Library of Harvard University. For a transcription of the contracts see Zechner 2017a, pp. 237–242.
9 The contract contains a standardized printed text with gaps to fill in the exact names and conditions of the engagement.
10 Roccatagliati states that only Severini/Robert, with the help of Rossini, executed the recruitment of still unknown but talented singers from Italy. Laporte had to rely on their judgement. His requests for accompanying the *directeurs* for their scouting trips to Italy were turned down (see 2002, pp. 204–205).
11 Mario, Grisi's partner, substituted the tenor Rubini after the end of his career, and in 1847, this group of singers (with the exception of Lablache) left Lumley and Her Majesty's Theatre for Gye's enterprise in Covent Garden.
12 Lumley held the management of Her Majesty's Theatre from 1842 to 1852 and from 1852 to 1856.
13 Through the conclusion of long-term contracts these *impresari* often worked as agents of the Italian opera market on an international scale. See Rosselli 1984, pp. 147–148.
14 For an overview of the reasons why Ronconi was dismissed from the management see *Revue et gazette musicale* (17 [1850], p. 331). Ronconi acted as the Théâtre Italien's manager only in 1849 and 1850.
15 'to give the Parisian Italian scene back all its splendour and influence of its glorious past' (translation by the author).
16 There is also a blank contract (held at the Houghton Library, Harvard University) of Frederick Gye from the Royal Italian Opera from the 1870s for a tour to the United States.
17 In the 1850s the government subsidy comprised about 100,000 francs, although it had been much higher in the first decades of the century. See Walter (1997, p. 70). Thus it is clear that the French government wanted to have influence and insight in the planning and production process. See Lumley (1864, p. 292).
18 For necessary reports to the government for the directors of the Parisian opéra see Walter (1997, pp. 56–59).
19 'Seit mehreren Wochen zischelte man sich allerlei in die Ohren, was wenn nicht auf einen offenbaren Bruch, doch auf eine bedeutende Missstimmung zwischen Frau H. Sontag und Herrn Lumley schliessen liess. Man sprach von nicht gelösten Verbindlichkeiten des Direktors, von nicht befriedigten contractmässigen Forderungen der berühmten Sängerin, anderer noch abgeschmackter[e]n Gerüchte zu geschweigen. Alles das erhielt dadurch, dass die Sontag in der That nicht auftrat, eine scheinbare Bestätigung. Und Alles war Comödie! [...] Nun auf einmal wird durch ebenso geschickte Organe die belebende Nachricht von der Versöhnung der Frau Sontag und des Herrn Lumley verbreitet. [...] Man reisst sich um die Billets, alle Logen sind bereits vergriffen, die Guinee-Plätze steigen bis zu zehn Guineen – und der schlaue Direktor hat der Sängerin frische Lorbeeren und seiner Kasse einen fruchtbaren Goldregen verschafft!'
20 For the different legal systems of theatrical law see Walter (2016, pp. 221–228).
21 'There is nothing more cosmopolitan than the Théâtre Italien in the management of Lumley' (translation by the author).

Bibliography

Bledsoe, R., 1998. *Henry Fothergill Chorley: Victorian Journalist*. Aldershot: Ashgate.

Chorley, H., 1862. *Thirty Year's Musical Recollections*. 2 Vols. London: Hurst and Blackett.

Cox, J., 1872. *Musical Recollections of the Last Half-Century*. Vol. 1. London: Tinsley Brothers.

Davis, J. and Emeljanow, V., 2001. *Reflecting the Audience: London Theatregoing, 1840–1880*. Hertfordshire: University of Hertfordshire Press.

Ellis, C., 1995. *Music Criticism in Nineteenth Century France: 'La Revue et Gazette Musicale de Paris' 1834–1880*. Cambridge: Cambridge University Press.

Fisc, A. and Wharton, H., eds., 1853. *The American Law Register*. Vol. 1. Philadelphia: D.B. Canfield.

Fouque, O., 1881. *Histoire du Théâtre Ventadour 1829–1879*. Paris: G. Fischbacher.

Gerhard, A., 1992. *Verstädterung der Oper: Paris und das Musiktheater des 19. Jahrhunderts*. Stuttgart: Metzler.

Hall-Witt, J., 2007. *Fashionable Acts: Opera and Elite Culture in London, 1780–1880*. Durham: University of New Hampshire Press.

Leech, J. and Smith, A., 1851. *The Month: A View of Passing Subjects and Manners*. London: Month Office.

Levin, A., 2009. 'Appendix: A Documentary Overview of Musical Theatres in Paris, 1830–1900', in Fauser, A. and Everist, M. (eds.) *Music, Theatre and Cultural Transfer: Paris, 1830–1914*. Chicago: The University of Chicago Press, pp. 379–402.

Lumley, B., 1864. *Reminiscences of the Opera*. London: Hurst and Blackett.

Maretzek, M., 1855. *Crotchets and Quavers: Revelations of an Opera Manager in America*. New York: S. French.

Osterhammel, J., 2010. *Die Verwandlung der Welt: Eine Geschichte des 19. Jahrhunderts*. Munich: C. H. Beck.

Preston, K., 2001. *Opera on the Road: Travelling Opera Troupes in the United States, 1825–60*. Urbana: University of Illinois Press.

Roccatagliati, A., 2002. 'Parigi-Londra andata e ritorno: musiche, cantanti e faccendieri fra i teatri d'opera italiana (1830–38)', in La Via, S. and Parker, R. (eds.) *Pensieri per un maestro: Studi in onore di Pierluigi Petrobelli*. Turin: EDT, 193–209.

Rosselli, J., 1984. *The Opera Industry in Italy from Cimarosa to Verdi: The Role of the Impresario*. Cambridge: Cambridge University Press.

Spillan, H., 1852. *The Rival Operas in London in 1852: An Art Memoir*. London: Dix & Co.

Tyldesley, W., 2003. *Michael William Balfe: His Life and His English Operas*. London: Routledge.

Von Olenhusen, G., 2014. 'Die "Casta Diva" und der "König des Humbugs" (Jenny Lind und P.T. Barnum). Zum Vertragsrecht und Vertragsbruch von Sängerinnen im 19. Jahrhundert in Europa und den USA', *UFITA Archiv für Urheber- und Medienrecht* 2, pp. 456–465.

Walter, M., 1997. *Die Oper ist ein Irrenhaus: Sozialgeschichte der Oper im 19. Jahrhundert*. Stuttgart: Metzler.

Walter, M., 2016. *Oper: Geschichte einer Institution*. Stuttgart: Metzler.

Zechner, I., 2015. 'Die Rolle der viktorianischen Zensur bei Aufführungen von Giuseppe Verdis Opern in London', *Archiv für Musikwissenschaft* 72/2, pp. 124–145.

Zechner, I., 2017a. *The English Trade in Nightingales: Italian Opera in Nineteenth-Century London*. Translated by Rosie Ward. Retrieved 23 May 2018 from https://e-book.fwf.

ac.at/o:1090. Published in German as: *Das englische Geschäft mit der Nachtigall: Italienische Oper im London des 19. Jahrhunderts*. Vienna: Böhlau.
Zechner, I., 2017b. 'London's Italian Opera as a Topic of Interest to International Nineteenth-Century Music Criticism', in Cascudo García-Villaraco, T. (ed.) *Nineteenth-Century Music Criticism*. Turnhout: Brepols, pp. 59–75.
Zicari, M., 2016. *Verdi in Victorian London*. Cambridge: Open Book Publishers. Retrieved 23 May 2018 from https://doi.org/10.11647/OBP.0090.

Historical periodicals

Jurisprudence générale: Recueil périodique et critique de jurisprudence, de législation et de doctrine
Neue Zeitschrift für Musik
Revue et gazette musicale
Rheinische Musik-Zeitung
Süddeutsche Musik-Zeitung
The Athenæum
The Harmonicon
The Musical World
The Spectator
Wiener Modespiegel

3 Carl Goldmark and cosmopolitan patriotism

David Brodbeck

> You can be cosmopolitan – celebrating the variety of human cultures; rooted – loyal to one local society (or a few) that you count as home; liberal – convinced of the value of the individual; and patriotic – celebrating the institutions of the state (or states) within which you live.
>
> – Kwame Anthony Appiah, 'Cosmopolitan Patriots'

In his own day, if no longer in ours, Carl Goldmark (1830–1915) was widely recognized as one of the leading composers of Central Europe. A child of small-town Hungary, where his pious, Polish-born father made a modest living as a cantor and notary, Goldmark spent most of his life in Vienna, eventually rising to a position of prominence rivalling that of his friend Johannes Brahms. A Jew by heritage, although not by observance, he was, despite his Hungarian birth, a German by language and culture. And he had no sense of belonging to any ethnonational fatherland. In short, Goldmark was the very model of the late Habsburg Jewish cosmopolitan, loyal to the dynasty, devoted to liberal politics and 'universal' German high culture, and nationally indifferent.[1]

The composer's working life was roughly coterminous with the period of the Dual Monarchy of Austria-Hungary (1867–1918). This sprawling polity was established in May 1867 when the Austrian emperor, Francis Joseph I, ratified the so-called Compromise of 1867 and agreed to accept the crown as King of Hungary. Eleven officially recognized nationalities were now spread over two largely independent constitutional states under one monarch (Figure 3.1). Francis Joseph continued to reign as emperor in the Austrian half of his newly configured realm but now also undertook his separate reign as the Hungarian king. The liberal framers of the Austrian constitution were Germans, who formed a plurality but not a majority of the Austrian population; the liberal framers of the Hungarian constitution were Magyars, who likewise formed a plurality, but not a majority of the Hungarian population. Both constitutions guaranteed certain rights to members of all nationalities, although, significantly, in Hungary those rights were afforded only within the strict framework of a Magyar state.

Figure 3.1 Map of nationalities within Austria-Hungary.

Both constitutions also guaranteed full religious equality under the law. Something of the excitement and astonishment felt by the Jews at this turn of events is captured in a letter of 21 January 1868, in which Rubin Goldmark, the composer's father, conveyed the good news to several members of his family who had emigrated to New York:

> You will have learned from the newspapers and telegraph dispatches that the Hungarian Jews have been fully emancipated and that by decision of the Reichstag all faiths made equal, and also that in Vienna a new ministry made up of boisterous commoners was formed by the Reichsrat. Who in the remotest would have thought such a light would break in from dark and authoritarian Austria? Who would have ever thought that ... such a glorious and morally strong Austria would arise. Austria is the only state governed on an enlightened constitutional basis. Francis Joseph – whoever would have believed it – is the beacon of light of his century.[2]

It is obvious that the affection Goldmark's father shows here for Francis Joseph was, in the first instance, rooted in the monarch's support of Jewish emancipation. This was entirely typical of the Habsburg Jews, who became the Habsburg state's most fervent supporters. It's no secret why: the rationale for Habsburg patriotism was multinational rather than ethnonational, making Jewish participation, at least in principle, unproblematic.[3] It should be noted as well that when Rubin Goldmark writes about Austria in this letter, he is clearly referring to both halves of the newly established Dual Monarchy. This was not unusual in the years after 1867. A slightly later example can be seen in a claim Goldmark made in a letter to Eduard Hanslick written in January 1873: 'I am the only Austrian composer – Brahms and Volkmann do not count as such – whose compositions are to be found everywhere.'[4] Urging Hanslick to use his influence to help him bring about the première, at the Vienna Court Opera, of *Die Königin von Saba*, Goldmark reminded the critic that he was an *Austrian* composer in a way that Johannes Brahms (a resident of Vienna but a native of Hamburg) and Robert Volkmann (a resident of Budapest but a native of Saxony) were not. Austria is synonymous here, as it had been since 1804, with the entire multinational Habsburg realm.

Habsburg patriotism was only one aspect of Goldmark's social identity, however. He was also a modern Germanized Jew. In this regard, let us focus our attention for the time being on the Austrian half of the monarchy, where Goldmark lived for most of his life from the age of 14, primarily in Vienna but, in later years, also in his summer residence in Gmunden, in the Salzkammergut. Although the educated bourgeois liberals who came to power in Vienna in 1867 – those 'boisterous commoners,' as Goldmark's father called them – were German cultural elitists, they were not German ethnonationalists. They might be described more accurately as nationalist cosmopolitans, to borrow a notion developed by the historian Michael Steinberg for use in connection with a somewhat later period of Austrian history. Nationalist cosmopolitanism, as Steinberg notes, was based on the belief that 'enlightenment and even more specifically cosmopolitanism are German virtues' (Steinberg 2000, p. 86). In Habsburg Austria, with its emerging ethnonationalist movements, this nationalist cosmopolitanism embodied a 'civilizing' mission. As the liberal lawyer and politician Johann Nepomuk Berger put it in 1861: 'The Germans in Austria ... should strive not for political hegemony, but for cultural hegemony among the peoples of Austria.' They should 'carry culture to the east, transmit the propaganda of German intellection, German science, German humanism' (quoted in Schorske 1981, 117). Fourteen years later, when Theodor Billroth, a noted surgeon and professor at the Vienna Medical School, lamented the influx into Vienna of poorly schooled, disproportionately Jewish, and often non-German speaking students from Hungary and Poland seeking medical degrees, he was upbraided by an anonymous writer for Vienna's *Neue Freie Presse* for his seeming failure to recognize that, in his adopted home, it was 'a mission of German scholarship to make the sons of those lands familiar with the blessings of German scholarship.' (Like his friend Brahms, Billroth was a North German immigrant to multinational Austria.) And this writer goes on to note approvingly that, by seeking their education in Vienna, these young men from the East would 'avoid ... the high pressure of Hungarian and Polish national agitation' (Anon. 1875, p. 4). What we see here is evidence of how, as historian Pieter M. Judson has shown, traditional Austro-German liberals aimed to bring about a 'public integration in Central and Eastern Europe ... that would ... wipe away the backward and particularistic attitudes held by uneducated peasants and Slavs [and join] them all in a great German Liberal nation.' With respect to public and institutional life (private life was of less concern here), the liberals aimed, in other words, to assimilate the various non-German nationalities in their midst to what they saw as their own superior 'cosmopolitan German values' of education and humanism (Judson 1996, p. 385).[5]

No large social group in Austria was more receptive to this ideology than the upward-striving Jews, who were eager to modernize and shed Jewish particularisms, and to embrace German culture and liberal politics along with the Habsburg dynastic loyalty they shared with their more orthodox co-religionists (Rozenblit 1992, p. 160). Although he had little formal schooling, Goldmark was a diligent and lifelong autodidact. The many quotations from and allusions to works by the likes of Lessing, Goethe, and Schiller found in his correspondence and other writings attest to his hard-won *Bildung*.[6] And when, in a letter of 1877 to Franz von Holstein, he wrote, 'Let us never forget that we are poor German composers,' he was staking his forthright claim to cosmopolitan German culture (Goldmark 1877, quoted in Kohut 1900–1901, vol. 1, p. 19). Notably, this letter was written shortly after the première of *Die Königin von Saba* (1875), an opera set in ancient Palestine that was widely assumed, much to the composer's irritation, and partly on the basis of its use of so-called 'Jewish-Oriental triplets' in certain melismatic passages, to embody his Jewish heritage. Goldmark rejected all such claims and in fact thought of the opera as an essay, not in Jewish identity, but in the kind orientalism that was fashionable at the time, in this case written from the point of view of a cultural German (see Brodbeck 2014, pp. 70–105).

If Goldmark, then, like German liberals more generally, conflated the values of enlightenment and Germanness, cosmopolitanism and nationality, the new racialist antisemites who began to emerge in German Central Europe around 1880, sought to sever those ties. Inspired to a great degree by Wagner's writings, they viewed *Deutschtum*, not as a matter of bourgeois cultural values accessible to all who strove to attain them, but as a far more circumscribed matter of race or what we would call ethnicity. Instructive of Goldmark's reaction to this unwelcome development is his remarkable letter of 17 January 1885 to the conductor Otto Dessoff, one of his earliest Viennese champions: 'The charming antisemites have nothing to object to about my talent but everything to object to about my nose.' Here the composer is responding to Dessoff's inquiries regarding the work that Goldmark was then completing, his second opera, *Merlin*, on an Arthurian-themed libretto by Siegfried Lipiner (a friend of Gustav Mahler and, like Mahler and Goldmark, an acculturated German Jew). As suggested earlier, the composer had been greatly annoyed that *Die Königin von Saba* was assumed by many somehow to be a 'Jewish opera.' Reporting in an ironic vein, Goldmark assured Dessoff that in his new opera he had 'righteously endeavoured to avoid as much as possible [any] conscious triplets, and to be truly Christian-Norman-Celtic, as required by my libretto.' Upping the irony, he goes on to write: 'Whether I have succeeded completely, I can scarcely dare to decide – the damned triplets are in the blood, in the race.' And he wonders aloud about his prospects for a performance in Vienna, not only because he couldn't be certain of the full-throated support of Hanslick and other 'half-hearted friends,' but because of Vienna's 'zealous Wagnerians,' including those 'charming antisemites' who were more concerned with his physiognomy than with his talent.[7] By the antisemites' lights, Goldmark was a cosmopolitan, not because he embraced liberal 'cosmopolitan German values,' but only in the negative sense used by Wagner in arguing that the 'Jews have no authentic culture of their own and [thus] constitute a transnational category of cultural parasites, merely imitating the various cultures in which they live' (Loeffler 2009, p. 2).

We can illustrate this Wagnerian claim with a brief passage from August Püringer's review of Goldmark's opera *Das Heimchen am Herd* (1896) for Vienna's radical German-nationalist and antisemitic *Ostdeutsche Rundschau*. Here we find all Wagner's negative associations with Jewry – imitation in place of creativity, cunning in commerce and in the marketplace, and so on. But the critic is especially outraged by what he takes to be Goldmark's untoward quotation in the third act of the German folksong 'So viel Stern am Himmel stehen.'[8] 'We could not believe our ears,' he writes. 'We have seldom experienced a greater tastelessness and absurdity! It shows what understanding Herr Goldmark possesses for our folksong!' For Püringer, as it would have been for Wagner, it was utterly impossible for this composer to lay any legitimate claim to German culture, a racially distinct culture of which he could never be a part. Goldmark may have thought of himself as a cultural German, but he was not allowed to forget that he was a Jew (Brodbeck 2014, pp. 236–248 and 290–308).

Loyal imperial subject, cultural German and ethnic Jew in a period of increasing racialist antisemitism – to these three strands of self-perception and identity we must add a fourth, one reflective of Goldmark's birth and childhood in Hungary.[9] By contrast to their German liberal counterparts in Austria, the founding fathers of constitutional Hungary were decided ethnonationalists. These Magyar liberals equated the Hungarian state they were building with what they called *a magyar nemzet* (the Hungarian nation) and undertook a vigorous programme of Magyarization of the country's substantial populations of Germans, Slovaks, Romanians and Croats, aiming to create a genuine Hungarian nation-state where one had not existed before (see Figure 3.1). Towards this end they were abetted by a linguistic ambiguity. In Hungarian, the word *magyar* expresses two very different conceptions of belonging – both the broad category based on territorial boundaries (what in German is called *Ungar*; in English, Hungarian) and the narrow one that referred to members of Hungary's largest but by no means majority ethnic group (called *Magyars* in both German and English as well as in Hungarian). This semantic imprecision made it easy for the ethnonationalists to conflate *Magyar* ethnicity with membership in the united *Hungarian* nation.[10] Although controversial, the Magyarization campaign was remarkably successful, most notably with the Hungarian Jews, who rightly sensed that their best interests no longer lay with the Germans, as had been the case earlier in the century with older Hungarian-born Jews such as Goldmark, but with the rising Magyar elites.

It did not take long for Goldmark to experience the consequences of these developments. As a Hungarian citizen, he was now strictly speaking a foreign national living in Vienna and therefore no longer eligible, as he had been before 1867, for support of his music from the institutions of the Austrian state.[11] In 1869 he applied for and was awarded a stipend from the new Hungarian Ministry of Education. This did not go over well with the ethnonationalists, as reported in June of that year in the *Vasárnapi Újság* (*Sunday News*):

> That the Minister of Education is championing the young cause of our artistic production has met with general approval. Only the assistance given to Mr. Goldmark has been censured. He is said to be a talented composer, but not exactly Hungarian; the circumstance that he happens to have been born here does not make him Hungarian, and one doesn't understand how a Viennese German composer may receive Hungarian state support.[12]

In fact, it was not until the 1890s, by which time the composer had become world-famous and the Hungarian nation-state was largely a fait accompli, that Goldmark was embraced by the very ethnonationalists who had once shunned him as an outsider. And even if they knew that he was no real Magyar (he never learnt to speak Hungarian, for one thing), they could reap the benefits of association with his considerable international cultural prestige at no risk to their now fully secure national project. Hungarian elites increasingly put Goldmark forth as a representative of Magyar greatness and cultural achievement.

In February 1895, in an early manifestation of this belated veneration, the composer was honoured with a three-day festival in Budapest. This included performances of his chamber music, *Die Königin von Saba*, and several orchestral works, and it was capped by a large banquet held in Goldmark's honour at the conclusion of the final concert.[13] August Beer, the music critic for the *Pester Lloyd*, Budapest's leading German-language newspaper, summed up the nationalist mood that prevailed throughout the proceedings in an effusive feuilleton that began as follows:

> 'It is good everywhere, but it is best at home.' The age-old saying must pass through the mind of Maestro Goldmark as soon as he arrives in the Hungarian capital and encounters a roar of enthusiasm wherever he appears in public. ... From every salvo of applause, from every toast, he hears: 'You are with us, are at home, are a son of our fatherland. Your residence [*Heim*] is in Vienna, but your homeland is the Hungarian land [*Deine Heimath ist das Ungarland*], and your cradle stood on a patch of earth to which the mighty Balaton sent its green waves with rushing salutation'.
>
> (Beer 1895, pp. 5–6)

As the article continues, Beer not only reports on the attitudes of the Budapest public; he also claims to speak for the composer himself:

> Maestro Goldmark feels at home whenever he crosses the Hungarian border. Like a Liszt, like a Munkácsy, Goldmark too was taken by fate at a young

age to a foreign land; they all laid claim to cosmopolitanism in art; each in his own way has become a citizen of the world in the artistic sense [*Weltbürger in künstlerischem Sinne*], but they have not forgotten their Hungarian thinking and feeling and even under foreign skies have felt like children of their Magyar homeland [*Kinder ihrer magyarischen Heimath*].[14]

(Beer 1895, pp. 5–6)

Twenty years later, Countess Róza Cebrián, whose husband, Jenő Hubay, had performed Goldmark's Violin Concerto (Op. 28) at the final concert of the festival, may well have drawn on Beer's feuilleton when telling of the speech the honoured guest had given at the concluding banquet. This report is found in a reminiscence published in the Hungarian music journal *Zeneközlöny* shortly after the composer's death; its most notable passage attributes to Goldmark these words: 'My parents repose in this earth, my cradle stood here. I say to everyone with pride from my heart: I am a Hungarian [*Magyar vagyok*]!' (Cebrián 1915, p. 6).[15] Even if Cebrián's memory, whether prompted by Beer's feuilleton or not, served her well, her transcription into Hungarian of the German-speaking composer's putative final utterance gave her readers a false impression, precisely because of that linguistic ambiguity noted earlier.[16]

Rather than relying on Cebrián's memory and her retelling of the story in Hungarian, we would do better to consider the contemporaneous account of the banquet speech given by an anonymous reporter for the *Pester Lloyd* (Anon. 1895, p. 5). According to this report, Goldmark began his dinner remarks by assuring those in attendance that, although he could not speak Hungarian, he was a 'true son of the fatherland.' After all, as the newspaper reported, 'here is found the grave of his parents, here he spent his childhood, here as a mature man he has been appreciated, and these many bonds can never be severed.' Evidently the attachments Goldmark described in his speech were limited to the categories of the familial and personal; he seems to have said nothing about any feeling for the Hungarian nation-state. 'Ich bin ein Ungar!,' he might well have exclaimed, but surely not 'Ich bin ein Magyar!'

The same failure to speak of his relationship to Hungary in terms of the nation-state can be said about the remarks attributed to Goldmark by the *Pester Lloyd* 15 years later in its report of a banquet held in his honour on the occasion of his eightieth birthday in Keszthely, the small town on the shores of Lake Balaton where Goldmark was born and lived until he was four years old (Anon. 1910, p. 9). Goldmark began by sharing memories of the home town in which he had not set foot for 76 years – the house of his birth, the street on which it was located, the banks of the Plattensee (as Lake Balaton is known in German) and even the terrifying day when he was sent to the doctor to be vaccinated against smallpox. After commenting that only a man with a heart of stone would not hold dear the spot where his cradle had stood, and that this homecoming day counted among the most joyous and beautiful in his long life, he concluded with a toast to the health of his birthplace and its people [*auf das Wohl der Heimat und ihrer Bevölkerung*].

The word *Heimat*, a particularly German concept, has no direct semantic equivalent in other languages. It can sometimes refer to one's native country but is typically used more narrowly to refer to one's native region (a village or town, for example), often together with its associated landscape, customs, traditions and so forth, and it was in this narrower sense, I believe, that Goldmark made use of the term in Keszthely.[17] Yet *Heimat* can also be any place where one has planted deep roots or feels at home for whatever reason. However it is used, the word tends to express an emotional bond and has little or nothing to do with national identity.

Around the time of his Keszthely toast, Goldmark set to work on his memoirs, and at one point in that text he again invoked the idea of *Heimat*, albeit this time with a wider range of meanings than before. The passage in question was prompted by Goldmark's retelling of the day in the early 1860s when, for the first time in many years, he paid a visit to his childhood home of Deutschkreuz, in a largely German-speaking region nestled alongside the border with Austria about 80 kilometres south of Vienna. The recollection of this episode some 50 years later prompted the composer to reflect in a telling way on the matter of his self-perception:

> The Hungarian newspapers have frequently denied me, not only my right of residence [*Heimatrecht*], but also my patriotism [*Heimatgefühl*] because I do not speak Hungarian and have lived for so long outside the country. Indeed, I have lived sixty-seven years in Vienna, have educated myself from German sources in science and art, and in this sense count myself among the Germans. I love this, my second home, where I came of age [*zweite Heimat des Wachsens und Werdens*], to which I owe everything that I am and stand for. But all that has not extinguished my strong deeply rooted patriotism [*Heimatgefühl*]. Only a man with a heart of stone would fail to hold dear the soil on which his cradle stood and all the sweet recollections of childhood. In this sense, I have remained true to the place of my birth [*Geburtsheimat*].
>
> (Goldmark 1922, pp. 82–83)[18]

Of this passage's many references to *Heimat*, the first stands apart from all the others, in that it refers to a concrete legal principle. In citizenship law in both halves of the Dual Monarchy, *Heimatrecht* denoted the right to reside in a particular municipality – often but not always the place of birth – and to be entitled to poor relief by its public authorities in case of need. As it happens, extant official documents give conflicting evidence on whether Goldmark was *heimisch* in Keszthely (where he was born) or in Deutschkreuz (where he spent most of his childhood).[19] In any event, it is clear that Goldmark felt a similar emotional bond – warm *Heimatgefühl* – for both his birthplace and his boyhood home.

Again, we must distinguish between the ideas of *Ungartum* and *Magyartum*. Goldmark's was a patriotic but not a nationalist attachment to Hungary, a love of *patria* but not an identification with *natio*. (Beer's claim that Goldmark had felt himself to be a child of his Magyar homeland [*ein Kind seiner magyarischen*

Heimat] seems especially misleading in this regard; Beer 1895, p. 5). At the same time, the composer made no secret that his mature cultural work sprang from the 'German soil' of Vienna. He was explicit on this point in an essay published in 1911 but originally drafted in 1896 in response to the review by August Püringer quoted earlier in which he had been dismissed as a Jewish cultural parasite: 'I wrote ... German music. That is proved by all my chamber and orchestral works, as well as by all my operas.' He then goes on to add that he not only had lived among Germans in Vienna since childhood but also owed 'his entire artistic *Bildung* to German art' (Goldmark 1911). The locution 'living among Germans in Vienna' is telling: it reminds us that Goldmark was an acculturated German, not an ethnic one. In this case, however, he did have an attachment to the nation – to the German *Kulturnation*, not the German *Volksnation*. And the distinguishing product of the former, as suggested, was an enlightened culture – *Bildung* – that was cosmopolitan in nature.

What are we to make, finally, of the many aspects of Goldmark's identity and self-perception I have recounted here? The idea expressed in my epigraph, taken from an essay by the contemporary philosopher and cultural theorist Kwame Anthony Appiah, may point us in the right direction (Appiah 1996/1997, p. 633). To be sure, Appiah's claim that one can be cosmopolitan and rooted, liberal and patriotic, all at the same time, generalizes from a post-colonial personal story whose circumstances do not align perfectly with those of the late-nineteenth-century, Central European, historical moment in which Goldmark lived. Still, and especially if we imagine multinational Austria-Hungary as a microcosm of the entire world of diverse peoples, the story of the composer's life shows something similar to the condition the philosopher sought to describe – the possibility that one can exemplify multiple ways of belonging all at once, and that none of these must necessarily give primacy to or even really involve a nation-state.[20] Seen in this way, Goldmark, a late Habsburg Jewish cosmopolitan par excellence, may well also be judged the very model of what in a later time and place Appiah would call a cosmopolitan patriot.

Notes

1 On Jewish cosmopolitanism, see Malachi Haim Hacohen, 'Dilemmas of Cosmopolitanism: Karl Popper, Jewish Identity, and "Central European Culture,"' *Journal of Modern History* 71 (1999): pp. 105–149; idem, *Karl Popper – The Formative Years, 1902–1945: Politics and Philosophy in Interwar Vienna* (Cambridge: Cambridge University Press, 2000), pp. 46–53; and idem, 'Popper's Cosmopolitanism: Culture Clash and Jewish Identity,' in *Rethinking Vienna 1900*, ed. Steven Beller (New York and Oxford: Berghahn, 2001), pp. 171–194. On national indifference, see Pieter M. Judson, *Guardians of the Nation: Activists on the Language Frontiers of Imperial Austria* (Cambridge, MA: Harvard University Press, 2006); Tara Zahra, *Kidnapped Souls: National Indifference and the Battle for Children in the Bohemian Lands, 1900–1948* (Ithaca: Cornell University Press, 2008); and the articles by Robert Nemes, Rok Stergar, Caitlin E. Murdoch, Tatjana Lichtenstein, Roberta Pergher and Pamela Ballinger included in the special section 'Sites of Indifference to Nationhood,' edited by Judson and Zahra, in *Austrian History Yearbook* 43 (2012). As Zahra notes, 'national

indifference' is in some ways merely a new label for categories of analysis that have long circulated under other names, including, what is most relevant for Goldmark, cosmopolitanism. See Tara Zahra, 'Imagined Noncommunities: National Indifference as a Category of Analysis,' *Slavic Review* 69 (2010): pp. 93–119.

2 'Daß die ungarischen Juden vollständig emancipirt und mittels Reichstagsbeschluss allen Confessionen gleichgestellt sind, wie auch daß in Wien vom Reichsrath ein neues Ministerium aus lauter Volksmänner gebildet wurde, werdet Ihr wohl schon aus den Zeitungen und telegrafischen Depeschen erfahren haben. Wer hätte nur im Entferntesten daran denken können, daß sein solches Licht, von dem finsteren absoluten Oestreich [sic] hereinbrechen wird? ... Wem wäre es nur im Entferntesten eingefallen, daß ... ein so herrliches und moralisch gekräftigtes Oestreich hervorgehen wird? Oestreich ist der einzige Staat der nach den freisinnigsten constitutionellen Basis regiert wird. Franz Josef[,] wer hätte je gedacht, ist der Leuchtstern seiner Jahrhundert.' Unpublished letter of 21 January 1868 from Rubin Goldmark to Leo Goldmark, Goldmark Family Collection, Leo Baeck Institute, New York, Series 1, Box 1, Folder 1. Following the Compromise, the Hungarian Diet was raised to the rank of Reichstag; the Reichsrat, originally formed in 1861, continued as the legislature in the Austrian half of the monarchy. The 'new ministry' formed by the Reichsrat in 1867, to which Rubin Goldmark refers here, came to be known as the *Bürgerministerium* because the majority of its members were commoners.

3 The classic study in English of this 'golden age' in the history of Viennese Jewry is Robert S. Wistrich, *The Jews of Vienna in the Age of Franz Josef* (Oxford and New York: Oxford University Press, 1989).

4 Letter from Goldmark to Hanslick of January 1873, quoted at length in Eduard Hanslick, *Aus neuer und neuester Zeit (der modernen Oper IX. Teil): Musikalische Kritiken und Schilderungen* (Berlin: Allgemeiner Verein für Deutsche Litteratur, 1900), pp. 10–17 (here at pp. 13–15); slightly abridged in Goldmark 1922, pp. 122–124; Eng. trans. Brandeis 1927, pp. 220–223.

5 After 1867, of course, this imperative no longer applied to the Hungarians, but it remained operative for some time thereafter with respect to the Monarchy's many Slavic nationalities.

6 See in this connection Goldmark's letter of 1 January 1867 to his brother Joseph, quoted in David Brodbeck, 'A Tale of Two Brothers: Behind the Scenes of Goldmark's First Opera,' *Musical Quarterly* 97 (2015): pp. 499–541 (at pp. 506–509).

7 'Was nun die bewußte Triole anbelangt, so war ich rechtschaffen bemüht ihr so viel als möglich aus dem Wege zu gehen, und echt christlich-normänisch-celtisch zu sein, wie es ja mein Textbuch (Merlin) verlangt. Ob es mir aber vollständig gelungen ist, wage ich kaum zu entscheiden – die verfl[ucten] – Triole steckt nun einmal im Blute, in der Race. – Ich hoffe im nächsten Winter damit in Wien herauszurücken. Offen gestanden gruselt mich schon heute davor. Ich habe zwar dort recht viele laue Freunde, an deren Spitze Hanslick steht; zu diesen gesellen sich die eigentlich zelotischen Wagnerianer, und im Hintergrunde noch die lieblichen Antisemiten, die zwar nichts gegen mein Talent, aber Alles gegen meine Nase einzuwenden haben.' Unpublished letter of 17 January 1885, to the conductor Otto Dessoff, Vienna, Wienbibliothek im Rathaus. I am grateful to Thomas Aigner for drawing my attention to this letter.

8 For a fuller discussion of this review, see Brodbeck, *Defining Deutschtum*, pp. 293–295.

9 The following discussion is adapted from my essay, '*Heimat* is Where the Heart Is; or, How Hungarian was Goldmark,' *Austrian History Yearbook* 48 (2017), pp. 235–254.

10 For a still useful discussion of all the issues raised here, see Scotus Viator [Robert William Seton Watson], *Racial Problems in Hungary* (London: Archibald Constable, 1908), pp. 135–160. As Seton Watson put it (ibid., 148–149): 'The ambiguity of the phrase becomes apparent when the political unity of *a magyar nemzet* (the Hungarian nation) is under discussion; for the attempt has often been made to define "a mag-

yar nemzet" as "az uralkodó nemzet," in other words, as "the ruling race," not as the Hungarian nation.'
11 In 1863 Goldmark was the first composer to be awarded an Austrian state stipend in support of talented artists of limited means. See Ed. H. [Eduard Hanslick], 'Karl Goldmark (Zum 18. Mai 1900),' *Neue Freie Presse* (18 May 1900), 1–2; rpt. with slight emendations as '*Die Königin von Saba*: Festvorstellung zu Goldmarks 70. Geburstag [18. Mai 1900],' in Eduard Hanslick, *Aus neuer und neuester Zeit (der modernen Oper IX. Teil): Musikalische Kritiken und Schilderungen* (Berlin: Allgemeiner Verein für Deutsche Litteratur, 1900), pp. 10–17 (at pp. 10–11).
12 'Irodalom és művészt' (Művészek), *Vasárnapi Újság* (27 June 1869), p. 357.
13 On the various Goldmark performances, see A.B. [August Beer], 'Goldmark-Soirée,' *Pester Lloyd* (12 February 1895), p. 7; and idem, 'Königliches Opernhaus,' *Pester Lloyd* (13 February 1895), p. 7.
14 'Cosmopolitanism' should not be equated here with Jewishness, as with the case of the antisemites, since Beer uses the same term to describe the 'international' artistic styles of Franz Liszt and Mihály Munkácsy, Hungary's most celebrated painter, neither of whom were Jews.
15 I am grateful to Ferenc János Szabó (Franz Liszt Academy of Music) for drawing my attention to this article.
16 In a particularly misleading statement made in his feuilleton of 14 February 1895, Beer refers to Goldmark's 'magyarische Heimat'; see Beer 1895, p. 5.
17 On *Heimat*, see Celia Applegate, *A Nation of Provincials: The German Idea of Heimat* (Berkeley, Los Angeles and London: University of California Press, 1990); Alon Confino, 'The Nation as a Local Metaphor: Heimat, National Memory and the German Empire, 1871–1918,' *History & Memory* 5 (1993): 42–86; and Heimat, *Nation, Fatherland: The German Sense of Belonging*, ed. Jost Hermand and James Steakley (New York: Peter Lang, 1996).
18 Goldmark uses both the older spelling with the genitive and the plural form 'Heimatsrechte' and 'Heimatsgefühle' for 'Heimatrecht' and 'Heimatgefühle.'
19 This may explain why he used the plural *Heimatsrechte* (rights of domicile), even though one could be *heimisch* in only place at a time. On the documentary evidence, see Brodbeck, '*Heimat* is Where the Heart Is,' p. 248n.
20 On Austria-Hungary as the world in microcosm, see von Hofmannsthal, 'Krieg und Kultur,' p. 417; quoted in Moritz Csáky, 'Culture as a Space of Communication,' in *Understanding Multiculturalism: The Habsburg Central European Experience*, ed. Johannes Fechtinger and Gary B. Cohen (New York and Oxford: Berghahn, 2014), pp. 187–208 (at pp. 191–192).

Bibliography

Anon., 1869. 'Irodalom és művészt' (Művészek), *Vasárnapi Újság* (27 June 1869), p. 357.
Anon., 1875. 'Billroth über das medicinische Studium [part] II,' *Neue Freie Presse, Abendblatt* (18 November 1875), p. 4.
Anon., 1895. 'Goldmark-Banket'. *Pester Lloyd* (14 February), p. 5.
Anon., 1910. 'Die Goldmark-Feier in Keßthely'. *Pester Lloyd* (22 May), p. 9.
Appiah, Kwame Anthony, 1996/1997. 'Cosmopolitan Patriots'. *Critical Inquiry* 23, pp. 617–639.
Applegate, Celia, 1990. *A Nation of Provincials: The German Idea of Heimat*. Berkeley, Los Angeles and London: University of California Press.
Beer, August, 1895. 'Karl Goldmark'. *Pester Lloyd* (14 February), pp. 5–6.
Beer, August, 1895a. A. B., 'Goldmark-Soirée,' *Pester Lloyd* (12 February), p. 7.
Beer, August, 1895b. 'Königliches Opernhaus,' *Pester Lloyd* (13 February), p. 7.
Beer, August, 1895c . 'Karl Goldmark,' *Pester Lloyd* (14 February), pp. 5–6.

Brandeis, Alice Goldmark, 1927. *Notes from the Life of a Viennese Composer*. New York: Albert and Charles Boni. (Eng. trans. of Goldmark 1922.)

Brodbeck, David, 2014. *Defining Deutschtum: Political Ideology, German Identity, and Music-Critical Discourse in Liberal Vienna*. New York: Oxford University Press.

Brodbeck, David, 2015. 'A Tale of Two Brothers: Behind the Scenes of Goldmark's First Opera'. *Musical Quarterly* 97, pp. 499–541.

Brodbeck, David, 2017. 'Heimat is Where the Heart Is; or, How Hungarian was Goldmark?' *Austrian History Yearbook* 48, pp. 235–254.

Cebrián, Countess Róza, 1915. 'Visszaemlékezés Goldmark Károlyra' (Reminiscence of Carl Goldmark). *Zeneközlöny* 13/1 (15 March), pp. 5–9.

Confino, Alon, 1993. 'The National as a Local Metaphor: Heimat, National Memory and the German Empire, 1871–1918'. *History & Memory* 5, pp. 42–86.

Csáky, Moritz, 2014. 'Culture as a Space of Communication'. In *Understanding Multiculturalism: The Habsburg Central European Experience*, ed. Johannes Fechtinger and Gary B. Cohen. New York: Berghahn, pp. 187–208.

Goldmark, Carl, 1867. Letter to his brother Joseph of 1 January 1867, partially quoted in Brodbeck, 2015.

Goldmark, Carl, 1877. Unpublished Letter to Franz von Holstein of 18 April, partially quoted in Kohut 1900–1901, vol. 1, p. 17.

Goldmark, Carl, 1887. Unpublished letter to Otto Dessoff of 17 January. Vienna, Wienbibliothek im Rathaus.

Goldmark, Karl, 1911. 'Gedanken über Form und Stil (Eine Abwehr)'. *Neue Freie Presse* (16 April and 4 June).

Goldmark, Carl, 1922. *Erinnerungen aus meinem Leben*. Vienna: Rikola Verlag. (Eng. trans. Brandeis 1927.)

Goldmark, Rubin, 1868. Unpublished letter to Leo Goldmark of 21 January. Goldmark Family Collection, Leo Baeck Institute, New York, Series 1, Box 1, Folder 1.

Hermand, Jost, and James Steakley, eds., 1996. *Heimat, Nation, Fatherland: The German Sense of Belonging*. New York: Peter Lang.

Hofmannsthal, Hugo von, 1979. 'Krieg und Kultur'. In *Hugo von Hofmannsthal. Reden und Aufsätze II (1914–1924): Gesammelte Werke in zehn Einzelbänden*, ed. Bernd Schoeller and Rudolf Hirsch. Frankfurt a.M.: Fischer, p. 417.

Judson, Pieter M., 1996. 'Frontiers, Islands, Forests, Stones: Mapping the Geography of a German Identity in the Habsburg Monarchy, 1848–1900'. In *The Geography of Identity*, ed. Patricia Yaeger. Ann Arbor, MI: University of Michigan Press, pp. 382–406. Also in Judson, *Exclusive Revolutionaries: Liberal Politics, Social Experience, and National Identity in the Austrian Empire, 1848–1914* (Ann Arbor, MI: University of Michigan Press, 1996), pp. 269–270.

Kohut, Adolph, 1900–1901. *Berühmte israelitische Männer und Frauen in der Kulturgeschichte der Menschheit. Lebens- und Charakterbilder aus Vergangenheit und Gegenwart*. 2 Vols. Leipzig: A. H. Payne.

Loeffler, James, 2009. 'Richard Wagner's 'Jewish Music': Antisemitism and Aesthetics in Modern Jewish Culture'. *Jewish Social History: History, Culture, Society* 15/2, pp. 2–36.

Rozenblit, Marsha L., 1992. 'The Jews of the Dual Monarchy'. *Austrian History Yearbook* 23, pp. 160–180.

Steinberg, Michael P., 2000. *Austria as Theater and Ideology: The Meaning of the Salzburg Festival*. Ithaca, NY: Cornell University Press.

Wistrich, Robert S., 1989. *The Jews of Vienna in the Age of Franz Josef*. Oxford and New York: Oxford University Press.

4 The cosmopolitan muse

Searching for a musical style in early nineteenth-century Latin America

José Manuel Izquierdo König

> Our composers have genius, and have to their favour the national character and the softness of our language, and they are excellent performers; So ... Why do their works not stand up to the Mozarts and Beethovens?
>
> (Elízaga, 1823)[1]

This quotation appears in Mariano Elízaga's 1823 *Elementos de Música*, one of the first books on music published in Latin America, and – as far as we know – the first one to be published after the collapse of the Spanish Empire in the region. Elízaga was then the foremost composer and pianist in Mexico, a child prodigy who had arrived from the provincial Valladolid (now Morelia), becoming the most sought-after private teacher in the capital. Agustín de Iturbide, the tragic first ruler and emperor of independent Mexico, chose Elízaga (then the piano teacher of his wife) as his Imperial chapelmaster in 1821. Elízaga thus gained the influence to publish music editions, campaign for a conservatoire, and establish a philharmonic society, sharing some of his ideas on the subject in this little book two years later (Miranda, 1998).

It seems obvious that the book appeared in print because he was at the height of his career, and the quotation should first be understood in that context. What could be another statement about celebrated European composers, thus becomes something rather different: Mexico, like many new nations in Latin America, was just becoming independent, still menaced by the Spanish armies stationed in Peru or Cuba. But Elízaga's quote seems to deny the postcolonial spirit we certainly expect at such an historical threshold: his wording merges organically both nationalist ideas ('our composers have genius') and extremely Europeanist models (comparing those supposed local 'geniuses' unfavourably to Mozart and Beethoven), in a language that feels distinctly canonical, but also curiously fresh.

In several ways, this essay is about that quotation, and the layers of meaning that have been lost to our contemporary understanding of what we mean by 'Latin American music'. In fact, I would argue that it is difficult for us to fully appreciate the ways in which the quote might have been read by Elízaga's contemporaries. Similar comparisons and exercises can be found one or two decades earlier in Mexico's first newspapers. Haydn, for example, was more of a model than Mozart or Beethoven for the very first comparisons between 'European' and 'Mexican' music at the turn of the century. In 1806, *El Diario de México* discussed the music of José Miguel Aldana, violinist in the local cathedral and the main urban theatre, *El Coliseo*, and proposed that Aldana might be 'the American Haydn; since we do not know of any other composers better than Aldana' (*Diario de México*, 18 November 1806).[2] A year later Manuel Delgado, a pianist whose works circulated among members of the elite in Mexico, was celebrated for one of his new works, considered 'full of merits [and] show[ing] that the author is saturated with the ideas, fantasy and fecundity of Haydn' (*Diario de México*, 14 May 1807).[3]

At first sight, it seems like Elízaga is following that same trend with his active comparison to a certain European notion of 'great' music (the appearance of Haydn, Mozart and Beethoven might seem too canonical to be true). But this is not entirely true. He is not searching for the 'local Haydn', as the *Diario de México* did, but rather ascertaining that, while there are good musicians in Mexico (even 'geniuses'), their works do not compare with the works of their European counterparts. The question of 'standing up' is not about the talent of the musician, but something else, more extensive and inclusive on the one hand, but also more focused on the other: it is really about works, and their stature as objects. We need to ask ourselves what makes a Mozart or a Haydn relevant as a composer-model (and work-model) in Mexico in the 1820s, and how Elízaga was publicly speaking to his peers and future students of music, to understand how this quotation shows how the way to think about music was being reshaped in this important period of Latin American history.

We need to find other clues in Elízaga's book. Another key moment, in my opinion, is when he states his hopes in reproducing in Mexico 'the Jomelis, Tartinis, Dueros, Aydens and others that *have been* the admiration of Italy and other states of civilized [*culta*] Europe' (Elízaga, 1823).[4] This idea is also an extension of the previous ones. Tartini or Haydn are not quoted here in terms of comparative quality or value, but rather in terms of 'social-political' relevance. Elízaga thinks, in other words, that Mexico needs local composers who can serve a similar purpose to the one served by European composers in their own lands. The thought is extended, surprisingly, by another writer in Elízaga's own obituary published in 1842: 'Let England celebrate its Handels, France its Dufais, Germany its Orlandos, Spain its Beloachagas, Ramos and Salinas, Italy its Palestinis [sic, probably Palestrina], Galileis and Rossinis, and Florence its Rues, and Catania its Bellinis; Morelia also sings its Elízaga' (*El Siglo Diez y Nueve*, 29 October 1842). Elízaga's standing is situated in a series of crossroads, the national with the local, the global with the national, tradition against novelty, or the sacred and secular.

This is a central question to Elízaga's discussion, because it goes beyond our assumptions of quality and traditional points of reference (our ideas of value), to the problem of social and historical relevance. The question Elízaga proposes, I believe, is informed by a belief in the cosmopolitanism of contemporary music-making, a belief shared by virtually all his contemporary colleagues in Latin America around those decades, at the end of three hundred years of colonial rule. While we might expect, using our own values, that citizens of the independent

American nations would have wanted to break with everything European, what actually happened is the contrary. In Peru and Mexico in particular, where allegiances to Spain were the strongest (Hamnett, 2017a, p. 4), the search for republican opposition to the Spanish past was undeniably attached to the hope of new cultural, social and economic contacts with the wider world, including 'protestant' nations like England and Germany. It was, in many ways, a question of stature: of standing up to the concert of nations after years of perceived enslavement and lack of equal opportunities.

Elízaga is conscious of this dichotomy in his little book. For example, he speaks of the way in which 'gothic' ornaments pervade Mexican music, of the 'abundance of notes' and of bad taste that restricts the possibilities of developing a modern musical style (Elízaga, 1823). His use of the word 'gothic' is particularly intriguing. It can certainly be understood simply as 'baroque' or 'obtuse' in Spanish of the time, but in the 1820s it was often used to describe Spain and Spanish people (*godos*) in derogative terms. Was Elízaga's desire to foster a new style, on its own terms, also a projection of a desire to break with the Spanish mould?

That question is key to understanding Elízaga's actions: from an anglophone theoretical perspective, we tend to view the postcolonial (or the break with the colonial past), in terms of a division between the European and some kind of 'others', but this model, which might work well for parts of Asia and Africa, does not allow us to explain what was happening in urban centres and intellectual discussions in Latin America in this period (Klor de Alva, 1995, pp. 241, 268). American musicians in the new republics that sprang from the collapsing Spanish Empire had to adapt to the new problems of making music not for colonial subjects, but for citizens. The process was marked by new unexplored questions, many – but not all – of them shaped by problematic identities: What did it mean to be a 'Mexican', or 'Peruvian' or 'Argentinian' musician? Was there anything that could be regarded as 'Colombian' music? Reading newspapers, pamphlets and books of the period, questions of identity (when asked) are usually answered in cosmopolitan terms, much like Elízaga did in his book. It is not about writing Mexican, Colombian, Peruvian or American music, but rather of a shared global style that could be equally and equitably expressed by Mexican, Colombian, Peruvian or American musicians, both in performance and composition.

It is important to discuss such a perspective in terms of cosmopolitanism, even if the concept appears to have been rarely used in the period in Spanish. Cosmopolitanism takes us back to an idea of shared knowledge beyond frontiers, which is essential to the experience of Latin Americans in the nineteenth century, when frontiers were still very loosely defined. It also helps us to avoid the usual denomination of that kind of knowledge and practice as 'transatlantic', a term that obscures the north–south, Pacific and inter-American networks and discussions. I understand here cosmopolitanism in the words of Stefanie Stockhorst as an ideology that 'purposefully overrode not only social but also national and language boundaries [...] guided by universalist interests and [that] inherently possessed a dimension of transfer' (Stockhorst, 2010, p. 24). This inherent dimension of transfer considers the problem raised by William Weber, which is that cosmopolitanism seems to imply a sense of 'cultural authority' that has to be carried over through cultural transfers and appropriations (Weber, 2013, p. 211). However, the notion of 'cultural authority' can easily obscure the agency someone like Elízaga had in these issues, and the understanding of the problem of a shared cultural background that is both accepted and denied as an authority, as his quotes seem to imply.

This last point is particularly relevant to any discussion of Latin American music and intellectual productions in this period, because so much of contemporary critical research on cosmopolitanism and European cultural influence over Latin America is framed in terms of 'colonialism' and imperialism, without any layer of active agency on the part of those being colonialized. Such an approach, however, is on its own an extension of colonial ideas: the idea that history is essentially European (and 'Western') and that those beyond that framework only adapt to 'history' as passive receptors. To understand Latin American cosmopolitanism in the nineteenth century, we need to think both in terms of reception and of active engagement. Cosmopolitanism, beyond an epistemology of imposition, is an aspirational force, and for many in Latin America, aspiration is not a negative proposition: it is a central concept that shaped (and is still shaping) the lives of many, particularly non-indigenous groups in urban centres, which is exactly where we find our composers and their music, as far as it has survived in scattered archives.[5]

There have not been many studies of Latin American cosmopolitanism at the time of the Wars of Independence, in the first decades of the nineteenth century. There are even fewer studies of the Latin American Enlightenment (Alridge, 1971; Hamnett, 2017b), including those dedicated to the problematic application of the concept and word *cosmopolita*, which was only rarely used in Spanish until much later on. In 1865, the Mexican writer Bartolomé Robert used it to define a cosmopolitan person as 'an organized person, who is able to live freely [*según su libre albedrío*] in any country in the world' (Robert, 1866: 9), thus linking ideas of literacy, culture (being organized) and a social and intellectual world without frontiers. As Ronald Briggs discussed in his monographic study of Simón Rodríguez (a key Latin American intellectual of the period, and private teacher of Hispanic-American independence leader Simón Bolívar), notions of cosmopolitanism are relevant to the period in Latin America, but they are better understood as a form of 'organic cosmopolitanism', part of a deeper 'impulse to provoke transformative change' in the culture and society of Latin America, and thus – perhaps ironically – an extension of modern nation-building projects (Briggs, 2010, p. 188).

That notion of 'organic' cosmopolitanism is one I have found relevant to understanding music creation in this period in Latin America, accepting the unavoidable material and cultural differences of the region with other parts of the world, as well as what is shared and common. Sometimes, those differences are simply shaped by diverse material realities. For example, we have to take into account that printed music had sometimes a very different value in the Latin American nations, serving as a physical way to get in contact with Europe (and other parts of the Americas), similar to newspapers and books. In a region that until the 1810s was shaped by closed frontiers, and almost no personal mobility, the possibility of 'listening' to the world through scores was of particular importance, and Independence allowed for more internal and external exchange than ever before. In words of an anonymous writer published in the first number of the *Mercurio Venezolano* (a patriotic newspaper printed in Caracas in 1811), and only a few weeks before the declaration of the Independence of Venezuela: 'only recently the marvellous products by Haydn, Pleyel, Mozart and all the great Masters of Europe crossed the ocean and sounded in Caracas' (*Mercurio Venezolano*, January 1811).[6]

On the other hand, while markets and commerce were reshaped, the profession of the musicians remained mostly the same as it was since colonial times, ascribed to the Catholic church and – in major cities – to theatrical life. Changes happened slowly: with the arrival of political and economic independence, the Catholic church sustained a deep economic crisis, and only certain cities managed to keep their music chapels as extended as before. From the 1830s, the mobility of musicians became much greater, and many found jobs in opera companies or as private teachers. We need to take this into account when reading Elízaga, and his idea that we *need* to have composers that could become what Haydn or Mozart *had been* for their own countries. Producing local geniuses was not only a matter of stylistic prowess, but also of allowing for a local music scene that would grow enough to become self-sustainable, using a global (common) musical style without escaping the utmost desire for modern nation-building.

Andrés Bello, one of the foremost Latin American intellectuals of the period (Venezuelan and later founder of the *Universidad de Chile*), tried to abridge this aesthetic problem – of a global art in a national landscape – in terms of a global, shared 'Muse'. His *Biblioteca Americana*, a projected collection of literary articles published in the 1820s to foster cultural debates in the Americas, opens with a now-famous commissioned lithograph (by Richard Corbould of London) of a Muse in classical Greek attire, visiting an Indian woman and her children, who happily play with the gifts she brings: a globe, books, musical and scientific instruments. It is followed by a poem that would quickly gain canonical value, in which Bello states: 'It is now time for you [the Muse] to leave the enlightened Europe and fly to the great, new stages that the world of Columbus opens for you' (Bello, 1823).

To discuss Elízaga's quote is to think about that Muse, Euterpe if you want. It was, in Bello's terms, a cosmopolitan Muse that made the mistake of living for too long on one side of the Atlantic only, like a person who, being able to live anywhere in the world, decides to stay at home without exploring what the world has to offer. Bello invites Euterpe to become a cosmopolitan citizen. Cosmopolitanism, thus, could be understood in terms of style, but to become inherently cosmopolitan, it needed to be able to adapt to a new setting. This hypothesis constructs an interesting duality: the aesthetic conviction that there is a certain global style (a Muse), is understood side-by-side with the idea that the Muse has to be able to adapt and function in any kind of local setting, under local expectations. Composers quoted by Elízaga, appreciated thanks to scores and newspapers, sold and resold in music stores, presented a framework for that cosmopolitanism, both in professional and aesthetic terms.

We can be even more explicit: that cosmopolitan Muse came to the Americas in the form of what we call today 'the classical style', which creates some very interesting opportunities to discuss how we define such a style. It has long been discussed that the music of the late eighteenth century had a particularly cosmopolitan appeal, not only from its contemporaneity with cosmopolitan ideals in French and German culture, but also because of the material and cultural changes in the networks of music. As Heartz and Brown have put it in their *New Grove* article on 'classical': 'The interpenetration of French, Italian and German music during the last part of the 18th century [...] is indisputable' (Heartz and Brown, 2001). Even Haydn allegedly said that 'my language is understood throughout the whole world' (Head, 2005, p. 80), while Ivo Supičić discussed, years ago, that the increased production of printed music in the period implied an early form of mass and global culture (Supičić, 1981). If we accept this, following Neal Zaslaw, we should agree that, 'taking away the presence of musical genius [...] in theory, at least, one may learn as much about musical culture of this period from discussion of provincial Stockholm or Philadelphia as from discussions of cosmopolitan Vienna, Paris or London' (Zaslaw, 1989: 3).

But is that the case? What sounds on paper like an ideal cosmopolitan position, must be weighed against the balances of influences and power, as well as the social conditions for the making of music, which differed wildly from place to place. A certain cosmopolitan style (shared beyond frontiers and borderlines) functioned alongside the practicalities of making music in a certain place, with a certain national interest. Being a relevant musical voice in that global style reflects, thus, on the status of the nation (as part of a global order, a 'concert' of nations); and it is that symbiotic duality of the global and the national that sustains the notion of musical culture of someone like Elízaga.

Of course, such a hypothesis could not be sustained if this point was not made also by other musicians in this period. A year after Elízaga published his little book, the composer and flautist Juan Meserón did the same in Venezuela, with similar intentions and results. Again, and probably without knowledge of each other, Meserón suggested that his teachings of a global style of music could foster 'local' geniuses (Meserón, 1824). Much more explicit is José Escolástico Andrino, whose writings have been studied and edited by Igor de Gandarias (Gandarias, 2007). Andrino started his career in Guatemala before becoming a foundational figure for the music of Salvador. In the 1840s he mused on the thought that the names of composers 'are conserved and venerated' by each European nation, while locals 'are not able to cite our own national artists' (Gandarias, 2007, p. 4). 'A country doesn't shine only because of its politicians, soldiers and religious people', says Andrino, 'but also because of the professors in the sciences, and the artists' (Gandarias, 2007, p. 47). Andrino was proud of the many composers that 'flourished here between the 1780s and the 1820s', with no chances to study music beyond their own 'ability or genius' (Gandarias, 2007, p. 47). In Andrino's words: 'We need to convince ourselves that to give progress and honour to Guatemala we have to work adapting what needs to be modified, without leaving the fundamental [*cosmopolitan?*] groundwork, or fall into ridicule' (Gandarias, 2007, p. 5).

Elízaga, like Andrino and Meserón, found a way to promote this mixture of cosmopolitan 'groundwork' and national honour in the form of philharmonic societies, because it is in the concert, in the sound, that the cosmopolitan ideal is mostly and most successfully explored. The concept of *Sociedad Filarmónica* functions as an umbrella in Latin America in this period for a mixture of semi-public subscription concerts, dance sessions or private recitals, changing in their scope according to local traditions and laws. Of course, these societies were modelled on the 'philharmonic' notions that developed in Europe in the late eighteenth century, which guaranteed a series of performances in conditions where there was not enough power or economic resource to sustain a 'proper' concert season (see Weber, 2009). Elízaga himself considered the opportunities of a philharmonic society in a newspaper article of 1825, discussing how they served a 'postcolonial' function of both national and cosmopolitan relevance:

> this kind of project is unheard of in our lands, perhaps because of the 300 years of political imposition we suffered [...] There will be those that think that we should dedicate ourselves to more serious matters, but I will say to them [...] that music has its own philosophy, through harmony, which is rich and fecund. [...] Will we ever reach the degree in which music is accepted today in the cultivated Europe? This is precisely the objective of our Mexican philharmonic society.
>
> (*El Sol*, 28 April 1825)

The space of the philharmonic society allowed for the creation of new music that would be both national *and* grounded on the notion of a cosmopolitan, global style and practice of music. Sadly, we still know very little not only about the music of this period, but specifically about the role of philharmonic societies, what they shared and their differences. Concert programmes of the 1820s and 1830s are full of instances where the local and the 'European' become interrelated, as if they were sharing the exact same virtual musical space, one that could only have been sustained by a certain notion of music cosmopolitanism. The *Sociedad Filarmónica de Lima* (or *Academia de Música de Lima*), conducted and organized by Manuel Bañón, included the following works in one of their concerts in August 1831 (*Mercurio Peruano*, 2 August 1831):

Obertura del Otelo a toda orquesta	[Giacomo] Rossini
Cuarteto de flauta, violin, viola y violonchelo	[Pedro Ximénez] Abrill
Trio de flauta, violin y guitarra	Gatages
Dúo de flautas	Hummer [Hummel?]
Dúo de guitarras	Aficionado
Obertura a toda orquesta	Hayden [sic]
Trio de flauta, violin y violonchelo	Davienne [Francois Devienne]
Trio de guitarras	Aficionado [Amateur]
Canción nueva *La súplica*	[Manuel] Bañón

Of the nine pieces on the programme, two were explicitly ascribed to local composers (Bañón and Abrill), and two others were by anonymous – most probably local – musicians. What is important to note here is that, in sound, there was no division or fragmentation between the local and the 'foreign'; a sense of *camaraderie* is created between the works on both sides of the Atlantic, the geographical distance erased by the moment of the sounding concert when a musical style is shared. And from what we know of the music of Bañón and Ximénez, that is exactly what happened with their music.

The music written by composers working in this field of *philharmonic* endeavours is cosmopolitan in style, as well as in setting, practice and conceptualization of taste. The music written and performed in Latin America in this period has been scantily studied, since it is either lost or kept in manuscript in scattered archives, but what can be said is that it is mostly written without explicit national considerations in the way it is composed, unlike later repertoires (the famous works of Chávez, Villa-Lobos or Piazzolla). It is also quite unlike the exciting baroque reconstructions that today are perceived as the '*essential* style of Latin American postcolonial identity' (Baverley, 2008, p. 40). Written in the style of Mozart or Haydn, this is music that is difficult to accept for those who expect 'Latin American music' to be constructed in terms of difference, and thus repertoires from this period are often regarded as simple reproductions of the 'inspiration derived from a more sophisticated centre' (Mendoza, 2001, p. xiii). They are seen as peripheral works, a mere 'continuation of processes formulated outside the region', only valuable in the very rare cases in which they use local 'spices' and colour (Roldán and Caruso, 2007, p. 21).

As Leslie Bethell has written, critics and historians are usually '"disappointed" by what they find in the art and literature of Latin America of this period' (Bethell, 1998, p. 45). For Cristina Magaldi, exoticism has forced an approach by which the only interesting works are those that show 'some kind of 'cross-fertilization' with the local element' or when there was a conscious intention from scholars to 'construct a local canon […] midway between European "master works" and nationalistic pieces' (Magaldi, 2004, p. xv).[7] This has created a gulf between our expectations and those from someone like Elízaga. We have forced – or are constantly forcing – creators from this period to become what we expect of them (as it as actually happened, particularly from the perspective of concert programming and their inclusion in music histories).

It is only when we accept how the music was written, and how cosmopolitan ideals played a role in that writing, that we begin to appreciate what happened in those concerts across Latin America. Pedro Ximénez Abrill, who was one of the authors in that concert in Lima by Bañón, organized his own series of concerts in his home in Arequipa, the second largest city in Peru at the time. The newspaper advertisement for those concerts read:

> The famous artist D. Pedro Jimenes Tirado gathers in his home a philharmonic society every Tuesday evening, where the best European pieces are played along with some of his own. Entrance is free, and there are chairs in

the room. We would very much like for people with taste to meet here: perhaps measures could be taken to add more capacity to the salon, so that in the best taste the most delightful evenings could be organised more frequently; perhaps even if they had to charge something for the essential expenses.

(*Arequipa Libre*, 25 November 1828)[8]

This is almost the same wording as used by Manuel Bañón when describing his philharmonic society in Lima, performing music both local and from the 'main composers in Europe', as well as his own works (*Mercurio Peruano*, 20 February 1832). A shared, global style, implied that music like that by Ximénez or Bañón could in practice sit alongside those 'best European pieces', without any perceived contradiction or a forced sense of exoticism or difference. In fact, Ximénez's own collection of 'European' music shows such an approach, since it has partially survived in Sucre, Bolivia, and contains more than 150 scores by composers such as Haydn, Gyrowetz or Pleyel. When looking at the materiality of the sources, it is almost impossible to separate Ximénez from European works, as if the sources expanded on the notion that the Atlantic Ocean is not exactly relevant in the moment of the performance itself. In other words, in the materiality of the music he owned, in the ink and the paper, Ximénez is 'virtually' one amongst peers, a composer in a calligraphic illusion of his own cosmopolitan ideals and aspirations (see Figure 4.1 and Figure 4.2, from the collection of Andrés Orías Blüchner).

Ximénez's own symphonies number more than 30, less than a handful of which have been transcribed and performed (Izquierdo, 2016, pp. 153–184). That someone like Ximénez would write up to 40 symphonies (as he states in the catalogue of his works), only makes sense in relation to the field of philharmonic cosmopolitanism, and the symphony became a key genre in that construction of a 'cosmopolitan' composer (Izquierdo, 2017, p. 185). In Ximénez's obituary, his interest in the symphony, and the relation between the genre and a certain cosmopolitan comparison and competition, is explicitly recognized:

[Ximénez] has written [a] multitude of symphonies, most of them in four movements [*acuartetadas*], various in concertante fashion and a good number in the minor mode, which shows his preference [for this mode] in comparison with European composers, of which we see only rarely pieces in the minor, since writing a symphony in the minor mode is a task of particular difficulties.

(*La Nueva Era*, 25 June 1856)[9]

To understand such an output and the corresponding appreciation of it, it is important to focus on Ximénez as a member of a larger musical circle in which such pieces were composed, performed and listened, always in dialogue with those reputed 'best European pieces'. Not much of that repertoire has survived, but a few pieces from other Arequipenian musicians from the early nineteenth century can be found in Ximénez's personal collection, like a string quintet by Mariano Tapia, or a symphony by Lorenzo Rojas, 'no. 20'.[10] Something like a 'Symphony

Figure 4.1 Front page of MI37 (Sinfonia by Pleyel), score surviving in the private collection of Andrés Orías Blüchner.

Figure 4.2 Front page of MI47 (Ximénez's 7th Symphony), score surviving in the private collection of Andrés Orías Blüchner.

no. 20' invites us to imagine how much more music must have been lost in the region, considering how much philharmonic societies served to foster local creation. It is the same with the symphonies by Juan Meserón, of which only numbers 5 and 8 have been found, even if, at least, a 'number 9' was premiered in 1837 in Caracas, Venezuela (López, 2011).

I have been thinking about this problem a great deal in the past few years. Take, for example, the case of several overtures with descriptive titles performed in Lima in the 1830s, of which only one has been found in Peru: *La Americana* (1831) by Manuel Bañón (*Mercurio Peruano*, 27 June 1831), *La Limeña* (1838) by Pedro Zavala (Mendoza, 2001, p. 409) and *La Araucana* (c.1839) by José Bernardo Alzedo.[11] The titles invite us to think about this duality between cosmopolitanism and nation-building, between the desire to become part of a larger *concerted* global style, and the local fostering of cultural practices to develop national awareness in terms of 'civilization'. The same duality is expressed in works such as José Eulalio Samayoa's symphonies in Guatemala, written in the same period, where national considerations (his *Sinfonía Histórica* or *Sinfonía Cívica* are very explicit examples of this) work alongside classical formats, to the point where it is impossible to find what is meant to be 'civic' about his 'Civic' symphony (Gandarias, 2014).

Perhaps what had become 'civic' was the symphony itself, the sound of orchestral instruments playing together, the construction of a certain compositional style and performance practices as portrayals of a cosmopolitan culture that helped the nation to 'sound' global in what was perceived as a modern, civilized way. There is no need in this music for specific 'national' tunes or rhythms, or the search for some local 'identity markers' that people could recognize. It is music that embraces a dialogue beyond the local conditions of its creation, but without escaping those conditions either. It is not a fiction: this is music that was composed, performed and listened to. It is just that it was heard in other ways, different from the codes and expectations we have today.

The cosmopolitan music scene of the early nineteenth century in Latin America was shaped by many of the genres and styles being used in Europe and the United States during that same period, that Age of Revolutions (Hobsbawm, 2010; Hensel, 2003). However, we cannot listen to that scene globally today, using the same approaches for the entire region. Returning to Andrés Bello, the *Muse* could have been the same, but her life was drastically different from place to place, and we still do not know if her 'Latin American' sojourn was something more than a tropical holiday. Music histories seem to think in those terms, of course, with almost nothing from the Latin American music of this period being known or discussed. But, on the other hand, this is a repertoire that invites us to rethink the teleological notions of 'progress' and bordered constructions of 'identity' in the light of our own contemporary debates, of the deconstruction of both notions in the twenty-first century.

The scene where these symphonies were performed was a cosmopolitan one, defined as cosmopolitan not only because of the theoretical terms and debates, but because in the sounding sphere created by a succession of pieces, there does not seem to have been an explicit difference that would have allowed listeners to separate what was foreign from what was local. The construction of a cosmopolitan model, in this period, seems intrinsically related to an idea of synchronicity sounded through the scene of the public concert and the shared, global, repertoires. Of course, this positive reading of the phenomenon does not incorporate the very simple fact that a similar approach was not taken in correspondence, and that much of the music being written in Latin America in this period was not performed elsewhere, beyond the limits of the cities where it was composed and first performed.

Thus, this positive reading, somewhat aspirational and democratic, clashes with sustained ideas of centre and periphery, but also – undeniably – with a construction of music history defined solely as a chain of closely related influences and circles across a defined geographical plane. The music and ideas of those discussed in this chapter (Elízaga, Samayoa, Ximénez, Andrino or Meserón) are better understood in terms of cosmopolitanism, of a shared sphere of knowledge that can bridge people's imaginations across geographical and political frontiers.

Thus, we are finally confronted with a question that keeps returning in relation to the music of this period in Latin American history: In an age of revolutions, and with the weight of world-shattering independences, should not artists have been creating something transformative, new and radically different from the oppressing colonial powers? I hope that this chapter has been able to show how that kind of question fails to embrace the complex political and cultural relations of the period, and the fact that these composers were, in fact, doing something that was in its own terms utterly transformative and new, even if we are not entirely able to listen to that music as such today. Someone like Mariano Elízaga was, in my opinion, conscious of the revolutionary aspects of that cosmopolitanism and its weight.

Finally, I believe that, if we account for influence in terms of transformation, agency and appropriation that are conscious – and not just neutral or transparent – these developments in Latin America are meaningful in discussions about the extent of the globalization of music in the late eighteenth century and early nineteenth centuries, as well as on the criteria we have used – and still use – to define this period and its style as 'classical', coming solely from a restricted poietic geography and number of 'names' and compositions (Webster, 2001; cf. Murray, 2014). Might it be better to talk of a 'cosmopolitan' style? I would argue that such a concept fits better with contemporary approaches, debates and the global scale of its use, as well as with the discussions and definitions of music-making around 1800, particularly in terms of instrumental concert music. Certainly, from a Latin American perspective, there is no sense in reading the 'classical style' only in terms of a Viennese form of modernism or aesthetic, since I have found no traces of it being discussed as Viennese (and rarely even as German), but certainly there was plenty of discussion about its perceived learned universality: as music for a republic of letters or a concert of nations, to use concepts more akin to the language of the period, and perhaps more akin to a music history in a global perspective.

Notes

1 'Sus autores [de nuestras composiciones] están dotados de genio, tienen a su favour el índole naicional, la suavidad del lenguaje, son excelentes prácticos, y sin embargo de estos auxilios, ¿Por qué sus obras no pueden todavía ponerse al lado de los Mozares y Bethovenes?'
2 'Ningún inteligente ha quitado la primacia de la composicion al incomparable Haydn: el que mas ha dado el segundo lugar en la parte instrumental a su discipulo Pleyel, y en la vocal a Paisielo. Ahora bien ¿que compositores *americanos* tenemos? Los maestros de capilla de México y de Pueblo son *Europeos*. Por otra parte no se ha dicho que otro Pleyel, y acaso podria quejarse de que no se dijese que era el Haydn americano, porque no sabemos que haya otros compositor americano, mejor que Aldana. Podrá haberlo; pero no hemos oído sus producciones.'
3 'El dia de la Ascencion se celebró a la hora de nona en la Santa Iglesia Catedral con la solemnidad acostumbrada, tocandose por la orquesta [una] excelente composicion de D. José Manuel Delgado, primer violín de la Capilla [...] Es notoria la habilidad y destreza de éste profesor en éste, y otros instrumentos y el particular conocimiento y expresion con que executa la música del incomparable Haydn, y aunque sabíamos que era compositor, no podíamos asegurar, como ahora, que es buen compositor, a nuestro juicio. La produccion referida es sin duda de mucho mérito, y acredita que su autor está empapado en los pensamientos, en la fantasía, en la fecundidad de Haydn, tanto que parecen suyos muchos rasgos de aquella.'
4 Italics are mine. 'Tenemos genios a propósito para que en América se reprodujeran los Jomelis, Tartinis, Ducecs, Aydms, y tantos otros que han sido la admiración de la Italia y demás estados de la culta Europa.'
5 See, for example, the long discussion in Brazilian literature over cultural cannibalism (*antropofagia*, first proposed by Oswald de Andrade in 1928) as a form of appropriation, and its ramifications in modernism.
6 '[hacia fines del siglo XVIII] varias academias filarmónicas [...] empezaron a hacer oir los encantos de este arte; y bien pronto pasaron el océano y resonaron en Caracas, las maravillosas producciones de Haydn, Pleyel, Mozart y todos los grandes Maestros de la Europa: la execución no se limitó solo al violin; sino que [...] empesaron a familiarizarse con todos los demas instrumentos, hasta formar orquestas capaces de agradar a los oidos más delicados, y merecer la aprobación del conocedor mas exquisito.'
7 Cristina Magaldi, *Music in Imperial Rio de Janeiro: European Culture in a Tropical Milieu* (London: Scarecrow Press, 2004), XV.
8 'Un artista célebre D. Pedro Jimenes Tirado reúne en su casa en la noche de los martes de cada semana, una sociedad filarmónica, donde se ejecutan las mejores piezas de Europa, y otras de su propia composición. Se franquea la entrada gratis, y asientos en la propia sala. Desearíamos que algunos individuos de gusto, se reunieran: que se tomaran medidas para hacer mas capas el salón, y que regularisada por el estilo del mejor gusto, se proporcionase una divercion tan agradable con mas frecuencia, aunque se ecsigiera una corta recompensa, para los gastos indispensables.'
9 'multitud de sinfonías, las mas de ella acuartetadas, varias concertantes y muchas en tono menor: circunstancia que le da sin duda, la preferencia en este orden sobre los compositores europeos, de quienes vemos muy pocas obras de este género, pues la composición de una sinfonía en tono menor es de bastante dificultad.'
10 There is a second symphony by Rojas in the Biblioteca Nacional de Lima, but it has yet to be catalogued. It doesn't have a number nor title to identify it.
11 *La Araucana* is kept in the *Biblioteca Nacional del Perú* in Lima, in the collection of José Bernardo Alzedo.

Bibliography

Arequipa Libre (Arequipa): 25 November 1828.
Diario de México (Mexico City): 18 November 1806, 14 May 1807.
El Siglo Diez y Nueve (Mexico City): 29 October 1842.
El Sol (Mexico City): 28 April 1825.
La Nueva Era (Sucre): 25 June 1856.
Mercurio Peruano (Lima): 2 August 1831, 16 July 1831, 20 February 1832, 27 June 1831.
Mercurio Venezolano (Caracas): January 1811.
Alridge, A. Owen, 1971. *The Ibero-American Enlightenment*. Urbana: University of Illinois Press.
Baverley, John, 2008. 'The Colonial Baroque', in *A Historical Companion to Postcolonial Literatures: Continental Europe and its Empires*, ed. Prem Poddar, Rajeev Shridhar Patke and Lars Jensen. Edinburgh: Edinburgh University Press,536–41.
Bello, Andrés, ed., 1823. *La Biblioteca Americana*. London: G. Marchant.
Bethell, Leslie, 1998. *A Cultural History of Latin America: Literature, Music and the Visual Arts in the 19th and 20th Centuries*. Cambridge: Cambridge University Press.
Briggs, Ronald, 2010. *Tropes of Enlightenment in the Age of Bolivar: Simon Rodriguez and the American Essay at Revolution*. Nashville: Vanderbilt University Press.
Elízaga, Mariano, 1823. *Elementos de música*. Mexico: Imprenta del Supremo Gobierno.
Gandarias Iriarte, Igor de, 2007. *Escritos de José Escolástico Andrino (1817?–1862). Pedagogía, periodismo, crítica e historia musical centroamericana en el Siglo XIX*. Guatemala, Mexico: Universidad de San Carlos de Guatemala.
Gandarias, Juan Andrés, 2014. *José Eulalio Samayoa. Sinfonía Cívica - Sinfonía Histórica*. Guatemala: Editorial Universitaria.
Hamnett, Brian, 2017a. *The End of Iberian Rule on the American Continent, 1770–1830*. Cambridge: Cambridge University Press.
Hamnett, Brian, 2017b. *The Enlightenment in Iberia and Ibero-America*. Chicago: Chicago University Press.
Head, Matthew, 2005. 'Haydn's Exoticisms: 'Difference' and the Enlightenment', in *The Cambridge Companion to Haydn,* ed. Caryl Clark. Cambridge: Cambridge University Press, 77–92.
Heartz, Daniel and Bruce Brown, 2001. 'Classical', *Grove Music Online. Oxford Music Online*. Oxford University Press. http://www.oxfordmusiconline.com/subscriber/article/grove/music/05889 (accessed August 27, 2018).
Hensel, Silke, 2003. 'Review: Was There an Age of Revolution in Latin America? New Literature on Latin American Independence', *Latin American Research Review* 38/3, 237–249.
Hobsbawm, Eric, 2010. *The Age of Revolution. Europe 1789–1848*. London: Phoenix Press.
Izquierdo, José Manuel, 2016. 'Las sinfonías de Pedro Ximénez Abrill y Tirado: Una primera aproximación', *Anuario de Estudios Bolivianos Archivísticos y Bibliográficos* 22, 153–184.
Izquierdo, José Manuel, 2017. 'Transcripción y comentarios de la 'Lista de obras' de Pedro Ximénez Abrill, un catálogo de compositor latinoamericano a mediados del siglo XIX', *Resonancias* 41, 185–193.
Klor de Alva, Jorge, 1995. 'The Postcolonization of the (Latin) American Experience: A Reconsideration of 'Colonialism', 'Postcolonialism' and 'Mestizaje'', in *After*

Colonialism: Imperial Stories and Postcolonial Displacements, ed. Gyan Prakash. Princeton, NJ: Princeton University Press, 241–268.

López Maya, Juan de Dios, 2011. 'El primer movimiento de la Sinfonía N°5 de Juan Meserón: Una forma sonata ortodoxa en el repertorio sinfónico venezolano', *Musicaenclave* 5/1.

Magaldi, Cristina, 2004. *Music in Imperial Rio de Janeiro: European Culture in a Tropical Milieu*. London: Scarecrow Press.

Mendoza, Daniel, 2001. *Music in Ibero-America to 1850: A Historical Survey*. London: Scarecrow Press.

Meserón, Juan, 1824. *Explicación y conocimiento de los principios generals de la Música*. Caracas: Tomás Antero.

Miranda, Ricardo, 1998. 'Haydn en Morelia: José Mariano Elízaga', *Revista Musical Chilena* 190, 55–63.

Murray, Sterling E., 2014. *The Career of an Eighteenth-Century Kapellmeister: The Life and Music of Antonio Rosetti*. Rochester: University of Rochester Press.

Robert, Bartolomé, 1866. *El hombre ¿Es cosmopolita? ¿Puede o no aclimatarse sobre todos los puntos del globo?* Madrid: Imprenta de Antonio Peñuelas.

Roldán, Eugenia y Marcelo Caruso, 2007. *Imported Modernity in Post-Colonial State Formation: The Appropriation of Political, Educational, and Cultural Models in Nineteenth-Century Latin America*. Frankfurt am Main: Peter Lang.

Stockhorst, Stephanie, 2010. *Cultural Transfer through Translation: The Circulation of Enlightened Thought in Europe by Means of Translation*. Amsterdam: Rodopi.

Supičić, Ivo, 1981. 'Early Forms of Musical Mass-Culture and the Musical Publishing', *Musicological Annual* 17/2, 183–189.

Weber, William, 2009. *The Great Transformation of Musical Taste: Concert Programming from Haydn to Brahms*. Cambridge: Cambridge University Press.

Weber, William, 2013. 'Cosmopolitan, Regional and National Identities in 18th-Century European Musical Life', in *Oxford Handbook of the New Cultural History of Music*, ed. Jane Fulcher. Oxford: Oxford University Press, 209–227.

Webster, James, 2001. 'Between Enlightenment and Romanticism in Music History: 'First Viennese Modernism' and the Delayed Nineteenth Century', *19th-Century Music* 25/2–3, 108–126.

Zaslaw, Neil, 1989. *The Classical Era. From the 1740s to the End of the 18th Century*. London: The Macmillan Press.

Part 2
Music and cosmopolitanism in the twentieth century

5 An 'intricate fabric of influences and coincidences in the history of popular music'
Reflections on the challenging work of popular music historians

Franco Fabbri

What we now call 'popular music' is not simply the Anglo-American mainstream from the Tin Pan Alley era (or even the 1950s) onwards, with the optional addition of a handful of local genres, styles and scenes: it is an extremely varied set of music events that became visible and audible almost simultaneously in many places around the world since the early decades of the nineteenth century. If we accept this idea, then a popular music historian has to face a number of challenging questions. Which sources are available? How reliable are they? In which languages were they conceived, written or recorded? Within which theoretical framework can they be studied?

In the year 1878

Let me start by commenting on two pictures. The first is the famous photograph portraying Thomas Alva Edison and his tinfoil phonograph: it was shot in Washington in April 1878; Edison had patented his invention at the end of February.[1] In my courses on popular music history I always show this photograph, along with a short video demonstrating the phonograph's actual functioning, other images showing how recordings were made and technical details about the evolution of the 'talking machine' and of its rival, Berliner's gramophone. Usually, at this point of the course, students seem to be relieved, and to finally acknowledge that the course is *really* about popular music: even if recorded music they listen to every day mostly originates from digital files, they respect what they call 'the vinyl,' or even the CD (some of them identify the CD with any phonogram in history), and are interested in the origin of sound recording and reproduction. But, especially, they incline to identify popular music, and its history, with recorded sound. They are in good company: with the exception of those (and they are not few in number) who think that popular music coincides with the Anglo-American mainstream from the late 1940s on, many popular music scholars and musicologists seem to adhere to the commonplace that the history of popular music begins with Edison's invention, with very few precursors (often limited to Stephen Foster and the minstrel show).

The other picture is more problematic. It shows the Estudiantina Española, a *tuna* (an amateur string band formed by students) from the University of Salamanca, acclaimed by the crowds in Paris, on Mardi Gras, 4 March 1878, just a few weeks before Edison was photographed in Washington, and a few days after the phonograph was patented. More than one illustration can be found about the huge success of the Estudiantina during that visit, on the occasion of the Exposition Universelle.[2] The Expo that music historians usually remember is the one that took place in 1889, when the Eiffel Tower was completed, and a Javanese gamelan orchestra gave a performance, which a certain Claude Debussy attended and listened to attentively. But the Estudiantina Española's performances were no less influential: soon that ensemble of (mostly) plucked strings instruments and singers – seen and heard in the *ville lumière* – became the model for many other similar bands, which were called *estudiantinas* even if they were not amateur bands formed by students, but groups of professional entertainers whose most common instrument was not the Spanish *bandurria*, but the Neapolitan mandolin.

So, we come to the question: is the Estudiantina's picture as clearly relevant to popular music history as Edison's phonograph? *Tunas* had been in existence for centuries, long before concepts like 'popular music' were acknowledged, and this is a very good example to discuss the problematic issue of how popular music from the nineteenth century can be related to pre-existing traditions, be they rooted in 'folk' or 'art' music from the preceding centuries. If the tradition and the music of the tunas existed from the thirteenth century, does that mean that it isn't popular music? Or that popular music had been existing since then? The basic misunderstanding that creates such dualistic (and useless) interpretation lies in assuming that belonging to a class in a taxonomy (or a 'category', or a genre) is an essential quality of the music, rather than determined by the way music is conceptualized within a community, which is what actually happens. The key for understanding if and how the Estudiantina Española's music can be related to popular music is the process by which, in the eighteenth/nineteenth centuries, the ideas of 'classical music' and 'folk music' were invented, and 'popular music' became the conceptual space where music not belonging to the classical canon or to the Romantic idea of folk could be placed. In 1878 that process was well on its way.

Although canons later became an important feature of popular music as well, its origins as a *refugium peccatorum* – as music that obviously did not comply with the necessary features prescribed to be classical (of universally accepted value, composed by geniuses from the past, or in a similar style) or folk (peasant, illiterate, exotic) – made innovation (or novelty) and imitation two contrasting but equally important impulses for the creation of new material. The role of the Estudiantina Española's Parisian success can be understood within this framework. Success in Paris, at that time in history, meant success anywhere else in Europe (and beyond); on the other hand, anywhere else an estudiantina was new, for a while, compared to existing orchestras and repertoires. This has to be proven, though. A few methodological issues arise: which documents can we find, in order to demonstrate and understand the spreading of new ensembles, styles and genre conventions? Are such documents reliable? Historical musicologists are familiar with such issues, but popular music poses special problems here, as a kind of music that – by definition – does not need to be saved for the future: scores, photographs, posters, ads, magazines and records, are easily thrown away. Sure, there are collectors of such items, but usually they collect what remained after attics or cellars were 'cleared' from 'useless' stuff, at some point in the nineteenth or twentieth century. Only a few years ago, RAI (Italy's state radio and television) got rid of all singles' sleeves in its huge record library; and public libraries (in Italy, again) destroyed many collections of entertainment weeklies and youth magazines from the 1950s and 1960s. When a field of study has a low academic status, and its object is considered culturally and socially irrelevant, disdain percolates down to decision makers at all levels.

Such a shortage of original documents also explains why the Internet can be a good source only for certain periods in history: anything that was shown on television sooner or later ends up on YouTube, but printed matter (including photos) is much harder to find. It is easy to find, for example, television appearances of bands with two electric guitars, an electric bass, and a drum kit, around 1960. When I want to discuss with my students how The Ventures and The Shadows contributed to the canonization of that line-up, I have ways to entertain them.[3] But it is not as easy if the subject is plucked-string ensembles between the end of the nineteenth century and the beginning of the twentieth. Let me go back to two or three decades after the beginning of their international success, considering the repertories of Greek/Turkish *estoudiantínas*.[4] Such small orchestras were popular in Istanbul and Smyrna in the 1900s and 1910s. Mandolins and mandolas were their main instruments; they performed in cafés and in sporting clubs established by and for Levantines (Western European citizens, who lived and made business in Ottoman cities) and were chosen as performers during recording campaigns by Western European record companies. The success of some of those records and songs can be demonstrated by the fact that different recordings and matrices exist for the same title. One of those hits is 'Smyrniopoúla,' a song recorded in Istanbul for Odeon (58579) by the Smyrnaikí Estoudiantína Kostantinoúpoli (1908–1909) and in Smyrna for Gramophone (6-12688 and 6-12688X) by the Ellinikí Estoudiantína (1909). The former version is scored for violin and piano (or *santúri*, or cimbalom), the second for a small wind ensemble (brass was substituted for strings in many arrangements in the age of mechanical recording, even with bands who used strings for live performances of the same song). The (male) voice sounds lighter in the former, more operatic in the latter.

Information about *estoudiantínas* and their recordings can be found in *Σμύρνη. Η μουσική ζωή 1900/1922. Η διασκέδαση, τά μουσικά καταστήματα, οι ηχογραφήσεις δίσκων*[5] (Kalydiótis 2002), and one of the versions of 'Smyrniopoúla' is included on a CD that was sold with the book. 'Smyrniopoúla' is a Greek adaptation of 'Nanninella,' by Antonio Barbieri and Vincenzo Di Chiara, released by publisher Bideri: in Naples it had been a big success in Elvira Donnarumma's performances at the Eldorado theatre in 1906;[6] the song was also recorded by I Figli di Ciro (1909), a group of *posteggiatori* (three violin players and a mandolin player/singer) performing only in restaurants.[7] I have not been successful in my efforts to find a copy of I Figli di Ciro's recording (on Gramophone/Zonophone), neither was I able to determine if their recording was made earlier or later than the *estoudiantína*'s versions, although the most probable channel for the transmission of the song across the Mediterranean was the score. In the twentieth century Italian music publishers sold scores for voice-mandolin and/or accordion (just the melodic line and chords), which were known in the business and by musicians as *mandolini*.[8] So, to say that the mandolin was one of the most powerful media for the dissemination of popular music from the nineteenth century up to the mid-twentieth century should not raise eyebrows among music scholars.

Smyrna and Naples[9]

Let us go further with mandolins and *estoudiantínas* in the early decades of the twentieth century, namely with 'Tik-Tak,' one of the most popular songs from Smyrna, recorded for Orfeon Records in Istanbul around 1912 by the Estoudiantina Tchanakas Smyrne (Orfeon 11578) and covered since then by many important Greek musicians, from Markos Vamvakáris (1905–1972) to the Estoudiantina Néas Ionías (established in 1998) to Glykería (1953). The song is now credited as 'traditional' (παραδοσιακό). However, authors were not credited on records in Greece and Turkey until the 1920s (Kalydiótis 2002, p. 132), so any attribution of 'Tik-Tak' to anonymous authors is posthumous and is not based on any evidence. The authors of 'Nanninella' are not credited on the label of 'Smyrniopoúla,' but their absence does not make 'Smyrniopoúla' traditional. Of course, I am aware that suggesting a non-traditional and maybe foreign origin for 'Tik-Tak' – one of the songs that embody the feelings of a number of Greeks about Asia Minor's *katastrofí*[10] (as expressed in the comments of the several versions uploaded on YouTube, for instance) – can be very unpopular among Greeks. However, until the equivalent of 'Nanninella' is found, we can only observe some facts. First, when 'Tik-Tak' was recorded in Istanbul, 'Smyrniopoúla/Nanninella', recorded by an *estoudiantína*, it had been one of the greatest hits in Smyrna and Istanbul for three years. Second, like 'Smyrniopoúla', 'Tik-Tak' is based on a repeating progression from a minor mode verse to a major mode refrain. Third, verse and refrain (in both songs) are based on an alternating tonic-dominant pattern, respectively in the minor and major mode. Fourth, there are two similar melodic phrases, one at the end of the verse of 'Smyrniopoúla,' the other at the end of the refrain of 'Tik-Tak,' when the harmony shifts back to minor mode. Fifth, the main subject of 'Tik-Tak' (the heartbeat of a lover sounding like a clock) was common in European popular songs at the beginning of the twentieth century, one example being 'Tticchete ttì tticchete ttà,' a 1902 Neapolitan song composed by Vincenzo Di Chiara (the author of 'Nanninella') with lyrics by Giovanni Capurro (known for being the lyricist of ''O sole mio'). One can guess at least that the unknown authors of 'Tik-Tak' had been exposed to examples of Western European (including Neapolitan) popular song and that their work was influenced by them.

The harmonic-melodic character of 'Tik-Tak' is irreducible to Asia Minor's (makam-based) music styles. The song is described in the booklet of the

Estoudiantína Néas Ionías CD (*Smyrna*, EMI Music Greece 7243 5980462 0, 2003) as based on the 'makam Nihâvend with Tsargiah;' but the explanation in the next line, 'minor scale that changes to major,' is more convincing, especially if referred to the Estoudiantína Néas Ionías' performance itself. The same applies to the recording [of 'Tik-Tak'] Markos Vamvakáris made in the 1960s, although the addition of a diminished chord in the instrumental intro and breaks, played by an accordion, gives the song a more Slavic (*hasaposérviko*) flavour. But the minor-major verse-refrain progression and the alternate tonic-dominant patterns are there as well.

I was struck by the song's irreducibility to Greek 'oriental' modal styles even before I started considering the possible influence of Neapolitan models (Fabbri 2009, p. 189). On the island of Tilos, during religious festivals in the summer, at some point (certainly after the publication of the Estoudiantína Néas Ionías album) one distinguished member of the community, an amateur performer and an expert of local music traditions, asked the invited professional musicians to play and accompany 'Tik-Tak.' I was present at the event and knew the song already, and I wasn't surprised to hear that the musicians (a very competent trio resident in Rhodes who performed traditional songs and dances at festivals all around the Dodecanese) 'could not' play the song as I knew it. It was difficult for them to even conceive a dominant (fifth degree) to tonic (first degree) relationship of the kind that structurally informs 'Tik-Tak.' Usually, when they are requested to accompany a melody that suggests such a relationship, they use different 'dominants,' either on the second or on the flat seventh degree, but of course the harmonic flavour of the song changes accordingly. That's why the performance of 'Tik-Tak,' during Tilos *paniyiria*, never took off.

Of course, we have to consider Finnish musicologist Risto Pekka Pennanen's warning, when he writes that some researchers

> consider modal harmony without noticing that characteristic chord progressions for some makam-based *dhromoi* do not differ from those of common practice harmony. Apparently these researchers have not been able to identify these *dhromoi* and have taken them for Western major.
>
> (Pennanen 1997, p. 76)

But 'Tik-Tak,' in my opinion, is beyond the borderline, and I wonder if Pennanen's remark shouldn't be reversed here: why try to interpret 'Tik-Tak' as makam-based, when it is so clearly a Western-styled piece? Moreover, as I went on listening to the Tilian version of 'Tik-Tak' year after year, I realized that another reason for the uncertain melodic and harmonic shape of the song was the fact that the singer, after the second line of the section in major, went on with the melody and lyrics of *another* song, 'Dhen se thelo piá' (interestingly, another piece featuring in the Estoudiantína Néas Ionías album: it was originally recorded by the Ellinikí Estoudiantina in 1908). 'Dhen se thelo piá' is very similar to both 'Tik-Tak' and 'Smyrniopoúla': this made me wonder if the authors could be the same. But 'Smyrniopoúla' was originally 'Nanninella' by Antonio Barbieri and Vincenzo Di Chiara: what about the authors of 'Tik-Tak' and 'Dhen se thelo piá'?

My doubts about the origin of the two songs could not be solved by investigating local sources: their Greekness appeared to be unquestionable, there was something 'sacred' in their belonging to the pre-*katastrofí* Smyrna repertoires. The musicians of the trio from Rhodes maintained that 'Tik-Tak' had been brought to the islands by a 'viol player' from Nysiros; I didn't dare to reply, noting the coincidence of the song's arrival to Tilos with the publication of a CD. So, I finally decided to ask a distinguished scholar of Neapolitan song, Raffaele Di Mauro, who in the first instance could only confirm my suspicions, without any proof. But later he circulated the recordings of the two songs I had given him to a few record collectors; one of them, Ciro Daniele, recognized the songs immediately. Di Mauro then provided me with the scores and original recordings. The version of 'Dhen se thelo piá' with Neapolitan lyrics (i.e. the original), is 'Mbraccia a me', by Antonio Barbieri and Vincenzo Di Chiara, published in 1908 by Bideri, Naples.[11] The version of 'Tik-Tak' with Neapolitan lyrics is 'Questa non si tocca?,' by Antonio Barbieri and Vincenzo Di Chiara, published in 1910 by Bideri, Naples.[12] On the score, below the title, writing informs that the song was presented at the 'Tavola rotonda' contest during the 1910 Piedigrotta Festival.[13]

If we add the information provided by Kalydiótis (2002, p. 130) about 'Nanninella'/'Smyrniopoúla,' we find that three Neapolitan songs by the same authors, published by the same publisher, became hits in Smyrna, with Greek lyrics, in 1908, 1908–1909 and 1912. The fact that the names of the authors (either the original lyricist and composer, or the Greek translator/adapter) do not appear on record labels is not surprising, and does not imply unethical copyright practices, if we remember that phonomechanical rights were first introduced (in the US) only in 1909. Rather, the 'string of hits' of 1908–1912, if it is not the result of a very unlikely series of coincidences, suggests that in the 1900s–1910s (at least) a significant communication channel existed between Neapolitan publishers and Smyrnian musicians; we are informed by Kalydiótis that music shops in Smyrna were owned by Italian or French entrepreneurs, and that the majority of piano teachers for the rich Levantine families were Italian. Unfortunately, the great fire of 1922 must have destroyed all possible evidence of such musical exchanges.

We could even go further, at the risk of departing completely from the entire rebetiko scholarship. Let us consider a song composed and recorded in 1927 by Andónis Diamantídhis, aka Dalgás (1892–1945): 'Mánghas,' whose status in the canon of rebetiko is similar to that of 'Funiculì funiculà' in Neapolitan song. 'Mánghas' could easily pass for a Neapolitan song. Its melody and chord progression are similar not only to several Neapolitan songs, but also to songs in Neapolitan style composed in the 1950s and 1960s by singer-songwriters like Georges Brassens or Fabrizio de André, with their turnarounds in minor mode featuring changes to the major seventh (flattened) degree and third degree (relative major), like in the instrumental intro (and breaks) in 'Mánghas:' i – iv (= i – V – i) – bVII – III – V – i –V7 – i.

In this case, we are probably closer to the territory where Pennanen's remark is valid, although Philip Tagg's objections to conventional musicologists' dichotomy between 'tonal' and 'modal' should also be considered. According to Tagg, tonality is a concept that refers to all kinds of tonal relations, including modality; so, Western popular music can be described as 'tonal' only inasmuch as it is, largely, modal (Tagg 2009).

Again, we have to take into account a few musical and paramusical factors as well: Dalgás was born in Istanbul and became one of the best-known musicians in the Asia Minor exile community in the late 1920s; like these other musicians he had no familiarity with the bouzouki. In fact, his recording of 'Mánghas' does not feature bouzouki, with the result that one of the songs most closely associated with a canonic rebetiko character, the *mánghas* (the lyrics consist of a woman's complaint against a particular *mánghas*[14]) is not accompanied by that canonic rebetiko instrument, but by violin, *santúri* and guitar. As an Anatolian Greek, Dalgás was certainly familiar with Italianate *kantádhes* (a genre that included Italian operatic arias and parlour songs, as well as Neapolitan popular songs), no less than with more 'oriental' genres. So, the idea of 'Mánghas' as a hybrid shouldn't sound overly strange, but it would serve to date the influence of Neapolitan song on rebetiko back by a couple of decades.

Influence

But, what is 'influence'? It is a widely used critical concept in music journalism, and also adopted by artists and the recording industry. It connotes similarity, and so it functions like classification concepts such as genre, style, scene and school, as a workaround to avoid more specific descriptions of the lyrical or musical text, or of the way they are performed or recorded. Recommender systems on the Internet (Celma 2010) try to fulfil the same need (to create associations among similar items, without describing them). Influence appears as one of the recommendation factors in the iTunes Store.[15] There is also a recommender system fully based on influence, inflooenz.com, which promises to 'Discover who influenced your favorite artists.'[16] Influence adds a hint of causality, suggesting a reason for similarity, and this may explain the concept's success among music critics, who often seem to be aiming at a (rather trivial) rationalization of music history.

But influence is not a trivial concept. When similar content elements or stylistic traits are found in different texts, influence may be (or may not be) operating. Here I will concentrate on the poietic aspects of influence, rather than on its post factum effects. Harold Bloom elaborated a theory of influence in literature, developing the idea of anxiety generated in poets by the implicit challenge posed by precursors who influenced them; Bloom's *The Anxiety of Influence* (1973) was considered at the time of its publication as one of the foundations of a new approach to literary criticism. Bloom's insistence on hierarchic values, and on the opposition between 'strong' and 'weak' poets, as well as his faith in the dominance of the Western canon, make his theory old-fashioned in our age. However, some of Bloom's suggestions could probably be applied to songwriters, without implying any resemblance or identification with poets. The six basic concepts, or 'movements,' or 'revisionary ratios', developed by Bloom in order to explain various modalities of influence – *clinamen, tessera, kenosis, daemonization, askesis, apophrades* (Bloom 1973, pp. 14–16) – apply independently of their author's canonistic views. One of the most important suggestions we can draw from these categories is that influence is an *active* (rather than passive) process on the side of the influenced. In other words, the influenced is the agent of influence: which should be obvious, if we were not misled by the usage of a passive form. Also, to some respect 'to be influenced by someone' is a euphemism for emulating, imitating, copying or even stealing from someone. If we were to adopt Bloom's hierarchies, we could say that 'stronger' songwriters would admit they stole from someone, while 'weaker' ones would maintain they were influenced. Of course, the idea of influence as exerted actively by an influencer onto an influenced is implicit in constructs like acculturation, commercial and media dominance and cultural imperialism, but it must also be noted that often in music history processes of influence were initiated before influencers were massively visible/audible in the context of the influenced. A paradigmatic example is offered by Bob Dylan. It wasn't until the publication in 2004 of his *Chronicles* that Bob Dylan disclosed he had been strongly influenced by Bertolt Brecht, 'the antifascist Marxist German poet-playwright whose works were banned in Germany' (Dylan 2004, p. 272), and especially by 'Pirate Jenny,' one of the ballads in *The Threepenny Opera* (1928), to which he was exposed during an off-Broadway performance of Brecht songs in the early 1960s (Dylan 2004, pp. 272–276). After listening to that and other pieces, dismounting and reassembling them many times, for weeks, Dylan would compose and sing 'in a few years' songs such as 'It's Alright, Ma (I'm Only Bleeding),' 'Mr. Tambourine Man,' 'A Hard Rain's A-Gonna Fall,' and others: in 2004 he maintained that without Brecht's example those songs would never have been born (Dylan 2004, p. 287). In the same autobiographical book, Dylan wrote that he was also influenced by French existentialist playwright and novelist Jean Genet: 'The songs I'd write would be like that' (Dylan 2004, p. 89). None of Dylan's critics before 2004 ever dared to suggest an influence on Dylan by the best-known German communist poet in the twentieth century, or by one of the exponents of the Parisian intellectual scene that had produced *engagé* songs, such as Boris Vian, Georges Brassens and Léo Ferré. Models and their copies are created out of the desire that they be transported into a new context: as Borges said, 'poets create their precursors' (quoted in Bloom 1973, p. 19). Communities of any magnitude whose members adopt the conventions of a certain genre or style may be formed by and around examples offered by individual works (i.e. music events) or by other genres or styles (Fabbri 2012).

Displaying information

Usually, relations among genres, styles, scenes and individual artists are displayed visually using geographical maps (a good tool anyway, if one wants to show how the Romani people moved from Rajasthan to Andalusia, or how elements of Uruguayan candombe and Cuban habanera were incorporated in tango), or conceptual maps, where genres or styles are represented by bordering surfaces (a metaphor that became popular in music journalism in the 1980s, despite its limits

Influences and coincidences in popular music 85

and undesirable consequences, see Fabbri 2007), or by parallel flows (Cichowlas and Lam 2014), a system that looks very convincing, even when data are unreliable, or by 'bubbles', as in Paul Lamere's Music Popcorn.[17] But in my opinion the complexity of such relations can be represented more effectively by means of digraphs or directed graphs.[18] An elementary example is the digraph (Figure 5.1) that summarizes some of the relations among genres and individual artists I commented on in an essay on singer-songwriters (Fabbri 2016a).

A better-looking digraph, albeit probably far too complex, is the one created by the application Music Genre Mapper, based on Wikipedia.[19]

Finding ways to display visually the complex web of relations that constitutes the 'intricate fabric' of popular music history is very important for teaching. It is even more important nowadays, when students have easy access to all sorts of information on any kind of music, but often have no clue on how to relate those pieces of information to one another. And I would add that spatial metaphors – more than simply visual representations – have been the conceptual backbone of many historical accounts of the arts, and especially of music. For example, the

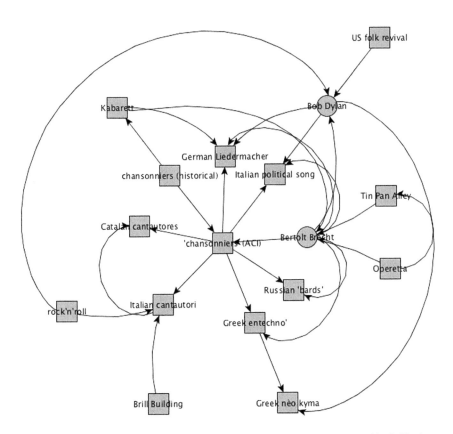

Figure 5.1 Digraph summarizing some of the relations between genres and individuals.

canon of European 'classical' music, since the mid-nineteenth century, has been based on the idea of a 'line,' progressing from Renaissance polyphony to the age of basso continuo, then to the 'classical style,' Romanticism and late-Romanticism, so-called atonality and expressionism, dodecaphony and serial composition, and so on, with names like Bach, Beethoven, Brahms and Boulez as points on the line. On the other hand, all critics of the idea of such a unidimensional music world have pointed their fingers at the incongruities of its underlying graphical representation, showing that there is music – also 'classical' music – outside the line, be it Italian and French opera, Sibelius, Ives, Bartók, Shostakovich, Britten or Cage (and we should not wonder if one of those critics was Adorno). Of course, there is a full multidimensional music world outside that line, which includes art music from non-European cultures, traditional music, jazz, popular music and whatever else communities in the world call 'music'. This is, I believe, the best contribution that individual musicological disciplines like ethnomusicology and music anthropology, jazz and popular music studies, could give to the development of musicology in general: showing that the music universe is multidimensional, and that the 'line' is an old scheme, created mainly for political reasons, which lost all its original heuristic value, if it ever had any. But this, of course, is not without consequences.

Conclusions: so-called popular music

In Italian official musicological circles, they now call it 'cosiddetta *popular music*,' so-called popular music (and 'popular music' is italicized, in order to clarify that it is a foreign expression). Schubert's Lieder are 'i Lieder di Schubert' (not italicized), Rossini's Ouvertures are not 'so-called' (nor are they translated into 'Aperture') and people in those circles would not say 'il cosiddetto *flamenco*,' nor 'il cosiddetto *jazz*,' nor even 'il cosiddetto *rock and roll*.' Some older musicologists, who until recently used to call popular music 'musica di consumo' (i.e. commercial music, which is only relevant because it is sold) or 'musica leggera' (using the same category officially adopted by Fascism for classifying radio programmes), are worried by the growth of popular music studies in the Italian academy. A well-known comment by one of those musicologists, uttered in 2002, was: 'What will happen when someone who graduated with a dissertation on rap holds a chair of music?' On the one hand, those musicologists, and ethnomusicologists, are still strongly influenced by old prejudices against popular music; on the other hand, the Italian academic system, based on the institutionalization of disciplinary fields, is still rooted in the nineteenth-century taxonomy of music studies, and allows for the existence of just two disciplinary fields, musicology (including Adler's historical musicology and music theory) and ethnomusicology. Popular music is not mentioned in the description of those disciplinary fields. Although the study of popular music is now possible in Italian conservatories (where only instruments and history are taught, however, and no research is carried out), the hostility against popular music studies in some musicological and ethnomusicological circles is commonly acknowledged. Once a cinema scholar met one of my PhD students, and told him: 'Alas, you are one of those who study popular music? In my department they burn them!'

If cosmopolitanism, as a critical concept, can be contrasted with universalism (Beck 2006; Scott 2018), then nothing is further apart from cosmopolitanism than the Eurocentric universalism of some Italian historical musicologists. Besides, historical studies seem to be outside the field of vision of most Italian ethnomusicologists. So, the issue is not popular music, but the fact that the very existence of popular music studies brings the blanks and omissions in conventional music studies to the surface. And this, I believe, is not happening only in Italian universities (for a comparative overview of conventional musicologists' attitudes towards popular music, see also Fabbri 2019).

Studying popular music implies considering a large body of music practices with a historical perspective, spanning over at least two centuries; it also implies considering those practices in relation to non-strictly musical practices and conventions; and it also implies considering music that could also be classified as 'classical' or 'traditional.' In short, studying popular music implies invading repeatedly the fields of existing musicologies, and this helps explain why most conservative musicologists are against popular music scholars, but not against sociologists or cultural studies scholars, most of whom avoid any reference to music as a structured language, and declare themselves incapable of dealing with the alleged 'technical' aspects of it; nor against media scholars, for similar reasons; nor against sound studies scholars, as they include music in the more general category of sound, but definitely not in a Cagean or music-anthropological perspective, the result being that – in many studies on sound – music as an independent concept seems to disappear; nor even against rock criticism, as the idea to confine popular music history and practices to the Anglophone mainstream from the 1950s onwards is, for conservative musicologists, soothing. Any music critic or scholar who is content with the hegemony of conventional musicology, and not willing to point at the inconsistencies of the discipline, is welcome. Popular music studies were established with an explicit reference to interdisciplinarity, as indicated in the Statutes of the International Association for the Study of Popular Music: 'The aim of the Association is to provide an international, interdisciplinary and interprofessional organization for promoting the study of popular music. A guiding principle should be that a fair and balanced representation of different continents, nations, cultures and specializations be aimed at in the policy and activity of the Association'. Whoever follows that guiding principle, it seems, is dangerous for the pre-existing hierarchies and disciplinary boundaries established in academia. And, I would add, is dangerous exactly in the same way as those who have been accused of cosmopolitanism in history, because they have no homeland, no faith, no obedience. In both cases, you will never hear or read an explanation for the resulting prosecution: one is cosmopolitan, therefore dangerous, as Ždanov would say; as a popular music scholar one is dangerous because one's ideas are dangerous, and they are dangerous because such ideas are the ideas of a popular music scholar.

So, it would make little sense for me to go any further than this, in order to show proofs of the obstacles popular music scholars find on their way, especially in Italy. When a system is based on the control of a territory and on a conspiracy of silence, evidence is hard to find and – when found – it is boring, or seemingly inconsistent (like that 'so-called', appended with suspect regularity to all references to popular music). Rather, I have followed a different and, I hope, more entertaining path to demonstrate my argument, that is, that the historical study of popular music implies the reference to an extreme variety of sources, which in turn demand responses to a variety of methodological issues, sometimes disturbing quiet assumptions established in the history of existing disciplines.

Notes

1 It can be seen here: https://en.wikipedia.org/wiki/Phonograph#/media/File:Edison_and_phonograph_edit1.jpg.
2 One picture can be seen here: https://commons.wikimedia.org/wiki/File:Estudiantina_Espagnola_défile_en_voiture_à_Paris.JPG.
3 See, for example, https://www.youtube.com/watch?v=owq7hgzna3E (The Ventures) and https://www.youtube.com/watch?v=C8COV_x7MB4 (The Shadows).
4 *Estoudiantína* is the transliteration of the Greek name for these orchestras (εστουδιαντίνα).
5 Smyrna. Music life 1900/1922. Entertainment, music shops, recordings.
6 According to Kalydiótis (2002, 130) the song – described as 'an Italian success from 1905–1906' – was recorded several times in Smyrna, and also in the USA.
7 About the success of 'Nanninella' in Naples, and about I Figli di Ciro, see Pesce 2005, 20, 89.
8 The writing under the title was: 'Canto – mandolino e fisarmonica', or 'Canto – mandolino o fisarmonica'.
9 This section is based partially on Fabbri 2016b.
10 Greeks usually call *katastrofi* the disasters of 1922–1923, from the killings and fire in Smyrna to the displacement of Ottoman Greeks that followed the Treaty of Lausanne.
11 A recording by Vittorio Parisi can be listened to here: https://www.youtube.com/watch?v=BUw8vby1QjY.
12 A 1916 recording by Amelia Bruno, with King's Orchestra conducted by Edward T. King, Victor matrix B-17664 (recorded in New York on 11 May 1916) is listed here: https://adp.library.ucsb.edu/index.php/matrix/detail/700002698/B-17664-Questa_non_si_tocca.
13 Piedigrotta is a traditional religious festival held annually in Naples in the night between 7 September and 8 September. In 1839 (some sources indicate 1835) a song contest was established, which lasted until 1860, and then from 1876 until the 1960s.
14 A *mánghas* is a ruffian or rogue.
15 Contents are provided by All Music Guide.
16 Developed by Argentinian programmer Hernán Gauna, Inflooenz is powered by APIs provided by Last.fm, YouTube and Rovi (by Rovi Cloud Services Documentation). Here is a comment on Inflooenz by recommender systems specialists: '… influence is a wider concept than similarity: while still related to a starting point (the favorite artist), the user can come up with new music that it's not (sic) "more of the same",' see http://www.programmableweb.com/mashup/inflooenz. Accessed 22 July 2018.
17 http://static.echonest.com/popcorn/. Accessed 22 July 2018.
18 https://en.wikipedia.org/wiki/Directed_graph. Accessed 26 July 2018.
19 http://blog.dr-ivan.com/2009/10/18/music-genre-mapper-now-available/. Accessed 22 July 2018.

Bibliography

Beck, U., 2006. *Cosmopolitan Vision*. Cambridge, MA: Polity Press.
Bloom, H., 1973. *The Anxiety of Influence. A Theory of Poetry*. New York and Oxford: Oxford University Press.
Celma, Ó., 2010. *Music Recommendation and Discovery. The Long Tail, Long Fail, and Long Play in the Digital Music Space*. Berlin and Heidelberg: Springer Verlag.
Cichowlas, A. and T. Lam, 2014. Explore the History of Pop -- and Punk, Jazz, and Folk -- with the Music Timeline. http://googleresearch.blogspot.it/2014/01/explore-history-of-pop-and-punk-jazz.html
Dylan, B., 2004. *Chronicles, Volume One*. New York: Simon & Schuster.
Fabbri, F., 2007. Browsing Music Spaces: Categories and the Musical Mind. In A. Moore ed., *Critical Essays in Popular Musicology*, 1st ed. Aldershot: Ashgate, pp. 49–62.
Fabbri, F., 2009. Ritorno a Tilos ('la musica che c'è'). In P. Bohlman, M. Sorce Keller and L. Azzaroni eds., *Antropologia della musica nelle culture mediterranee. Interpretazione, performance, identità*. Bologna: Clueb, pp. 181–190.
Fabbri, F., 2012. How Genres Are Born, Change, Die: Conventions, Communities and Diachronic Processes. In S. Hawkins ed., *Critical Musicological Reflections*. Aldershot: Ashgate, pp. 179–191.
Fabbri, F., 2016a. 'The Songs I'd Write Would Be Like That'. Transnational Influences between Poets, Composers, Singer-Songwriters. In I. Marc and S. Green eds., *The Singer-Songwriter in Europe. Paradigms, Politics and Place*. London and New York: Routledge, pp. 23–35.
Fabbri, F., 2016b. A Mediterranean Triangle: Naples, Smyrna, Athens. In G. Plastino and J. Sciorra eds., *Neapolitan Postcards*. Lanham, MD: Rowman & Littlefield, pp. 29–44.
Fabbri, F., 2019. Quelle musicologie pour la chanson? In P. Abbrugiati, S. Chaudier, S. Hirschi, J.M. Jacono, J. July, C. Pruvost eds., *Chanson. Cartographier un genre en mutation*. Aix-en-Provence: PUP.
Kalydiótis, A., 2002. *Σμύρνη. Η μουσική ζωή 1900/1922. Η διασκέδαση, τά μουσικά καταστήματα, οι ηχογραφήσεις δίσκων*. Athens: Music Corner & Tínella.
Pennanen, R.P., 1997, The Development of Chordal Harmony in Greek Rebetika and Laika Music, 1930s to 1960s. *British Journal of Ethnomusicology*, Vol. 6, pp. 65–116.
Pennanen, R.P., 1997. *Westernisation and Modernisation in Greek Popular Music*. Tampere: University of Tampere Press.
Pesce, A., 2005. *La Sirena nel solco. Origini della riproduzione sonora*. Naples: Alfredo Guida Editore.
Scott, D.B., 2018. Cosmopolitan Musicology. In E. Kelly, M. Mantere and D.B. Scott eds., *Confronting the National in the Musical Past*. Abingdon: Routledge, pp. 17–30.
Tagg, P., 2009. *Everyday Tonality. Towards a Tonal Theory of What Most People Hear*. New York and Montréal: The Mass Media Scholars Press.

6 Mapping musical modernism

Björn Heile

Western music, and modernist music in particular, is assumed to be universal, transcending its cultural and geographic origin. Open any history of twentieth-century music and you are likely to find chapters on prominent styles, techniques, composers and works in chronological order. Typically, there is an acknowledgement of sorts of 'the non-simultaneity of the simultaneous',[1] in that, for instance, many textbooks devote two parallel opening chapters to fin-de-siècle Paris and Vienna respectively and similarly cover events in Russia, Hungary and sometimes Britain or the USA in separate chapters. This happens, for instance, in Glenn Watkins's *Soundings* (1995), which devotes Part 1 to Vienna 1885–1915, Part 2 to Paris 1885–1915 and Part 5 to 'Emerging National Aspirations' (covering Hungary, Russia, Spain, England and the USA) and, with some idiosyncrasies, in Richard Taruskin's *Oxford History of Western Music* (2010). Paul Griffiths (2010, 1995, 1981, 1978) and Arnold Whittall (2003, 1999, 1977) largely prefer stylistic or thematic orderings more in line with straightforward universalism, although in Whittall's *Exploring Twentieth-Century Music* (2003, pp. 1–14) a concern for place is prominent in the first chapter.[2]

Typically, it is the achievements of individual composers, in these cases chiefly Alexander Scriabin, Béla Bartók, Manuel de Falla, Benjamin Britten and Charles Ives respectively, that appear to necessitate this recognition of cultural geography as an inconvenient fracturing of an imagined singular arrow of history. The standpoint from which the significance of composers and their works, which governs inclusion or exclusion, is judged is rarely questioned. After all, on what basis can we say that the work of de Falla or Britten is more important than that of Heitor Villa-Lobos or Alberto Ginastera, and that of Ginastera more than that of Juan Carlos Paz – to say nothing of Ruth Crawford, Lily Boulanger or Elizabeth Lutyens or, for that matter, Samuel Coleridge-Taylor? In any case, Europe and North America remain the limits of diversity: if any composers from outside 'the West' are mentioned – which is astonishingly rare – they are generally treated as individual exceptions, rather than as reasons to redraw the geographical purview. Indeed, none of the books discussed above has much if anything to say about music from Latin America, Asia or Africa, and there are no chapters on, say, Japan or Argentina on the model of those on Hungary or Spain. Paul Griffiths's *Modern Music and After* shuttles between Western (!) Europe and North America in its earlier chapters to settle into a mid-Atlantic mix for the remaining ones. Although he mentions a smattering of non-Western composers, even major figures, such as Toru Takemitsu (who also makes a brief appearance in Whittall's *Musical Composition*), Toshio Hosokawa, Unsuk Chin and Tan Dun, are mentioned only in passing; none of their music is discussed in any detail, never mind made the subject of a chapter or sub-chapter. Latin America and Africa remain entirely white spaces. Taruskin is entirely silent on the issue: the only mention of composers from outside what he explicitly defines as the West – Europe and North America – that I was able to find are passing references to Ginastera under the heading of the 'Chopinesque miniature' in the volume dedicated to the nineteenth century and to Tan Dun, in relation to a work composed when Tan had long settled in the USA. Robert P. Morgan's *Twentieth-Century Music* (1991) is virtually alone among textbooks in including a chapter on Latin America (possibly looking back to an earlier vision of pan-Americanism as indicated by its subtitle), and *The Cambridge History of Twentieth-Century Music* (Cook and Pople, 2004) devotes a chapter to African music, by Martin Scherzinger (2004) – which has only earned it deprecating remarks from at least one reviewer (Holloway, 2005, p. 338).

Maybe the work of the composers just mentioned, and many others, is not of sufficiently high quality, influence or prominence to warrant inclusion, but it is not as if Taruskin and Griffiths – to focus on the most recent publications – only concern themselves with household names (whether on the concert stage or in academic discourse) and avoid minor figures. Beyond the effects of ignorance, neglect or inertia, we cannot exclude that bias and exclusion play a role here. There appears to be still a reluctance to admit that what used to be known as 'Western (Art) Music' – a term that has become deeply problematic – is no longer the exclusive property of Europe and North America; indeed, in his introduction (reprinted in all volumes), Taruskin (2010, p. x), for one, explicitly restricts 'the West', which is so prominent in his title, to Europe and North America, so it is only consistent that he proceeds by ignoring the rest of the world. Acknowledging the importance of classical music of Western origin in the non-Western world would touch on anxieties about the nature of 'Western' art and culture and what distinguishes that heritage and therefore 'our identity' from others. The claim of universality has come back to haunt us.

Another issue that is being occluded by a historiography based exclusively on notions of artistic quality or influence is the complexity of the music-historical situation at any given time and place. It may well be that, from a universalist position, 'all that matters' about the music of, say, Spain and Hungary in the first half of the twentieth century are the works of de Falla and Bartók (possibly with Zoltán Kodály thrown in for good measure) respectively, but in their own contexts these composers typically represent only one of many competing centres, movements and positions. What about the 'other stories' that do not fit into the chronology of masterworks or the geography of national styles, such as, for instance, dodecaphony in Hungary or Spain, or, for that matter, Russia, Japan and Panama?

This is not to dismiss the importance of notions of, variously, quality, importance or influence, but to point out to what extent their assessment is dependent on the perspective of the observer, who is never neutral or objective, and that they are not the *only* issues that should matter. If musicology is to be more than connoisseurship, music history has to be more than a succession of masterworks. Musical culture, as practised and experienced by different people at specific times and in particular places, tends to be far more diverse and heterogeneous than a canonic history based primarily on stylistic innovation in composition. An understanding of musical developments therefore needs to be based on a broader appreciation of the various trends and forces at work in any moment and how they are mediated by diverse musical works and performances as well as their reception by audiences.

To be fair, national, local and regional music histories have generally provided fuller, more complex pictures of musical culture. The problem here tends to be a lack of a genuine comparative dimension: for one thing, national (or regional or local) musical cultures do not exist in isolation – and, in truth, hardly anyone claims that they do – for another, their specificity can only be shown through comparison – and what could act as an appropriate counterpart? Too often, it seems to me, national music cultures are directly compared to a notion of 'universal music history', which, at best, is a distillate of various national cultures that does not exist in this form anywhere.

It is not easy to conceive of alternatives to the 'view from nowhere' represented by universal histories on the one hand and the particularity of national, regional or local histories on the other. One approach, taken by the Balzan musicology project led by Reinhard Strohm, envisaged a 'global history of music'. As the blurb to the collected volume arising from the project explains (Strohm, 2018):

> The studies presented in this volume aim to promote post-European historical thinking. They are based on the idea that a global history of music cannot be one single, hegemonic history. They rather explore the paradigms and terminologies that might describe a history of many different voices.

This is an exciting, commendable approach; at the same time, however, it is also clear that it represents an ideal that can never be fully realised: note the multiple qualifications in 'explore the paradigms and terminologies that *might* describe …'. The amount of detail and the number of different, potentially competing voices would make this impossible to produce if not to read.

As I have argued elsewhere (Heile, 2019), the global diffusion of notions of musical modernism is itself an interesting story – the very stuff of music history – and one that hasn't really been told. It cuts across national histories, but it is also largely ignored by universalist histories, with their concentration on stylistic innovation and singular masterpieces that are overwhelmingly concentrated in a small number of centres. It is my contention that the peripheries and semi-peripheries are likewise the subject of music history, and not only in their local particularities but in their commonalities and in their relations to centres. How can we do justice to the multitude of places in which modernist music (or any other music for that matter) has been composed, performed, listened to, written and thought about? I have previously proposed a comparative approach, involving a selected number of case studies (Heile, 2019). On this occasion, I suggest mapping as another, complementary approach.

Mapping as method

Following the 'spatial turn', mapping has become a prominent approach in the arts and humanities (among others, Bodenhamer et al., 2010; Roberts, 2012; Stephenson et al., n.d.). Not surprisingly, it is more commonly used in subjects such as history, archaeology and anthropology (to say nothing of geography), but there is also increased attention in musicology. My own interest in using maps to illustrate music history was initially sparked by a number of articles by the literary theorist Franco Moretti in *New Left Review*. In 'Conjectures on World Literature' Moretti (2000) argues that the dominant concept of national literatures is deeply problematic since most innovations are rapidly emulated internationally, proving that authors look everywhere for inspiration and are not constrained by their own supposed national tradition. His method eschews the traditional close reading of individual canonic work but is instead based on analysing the bulk of literary or cinematic production according to simple identifying criteria, an approach he has termed 'distant reading'. His use of maps was illustrated in a series of articles entitled 'Graphs, Maps, Trees' (Moretti, 2003a, 2004a, 2004b) that was subsequently expanded into a book (Moretti, 2007). For example, he maps the 'percentages of the top-five box office hits' of US comedies in different countries around the world (Moretti, 2003a, p. 87, 2007, p. 25).[3] Within musicology, Sara Cohen's work on live music in Liverpool was pioneering (Cohen, 2012a, 2012b; Lashua et al., 2010); however, like most musicological mapping exercises, it concerns urban micro-geography, rather than global macro-geography, which is my focus here (which is not to diminish its importance). Another important source of inspiration were the maps produced by my colleague Eva Moreda Rodriguez. Her maps on Spanish exiled musicians, for instance, have a global dimension, but due to their focus on Francoist Spain remain comprehensible.[4]

Like other forms of visualisation, mapping can help to present complex and voluminous data in intuitively comprehensible ways. What is even more important for my purposes is that maps are (relatively) non-hierarchic and non-linear:[5] they allow users to explore data according to their own interests in ways that are not quite possible with written text, for example. Indeed, the idea of processing all the information contained in a map – as is common with books – does not quite make sense, at least for reasonably complex maps. We typically consult maps with a particular interest or question in mind and we go back to them frequently. To continue the comparison with writing (the most common mode of music historiography and hence the most obvious alternative), maps are more akin to encyclopaedias or dictionaries than other forms of historical writing. And just like encyclopaedias and dictionaries invite aimless browsing occasioned by the serendipitous randomness of the alphabetic succession of entries, so maps invite our eyes to wander (and our minds to wonder).

It goes without saying that only certain information can be shown on maps and that there are typically limited possibilities for contextual interpretation and evaluation or narrative elaboration. That is why maps are often best employed in combination with written text as a form of illustration. That said, online maps allow the integration of significant amount of text through hyperlinks and pop-up windows, and they also enable crowdsourcing by encouraging users to contribute items either directly, through Web 2.0 interfaces, or by contacting the map administrator.[6]

As previously mentioned, my intention was to illustrate the global dissemination of musical modernism. One immediate problem is that musical modernism is an abstract concept that cannot be directly shown. What does it mean for modernist music to reach a country, city or region and how can we tell: by the first performance(s) of modernist works, the first modernist compositions, the first discussions of the music in print or in private diaries and letters? And what counts as 'modernist music' on this occasion: atonality (by no means a clear-cut concept itself); non-periodic rhythm; the avoidance of traditional forms, textures and timbre combinations? The definition and nature of modernist music are hotly debated and in constant flux, and there are no hard-and-fast definitions or clear-cut criteria. Traditional music histories tend to employ a mixture of the criteria and categories mentioned, typically in an informal but ideally judicious manner. But while this approach works well at a national, regional or local level, it is not suited to the global dimension: again, the sheer amount of material – in principle, all national, regional and local histories combined – renders this an impossibility; universalist histories typically restrict themselves to an innovation history from the start.

For these reasons, maps can only show *aspects* of modernism in music, proxies as it were. Yet, on reflection, this is just common sense: places cannot 'be modernist'; they can only play host to musical activities that could be described as modernist, and the extent to which they do is not absolute but relative, according to certain criteria. The maps included here (see Map 6.1 and Map 6.2) and presented online (https://musicalmodernism.arts.gla.ac.uk/) are based on three categories: membership of the International Society for Contemporary Music (ISCM) (by date), the first dodecaphonic composition by country (with composer, date and title), and major conservatoires (typically the first by country). They were produced in phases and advertised on social media and musicological email lists and web forums, to crowd-source additions and corrections, which are listed in the 'Credits' section on the accompanying website.[7] Before explaining the different categories in more detail, it is important to reveal what may be the biggest problem. The only realistic possibility was to use a current political world map as a basis, which leads to a problematic 'presentism'. Using historical maps for different points in history or even a dynamic map would have been too complex, and historical change or fixed reference points are not the ostensible focus. The difficulty this creates in such cases as the Soviet Union or Yugoslavia and their respective successors or the two Germanies is obvious. This problem is not confined to mapping, however, but is shared with reference works, which likewise prioritise present-day states and institutions.

For the ISCM map, my solution was to count the entry date of the predecessor state, if, following its dissolution, the successor state remained a member or rejoined the organisation. Concretely, the Soviet Union joined the ISCM in 1924, and Russia and Ukraine retained membership, but Belarus and the Asian republics did not, so the former are assumed to have been members since 1924 (even if their individual membership is more recent), whereas the latter are assumed never to have been

Map 6.1 ISCM members: darker shading indicates earlier entry dates; hachures stand for former members, dots for non-members. The building symbols represent important conservatoires, darker shading indicating earlier foundation.

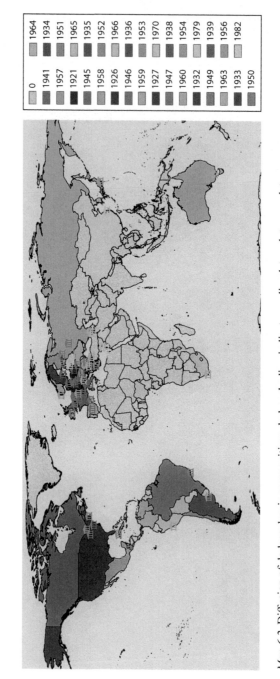

Map 6.2 Diffusion of dodecaphonic composition: darker shading indicates earlier dates; dots – no data.

members (although, as parts of the Soviet Union, they previously were). Of the Baltic states, only Lithuania was a member, having joined in 1936, before they were annexed by the Soviet Union in 1940;[8] all have retained membership or have rejoined the ISCM after independence. A similar solution was applied to former Yugoslavia (which joined in 1926) and Czechoslovakia (1922). For the mapping of dodecaphony, this was a smaller problem, although one could well ask whether it makes sense to conceive of the history of twelve-note technique in Russia, Ukraine and the Baltic states individually and separately from that of the Soviet Union. I have not covered the German Democratic Republic (although that would be interesting).

Categories

Membership of the International Society for Contemporary Music

The ISCM was and is an important – although seemingly somewhat unwitting – agent in the dissemination of musical modernism. Most national member sections previously functioned as associations, usually of composers, at the national or sometimes regional level. In many cases, which of several competing organisations would become the respective national ISCM section was hotly contested, involving both regional rivalries and aesthetic differences (particularly between relatively conservative and innovative factions). Thus, membership normally indicates the existence of an established infrastructure for contemporary music; conversely, although the fees appear to have been a serious obstacle, membership was evidently widely regarded as attractive and most national associations wanted to be represented. Although 'contemporary music' is not the same as modernist music and the Society famously refused to define the term – indeed retaining Internationale Gesellschaft für *Neue* Musik [*New* Music] as its official German title (Haefeli, 1982, pp. 262–284) – and although it supported a wide variety of styles and techniques, it is probably fair to say that the majority of work that was and is performed at its annual festivals (now World New Music Days) or supported by it in other ways can be considered broadly modernist. The data for Map 6.1 was taken from two main sources: a table in the appendix of Anton Haefeli's (1982) book on the Society and the ISCM's own website, which shows current members.[9] The problem is that the latter source does not indicate when sections joined, so there is no proper record for the period between 1982 (Haefeli's cut-off date) and the present. Likewise, many former members have since left, either deliberately due to disagreements or due to non-payment of fees. These are highlighted with hachures in the map. Similarly, a number of countries left the Society only to rejoin later; some famous examples include Germany and other axis or occupied countries during the Third Reich, Maoist China or South Africa under apartheid. Precise details will in many cases only (if at all) be available from a study of the ISCM's central archives or that of the member section(s) in question. In its present form, the map only shows entry dates and whether membership is current or has lapsed. Entry dates are depicted in a choropleth map where dark shading (dark blue in the online version, dark grey in the print version) represents early entries and light shading recent entry dates (with all entries since 1982 combined in a single category due to the lack of precise data). In the online version, clicking on a country reveals the exact entry date.

As Map 6.1 shows, the ISCM expanded rapidly in the inter-war years: from its founding in 1922 it encompassed large swathes of Western and Central Europe and North America by the mid-1920s. It is noticeable, for instance, that there was no perceptible difference between Western and Central Europe: Czechoslovakia (in its then incarnation) was one of the founder members in 1922; the Soviet Union followed in 1924, Poland in 1925 and (then) Yugoslavia in 1926. Indeed, there are more 'stragglers' in what would become the West (a concept that did not exist in the modern sense before the Cold War) than in the East: Portugal only joined in 1946, Greece in 1948, Finland in 1951, Canada in 1953 and Ireland only after 1982. While the Society was and still is dominated by Europe and North America, Latin America was well represented from early on, with Argentina joining in 1924 (well before Norway, by comparison), Cuba in 1932, and Colombia and Peru in 1933, for example. The expansion into Asia took a little longer, starting in Japan (1935), with China and India following in 1946 and 1948 respectively, for relatively brief periods (until 1951 and 1953 respectively) – although China has since rejoined and has indeed hosted the World New Music Days 2018. Australia joined as early as 1926, and the first African representative was Egypt in 1938, followed by South Africa in 1948 – both countries' memberships were suspended for long periods, but both rejoined.

In other words, the 'international' record of the Society is somewhat chequered: while it is represented on all five continents and has been from quite early on in its history, it remains clearly centred in Europe and North America, with Africa and the Middle East remaining mostly blank. Indeed, there is little indication that the Society was particularly interested in its more far-flung members or in expanding beyond 'the West'. Haefeli's book, for example, is practically exclusively devoted to the various conflicts between its European members (of which there were admittedly many during the interwar and Cold War periods). Conversely, however, the ISCM and the networking and international performance opportunities it represented, was and is crucial for many of its non-Western members.

National membership is only part of the story, however. As I suggested earlier, there were often many competing organisations, representing different regions, aesthetic persuasions or interest groups, and which one eventually formed the national ISCM section was frequently the result of political wrangles and internecine struggles. In Japan, for instance, composers were (and to an extent still are) divided between what could, with some simplification, be described as Western-modernist and traditionalist-nationalist factions; the Federation of Newly Rising Composers, founded in 1930, was able to unite representatives of both and it duly became the national ISCM member section in 1935 (Galliano, 2002; see also Herd, 2008; Kishibe et al., n.d.; Wade, 2014). This is just one example of the rich and complex histories being played out at the national and regional levels. Some of these are reflected in somewhat oblique ways in the current membership list, particularly since the ISCM also allows full associate and allied associate membership. It will come as little surprise that Belgium is represented by sections for Wallonia and Flanders respectively, but none for Belgium as a whole. China is represented by no less than five sections, for Beijing, Chengdu, 'Chinese Taipei' (!), Hong Kong and Nanning. The UK and Sweden both have two proper sections, the UK for Britain and, separately, for Wales (but not Scotland or Northern Ireland), and Sweden for Gotland as well as one for the nation as a whole. The USA is likewise represented by five organisations, although there is only one national section, with four additional full associate members (www.iscm.org/about/members). In many cases, one may well ask what led to these somewhat curious results. However, these details cannot be properly shown on maps. Then again, the idea is not for maps to replace more detailed, discursive histories, only to complement them. In other words, the map is not the territory.

Dodecaphony

The idea to represent the international dissemination of dodecaphony is perhaps the most contentious element of my maps. Maybe this should not come as a surprise, given that it is most directly inspired by Moretti's example – a stylistic feature acting as an analogue to Moretti's focus on genres – whose work has likewise proved controversial (cf. Moretti, 2003b). It is not my intention to argue that dodecaphony represents 'a necessary historical step' or that it is more properly modernist than other technical approaches or styles. There is undoubtedly a lot of modernist music that is not serial, and there are many modernist musical cultures that remained quite resistant to serialism. Having said that, as will become apparent, dodecaphony was more widely adopted than is usually realised, although it typically remained in an oppositional relation to the respective mainstream (normally even in its supposed heartlands). The reason it was chosen is simply that it illustrates the way ideas spread. Pretty much all examples of serial composition ultimately go back to Schoenberg's innovation (or 'discovery'); competing approaches, such as that by Josef Matthias Hauer, have generally not found imitators (cf. Krenek, 1953). Furthermore, whether a composition is dodecaphonic or not can generally be established quite clearly. It is sufficient for a composition to be intended and commonly regarded as dodecaphonic. There is no requirement for the technique to be adhered to strictly and consistently (which was quite rare in any case), although a minimum of rigour and pre-compositional planning can be expected. While there are borderline cases (as there are for any category), this is manageable, at least compared to other stylistic categories that one may wish to use, such as 'neoclassicism', 'atonality' or even 'modernism'.

There are other reasons why the choice of dodecaphony as the basis for a map might be problematic. Map 6.2 shows the first dodecaphonic compositions of each country as best as that could be established (on the online version, clicking on a country will reveal the composer, title and year of composition). There are no judgements of quality, influence or importance. Some of these compositions are well known, highly regarded and influential; others are obscure, relatively uninteresting and may have found no imitators. However, it seems to me that the (occasional) emphasis on otherwise unsung pioneers makes this approach an interesting alternative to the focus on canonic masterworks in most general histories. Finally, the framework focusing on nation-states and including just the first twelve-note composition per country is admittedly problematic (as should be clear in a publication devoted to cosmopolitanism in music). I am not going to defend this decision on principle; it was simply taken as the best available compromise. I had originally envisaged to associate dodecaphonic compositions with cities, not countries, but exact places were too difficult to establish. Furthermore, another decision would have to be taken whether what counts is the place of composition or that of performance (and what to do if a composer had written a piece while on holiday abroad or if the performance happened to occur in a different country or continent). Associating compositions firmly with countries was made more difficult by the fact that so many twelve-note composers were emigrants, often several times over (making them, in effect, 'serial emigrants'), which may not be purely coincidental.

In the case of emigrants, the compositions have generally been associated with the host country, not the composer's country of origin. In the case of composers going abroad for training, even for extended periods, the composition was generally associated with the country of origin. The rationale was to establish to which musical culture the composer in question made the more substantial and sustained contribution.

It is in this area that I made the most interesting discoveries, either in my researches or through the many suggestions I have received. It is impossible to list all these (although the credit section on the website may give an idea). I would highlight the work of the Panamanian composer Roque Cordero, who was instrumental in the propagation of modernist composition in general, and twelve-note technique in particular, in Latin America (Astor, 2008; Laufer, 2015, pp. 57–65), especially in its northern part (in the south, this role fell to the Argentine Juan Carlos Paz, who had begun using twelve-note technique in 1934, when it was largely unknown even across most of Europe, and later on Hans Joachim Koellreutter, a German immigrant who had settled in Brazil; Béhague, 1979, pp. 245–284; Paraskevaídis, 1984). It was through Cordero that Alejandro Planchart in Venezuela learned about the technique. The person who brought dodecaphony to France appears to have been Erich Itor Kahn, a German refugee who settled for a while in Paris, before moving on to the USA. Kahn passed his knowledge on to René Leibowitz – another immigrant – who taught Boulez, among others, and published important books on dodecaphony (Allende-Blin, 1987; 'Erich Itor Kahn', 2017). Turning to the East, the musician who introduced knowledge of serialism to Russia (apart from home-grown experiments in the early parts of the twentieth century) was Philip Herschkowitz, a Romanian-born student of Webern (Lupishko, 1998). He is not credited directly here since he was more influential as an (often unofficial and informal) teacher than a composer, and most of his work remained unperformed, so Volkonsky's *Musica stricta* (1956) is the first definitive twelve-note composition in Russia. Finally, my correspondent Jun Zubillaga-Pow managed to track down the Festival of Britain award-winning dodecaphonic

Piano Sonata by William Rea, a Belfast-born composer who settled in Singapore ('A New Musical Language', 1952; Attenborough, 1952). As these examples show, there was a wide network of dodecaphonic composers, most of whom operated in relative obscurity and few of whom are recognised in established music histories. Nevertheless, their work is an important aspect of the history of musical modernism. Again, as can be seen on Map 6.2, twelve-note technique travelled further and earlier than is often realised. It, too, is by no means an exclusively 'Western' phenomenon, being widespread in Latin America by the 1930s and 1940s (well before large parts of Europe) and reaching Japan in 1951, at the same time as Finland.

Conservatoires

Finally, the point layer of conservatoires, included in both maps, was intended to draw attention to some of the enabling conditions of musical modernism – musical modern*ity* as it were (on the online version, clicking on the icon reveals the name and founding date of the institution in question). It seems clear that the development of musical modernism requires the prior establishment of the infrastructure and institutions of Western musical modernity: conservatoires, orchestras, broadcasters, record companies, publishers, etc. Not all of these can be included, but conservatoires appear to be the most essential. Again, the history of the conservatoire outside Europe and North America is astonishingly difficult to research. I have decided to focus on modern conservatoires, defined as institutions for the systematic training of professional musicians, which emerged largely with the Paris Conservatoire in 1795, a model that was emulated elsewhere, although some later variations of that model, such as the one in Leipzig of 1843, proved similarly influential (Weber et al., n.d.). As in the earlier categories, most ancient conservatoires are concentrated in Europe and North America, but the first outside these spheres begin to appear by the middle of the nineteenth century (so just after the influential German conservatoires) in Rio de Janeiro (1847), Mexico City (1866) and Tokyo (1879).

Conclusion

It was not my intention to correlate the different data sets; in other words, to compare ISCM membership with dodecaphonic composition or either or both with the presence of conservatoires. Nevertheless, early membership of the ISCM tends to go hand-in-hand with early adoption of twelve-note technique more often than not. This is true of most of Europe and North America, but almost more telling in Latin America and East Asia. The persistent embrace of modernism in Argentina and, a little later, Japan, are cases in point. Obvious exceptions are the Soviet Union and countries in its orbit, which joined the ISCM but which remained hostile to dodecaphony for largely political reasons. Countries on the European periphery, such as Spain and Britain, did join the ISCM but were slow to fully embrace dodecaphony (although the Spanish-born Roberto Gerhard employed the technique early on as Schoenberg's student in Vienna, but did not do so on his return to Spain or in his early years of British exile). Mexico, by contrast, has a distinguished tradition of modernist composition, but appears to have had relatively little interest in either the ISCM or twelve-note technique – but this is quite unusual.

These maps are only the beginning; more aspects of musical modernism can and should be mapped. Admittedly, however, the number and nature of categories that can be usefully mapped may be quite limited. However, I could envisage a greater emphasis on performance, rather than composition. For instance, it would be worthwhile to map all performances of Stravinsky's *Sacre du printemps*, as a composition that has been performed across much of the world. The difficulty in this case would not be the mapping itself (which would be quite easy), but the research needed to find all the data. Again, however, the potential of crowdsourcing would be promising. Another important cultural-geographical element in the history of musical modernism is mobility, both in terms of travel and migration. It would be very tempting to map the routes taken by influential composers, musicians and educators, the contacts they made and the networks they established. However, the number of potential candidates, travel routes and places is such that this would soon mean that the map would be covered in lines and dots.

I want to conclude with another reason why mapping can lead to a more cosmopolitan engagement with music history. World maps, such as I have made, have a levelling aspect: each blank space is a space to fill. For example, for my map on dodecaphony, it was equally important to get authoritative information on Colombia or South Korea as on Germany or France, and there is no temptation to add more details to the already burgeoning literature on the two latter countries. Thus, we may be drawn away from our habitual preferences and interests and gently persuaded to look elsewhere. Admittedly, however, my chosen criteria were inherently Eurocentric. It is my intention to show that ISCM membership, dodecaphonic composition and conservatoires all had a significant history outside Europe and North America, but they all originated in Europe and arguably remained centred there. It would be interesting to use categories that originated elsewhere. However, it is worth pointing out that, for his part, Moretti gives the idea of cultural influence from the periphery to the centre and even between peripheries short shrift. Although I do not fully agree with his reasoning, it is our task to describe and analyse music history as it has happened and continues to happen, not as we would like it to happen.

Notes

1 'Non-simultaneity of the simultaneous' (*Ungleichzeitigkeit des Gleichzeitigen*) is a phrase coined by the art historian Wilhelm Pinder that became central to the philosophy of Ernst Bloch (although, confusingly, as 'simultaneity of the non-simultaneous') and subsequent theories associated with Marxism, postcolonialism, globalisation, modernity and postmodernity. See, among others, Pinder (1926), Bloch (1990) and Jameson (1991, p. 307).
2 Both Griffiths' and Whittall's books have been used as textbooks in the UK (and beyond) and have gone through a number of editions and revisions. Whittall's

Exploring Twentieth-Century Music (2003) demonstrates a different approach to his earlier books. They all share a broadly universalist orientation and restriction to Europe and North America.
3 Here my memory was playing tricks on me. I thought there were plenty of relevant examples in Moretti's work, but this is the only instance of the kind of map I have been developing I can find (there are lots of other interesting things, but none is closely related to the ideas I am developing here).
4 https://musicinexile.wordpress.com/ (accessed 10 April 2018).
5 The centring of conventional world maps on Europe and the Northern hemisphere as well as the distortion produced by most map projections do of course create a – problematic – hierarchy. Nevertheless, this seems a lesser evil than the selectiveness of most music-historical writing, in which large parts of the world do not feature at all.
6 See www.mapyourbristol.org.uk/ (accessed 4 April 2018) and https://storymaps.esri.com/stories/2017/hip-hop/ (accessed 4 April 2018) for interesting examples of musical maps.
7 The maps were produced using QGIS (www.qgis.org/en/site/, accessed 4 April 2018), a freeware, open-source Geographic Information System (GIS) that is relatively easy to use for non-specialists (in either cartography or computer technology); the base layer was taken from Natural Earth (http://www.naturalearthdata.com/, accessed 4 April 2018).
8 I am grateful to Rūta Stanevičiūtė for clarifying this to me (private email).
9 www.iscm.org/about/members (accessed 10 April 2018).

Bibliography

Allende-Blin, J., 1987. *Erich Itor Kahn*. Liner Notes *Erich Itor Kahn*, New World Records, NWCR563.
Astor, M., 2008. Los ojos de sojo: El conflicto entre nacionalismo y modernidad en los Festivales de Música de Caracas (1954–1966) (PhD). Universidad Central de Venezuela, Caracas.
Attenborough, I., 1952. A Composer in Malaya. *Straits Times* 10.
Béhague, G., 1979. *Music in Latin America: An Introduction*. Prentice-Hall, Englewood Cliffs, NJ.
Bloch, E., 1990. *Heritage of Our Times*. Polity Press, Oxford.
Bodenhamer, D. J., Corrigan, J. and Harris, T. M., 2010. *The Spatial Humanities: GIS and the Future of Humanities Scholarship*. Indiana University Press, Bloomington, IN.
Cohen, S., 2012a. Live Music and Urban Landscape: Mapping the Beat in Liverpool. *Social Semiotics* 22, 587–603.
Cohen, S., 2012b. Bubbles, Tracks, Borders and Lines: Mapping Music and Urban Landscape. *Journal of the Royal Musical Association* 137, 135–170.
Cook, N. and Pople, A. (Eds.), 2004. *The Cambridge History of Twentieth-Century Music*. The Cambridge History of Music. Cambridge University Press, Cambridge and New York.
Galliano, L., 2002. *Yogaku: Japanese Music in the 20th Century*. Lanham, MD: Scarecrow Press.
Griffiths, P., 1978. *A Concise History of Modern Music from Debussy to Boulez, World of Art*. Thames & Hudson, London.
Griffiths, P., 1981. *Modern Music: The Avant Garde Since 1945*. Dent, London.
Griffiths, P., 1995. *Modern Music and After*. Oxford University Press, Oxford.
Griffiths, P., 2010. *Modern Music and After*, 3rd ed. Oxford University Press, Oxford.

Haefeli, A., 1982. *Die Internationale Gesellschaft für Neue Musik*. Atlantis-Verlag, Zurich.

Heile, B., 2019. Musical Modernism, Global: Comparative Observations, in: Heile, B. and Wilson, C. (Eds.), *The Routledge Companion to Modernism in Music*. Routledge, London, pp. 175–198.

Herd, J. A., 2008. Western-Influenced 'Classical' Music in Japan, in: Tokita, A., Hughes, D. W. (Eds.), *The Ashgate Research Companion to Japanese Music*. Ashgate, Aldershot and Burlington, VT, pp. 363–381.

Holloway, R., 2005. Twentieth-Century (Light-)Blues. *Journal of the Royal Musical Association* 130, 327–339.

Jameson, F., 1991. *Postmodernism, or, the Cultural Logic of Late Capitalism, Post-Contemporary Interventions*. Verso, London.

Kishibe, S., Hughes, D. W., Ferranti, H. de, Adriaansz, W., Thompson, R., Rowe, C., Berger, D. P., Malm, W., Waterhouse, D., Marett, A., Emmert, R., Koizumi, F., Tanimoto, K., Kanazawa, M., Fujie, L. and Falconer, E., 2001 Japan. *Grove Music Online*. 12 May 2019. https://www-oxfordmusiconline-com.ezproxy.lib.gla.ac.uk/grovemusic/view/10.1093/gmo/9781561592630.001.0001/omo-9781561592630-e-0000043335.

Krenek, E., 1953. Is the Twelve-Tone Technique on the Decline? *Musical Quarterly* 39, 513–527.

Lashua, B., Cohen, S. and Schofield, J., 2010. Popular Music, Mapping, and the Characterization of Liverpool. *Popular Music History* 4, 126–144.

Laufer, M., 2015. Reinscribing Modernism: Selected Episodes in Venezuelan Composition after 1950 (PhD). New York University, New York.

Lupishko, M., 1998. A Pupil of Webern in the USSR: The Writings of Philip Herschkowitz (1906–1989). Ex Tempore IX. no. 1 (1998). http://www.ex-tempore.org/ExTempore00/Hershkowitz.html

Moretti, F., 2000. Conjectures on World Literature. *New Left Review* I, 54–68.

Moretti, F., 2003a. Graphs, Maps, Trees - 1. *New Left Review* II, 67–93.

Moretti, F., 2003b. More Conjectures. *New Left Review* II, 73–81.

Moretti, F., 2004a. Graphs, Maps, Trees - 2. *New Left Review* II, 79–103.

Moretti, F., 2004b. Graphs, Maps, Trees - 3. *New Left Review* II, 43–63.

Moretti, F., 2007. *Graphs, Maps, Trees: Abstract Models for a Literary History*. Verso, London.

Morgan, R. P., 1991. *Twentieth-Century Music: A History of Musical Style in Modern Europe and America, Norton Introduction to Music History*. W. W. Norton, New York and London.

Paraskevaídis, G., 1984. An Introduction to Twelve-Tone Music and Serialism in Latin America. *Interface* 13, 133–147.

Pinder, W., 1926. *Das Problem der Generation in der Kunstgeschichte Europas*. Frankfurter Verlags-Anstalt, Frankfurt am Main.

Presto, 1952. A New Musical Language, *Singapore Free Press* 4.

Roberts, L., 2012. *Mapping Cultures: Place, Practice, Performance*. Palgrave Macmillan, London.

Scherzinger, M., 2004. "Art" Music in a Cross-Cultural Context: The Case of Africa, in: Cook, N. and Pople, A. (Eds.), *The Cambridge History of Twentieth-Century Music*. Cambridge University Press, Cambridge, pp. 584–613.

Stephenson, B., Zajanc, C., Sandes, A. and Owens, J. B. (Jack), n.d. *A Geographic Information Systems (GIS) Training Manual for Historians and Historical Social Scientists*. Accessed 5 December 2017. https://www.academia.edu/8438126/A_Geogr

aphic_Information_Systems_GIS_Training_Manual_for_Historians_and_Historical_Social_Scientists.
Strohm, R. (Ed.), 2018. *Studies on a Global History of Music: A Balzan Musicology Project, SOAS Musicology*. Routledge, London and New York.
Taruskin, R., 2010. *The Oxford History of Western Music*. Oxford University Press, Oxford.
Wade, B. C., 2014. *Composing Japanese Musical Modernity*. University of Chicago Press, Chicago.
Watkins, G., 1995. *Soundings: Music in the Twentieth Century*. Schirmer, New York and London.
Weber, W., Arnold, D., Gessele, C. M., Cahn, P., Oldani, R. W. and Ritterman, J., n.d. *Conservatories*. Grove Music Online. 12 May 2019. https://www-oxfordmusiconline-com.ezproxy.lib.gla.ac.uk/grovemusic/view/10.1093/gmo/9781561592630.001.0001/omo-9781561592630-e-0000041225.
Whittall, A., 1977. *Music since the First World War*. Dent, London.
Whittall, A., 1999. *Musical Composition in the Twentieth Century*. Oxford University Press, Oxford.
Whittall, A., 2003. *Exploring Twentieth-Century Music: Tradition and Innovation*. Cambridge University Press, Cambridge.

7 André Tchaikowsky (1935–1982)
A cosmopolitan in a closet

Anastasia Belina

Polish-born British pianist and composer André Tchaikowsky (1935–1982) had a complex personality, astonishing memory and erudition and prodigious literary talent. He was a brilliant pianist and a highly individual composer; he was a part of the history of the Holocaust and his traumatic path to survival made him highly volatile. He had a professional conflict of composer v. pianist, and a personal one: his sexual orientation caused him much self-doubt at various stages of his life. Although complicated and difficult, he was, by all accounts, unforgettable; many of those who knew him personally agree that he was probably a genius whose smile could light up a room as easily as his acid comment could break a heart.

Tchaikowsky received his formal musical training in Poland and Paris with Lazar Levy and Nadia Boulanger, and in Belgium with Stefan Askenaze. He came third in the Queen Elizabeth Competition in Belgium in 1956, which launched his career and took him to prestigious stages worldwide. He left the country of his birth at the age of 22, and eventually settled in England.

Having grown up in a family of cosmopolitan Warsawians, he did not consider himself to be Polish, British, or Jewish; he epitomised the saying 'being a Pole is being a cosmopolitan' (Shore 2006); he did not identify readily with any particular culture or nationality, spoke several languages, loved world literature, theatre, and music, and travelled extensively around the world throughout his performing career.[1] His diaries, letters, and his unpublished autobiography show that he rarely referred to himself in national terms. To the onlooker, Tchaikowsky's polyglot life, filled with international travel, would surely seem cosmopolitan, and his compositions would show an amalgamation of European musical heritage and traditions. But what is seen from the outside does not always, if ever, correspond to what is actually happening on the inside, and so it was with Tchaikowsky – his many internal conflicts stretched to all areas of his life.

This chapter will take a look at an intricate web of complexities and contradictions that made up Tchaikowsky's uneasy existence to determine if, and how, cosmopolitanism and cosmopolitan values manifested themselves in his life and creative output. Was he a reluctant or unwitting cosmopolitan, or a closeted one? Was he a cosmopolitan at all? One of the examples considered in this chapter is *The Merchant of Venice,* written to a libretto in English, adapted from Shakespeare's play. In fact, Shakespeare was the inspiration for a number of other Tchaikowsky's works, such as *Ariel* (1969, three songs from *The Tempest*), written for mezzo soprano and instrumental ensemble, and his song cycle *Seven Sonnets of Shakespeare* (1967).

To explore Tchaikowsky's personality and identity I use such primary sources as his diaries (published in part only), letters, and unpublished autobiography,[2] and find it useful to apply a theoretical model described by Simon Frith in his *Music and Identity* (2004). Frith believes that identity is embedded in cultural experience, and is a process of *becoming*; Tchaikowsky's case shows that he was in one continuous process of *becoming*: becoming comfortable with his own identity as a composer, homosexual, and, most importantly, a human being in a world of strangers. Such an approach to interpreting Tchaikowsky's creative output gains more weight in a world that increasingly turns to racial, ethnic, cultural, or social divisions, and where cosmopolitan values hold even more importance.

Cosmopolitanism: universality and difference

Thinking about Tchaikowsky in connection to cosmopolitan values, I found *Cosmopolitanism: Ethics in a World of Strangers* (2006) by Kwame Anthony Appiah most relevant to my argument. The author reminds us that human connection is at the core of cosmopolitan ethos, and cosmopolitanism begins 'with what is human in humanity' (Appiah 2006, p. 134). A cosmopolitan is aware of many connections, one of which, 'the one neglected in talk of cultural patrimony – is the connection not *through* identity but *despite* difference' (Appiah 2006, p. 135).

Tchaikowsky, when he was able to make connections, made them *despite* difference because he could not easily, if at all, connect *through* identity. Only in 1980, two years before he died, did he begin the process of identifying with his Jewish roots, for example. Many of his letters and diary entries point to his thoughts and feeling of being different and not being able to reconcile these differences or think that they would prevent him from making connections, or fitting in. But of course, a cosmopolitan knows that differences can still connect people.

Famous Russian actor and producer Theodore Komisarjevsky remarked in his memoirs about the cosmopolitan nature of art, and commented that an artist

> Must be a man of international culture. It is in art and science that all nationalities meet on friendly terms and through art and science they understand each other and assist each other's development. A great work of art is universal because of its content and national because of its details.
> (Komisarjevsky 1929, pp. 180–181)

So it was for Tchaikowsky: he was indisputably a man of international culture, at ease with the masterpieces of international languages and art, and a polyglot. When Komisarjevsky was questioned about his nationality and a sense of belonging in the world, he answered that nationality was 'a matter of what one feels oneself to be. For some people it is a matter of habit' (Komisarjevsky 1929, p. 103). When it came to Tchaikowsky's nationality, he would probably be unable to answer what it was easily, much like many global citizens in today's world, who are born in one place, but grow up, study, work, and live in various others.

A wandering Jew or a cosmopolitan on tour?

For almost his entire life, Tchaikowsky felt as if he belonged nowhere – in relationships, social contacts, and countries. He left Poland in 1957 for good and wandered around Europe for almost six years. In 1963, he arrived in England but never properly settled, having had to spend at least six months a year travelling to perform in concerts. He really did exist in a constant international and transnational state, geographically, politically, and in his own mind.

In 1968 he finally became a British citizen. His friend and assistant Judy Arnold (between 1963 and 1969 she looked after all his paperwork and some concert affairs) remembered that travelling so much for him meant endless applications for visas and copious amounts of paperwork, but applying for the passport was, in his mind, dangerous: he was homosexual and he thought he would, somehow, be found out. Only when the act was passed in 1968, he arranged for his British passport (*Rebel of the Keys* 2016). But there was another reason for this delay: he was not mentally ready to write down his birth name: Andrzej Krauthammer. The boy was still suffering inside the man, and his search for a safe place in the world would continue for the rest of his life.

But if a cosmopolitan is defined as someone who is at ease with other cultures, and who feels at home in foreign lands, then Tchaikowsky's case becomes complicated. Much like his namesake, Pyotr Tchaikovsky, who travelled the world and found fame across the globe in his lifetime but never felt at home anywhere but his native Russia, so André Tchaikowsky was continuously seeking for a place where he could settle. In 1974, he asked himself:

> Is it a fallacy to think I could accomplish more away from London, where there would be no distractions – no friends? Shall I try to sell this flat and get myself a place in the country, whether I do eventually emigrate to Australia or New Zealand or not? Wouldn't a fresh environment give me a boost? Somewhere on the seaside or at least a river. Or perhaps Cambridge? […] But enough of this city of ten million, nine and a half of which seem to be forcing themselves on me! A house in a village with one grocer's shop which sells everything and doubles up as post-office, some lovely scenery, and a 'phone I could plug out. No contact with the neighbours. The hordes of friends I've met everywhere on my tours all converge on London and make a point of looking me up, but would they follow me to Backwater-on-Sea?
>
> (Belina-Johnson 2013, p. 141)

It is clear that his identity was closely related to his sense of personal space, and to have the freedom to do what he wanted. But the peace within himself was often identified with making a human connection and to being loved. While he had numerous affairs and relationships, two of the most intense connections happened when he was in Australia and New Zealand in the 1970s, and neither of them could be called a relationship. He met two men who challenged his worldview, but most importantly, made him question how he viewed himself. One of the most striking diary entries was made in March 1977 in New Zealand, the country that for him became a kind of spiritual home:

> On Friday the 4th I became a conscious member of the human race.
>
> I had always been an outcast – or a prisoner. At first the confinement was quite literal, whether in the Warsaw ghetto or in a wardrobe; released from that, I actually sought confinement (which I then probably regarded as security) in claustrophobic relationships or the larger ghetto of the homosexual community (if that is the right word for a group whose members have so little else in common). The trouble was my *mind* was still in prison: I had been trained to forge my own handcuffs.[3] As for being an outcast, that also started in its most literal and drastic form: who can be more cast out than one whose very right to live has been denied? [...] Unable to merge, I undertook to stand out, and succeeded. Even *I* didn't at first suspect that the solitary position of a 'star' performer was not of my own choice. I performed on stage and in conversation, as an artist or as a clown: I might get no one's love, but I knew how to force their applause. I even performed when alone – was that because I couldn't love myself? I often courted dislike as much as admiration, and that proved even easier to get. What did it matter which reaction of the two it was, as long as I was *noticed*? I was making up for years of hiding.
>
> It took me a long time to notice the strain of that perpetual display. [...] To see oneself as an outcast is quite as damaging as to be one; perhaps more so, since a real one may yet eventually find acceptance, whereas I kept rejecting whatever was offered.[*] To my suspicious and black-and-white mind, it always seemed based on spurious grounds: I was accepted as a fellow Jew, a fellow queer, above all as a pianist: that made me interchangeable with any other specimen of the same group. It never felt enough just to be me.
>
> (Belina-Johnson 2013, pp. 187–189)

These are poignant words, written by man only five years away from his death, and an artist greatly admired by audiences, friends, and colleagues. How could a pianist who was admired and promoted by none other than Arthur Rubinstein feel so insignificant, and seek occasions and sharp words that would get him 'noticed'? The pianist Peter Frankl remembered a story, from Tchaikowsky's concert in Dallas during his 1957–1958 US tour, that illustrates this need to stand out. He was asked to speak at an after-concert party:

> I'm not a polite speaker at dinner parties. In fact, I'm not very good at dinner parties; in fact, I hate dinner parties. I didn't want to come to this party and

---

[*] For expecting a door to slam in my face, I was slamming it myself to get in first!

> I'm not suitable to this party because when I get excited, I get nose bleeds in public and I feel one coming on and will have to leave soon. You really don't want me at your party. I am a communist, I eat with my fingers, I never take a bath, I'm Jewish, I pick my nose, I believe in equal rights of whites and blacks, and, finally, I'm a homosexual.[4]

Taken in the context of mid-1950s America, when segregation was still observed, this was a reckless speech, and it was not the only one he delivered. Needless to say, his American career did not last – he burned bridges and slammed doors without ever looking back. Why would a man who was already a centre of attention do that? Would a cosmopolitan deliver such a speech? It is clear that in order to accept the world, Tchaikowsky felt the need to be accepted by the world first, no matter how he behaved. When he finally found a place where he felt more settled, it helped him to finally begin a process of establishing some inner peace:

> I now have a congenial environment to live and work in, a measure of solitude without loneliness, a feeling of being part of the place which I had experienced nowhere else: I have found a house. […] But the greatest progress has been in myself – I am steadier, more at peace with myself and therefore the world, capable of long stretches of happiness and not merely brief flashes of joy, more responsive in true relationships and more deft at avoiding fake ones. I find it easier to be frank with people, now that I've gained enough self-acceptance to dispense with theirs!
>
> (Belina-Johnson 2013, pp. 193–194)

He later wrote in a letter to his friend that 'One's sense of identity depends on being part of one's environment' (unpublished letter to Michael Menaugh dated 21 August 1978): obviously, the internal work was being done.

It was important for him to be left alone, even though he craved human contact and, even more, human connection and love. But as soon as that contact was found or established, he bolted away from the person next to him like a spooked horse, leaving the bemused companion, at best, lost for words, and at worst, feeling wounded. For those familiar with the writings of Portuguese poet Fernando Pessoa, his description of life's journey may seem apt to reflect an outlook of a cosmopolitan: 'In this world we're all travellers on the same ship that has set sail from one unknown port en route to another equally foreign to us; we should treat each other therefore with the friendliness due to fellow travellers' (Pessoa 2010, p. 149). But while Pessoa realised the importance of treating others in the same way as he would want to be treated himself (whether he managed to do so or not), Tchaikowsky had a somewhat different approach, to put it mildly.

And yet, he found it easy to find 'home' in other literary cultures. Tchaikowsky spoke several languages fluently, corresponding voraciously with his international contacts, and was able to quote extended passages from admired works of world literature. In fact, he felt so 'at home' in English literature that he reputedly decided to move there after reading *A Diary of a Nobody* by George

Grossmith, because he thought the people in England truly lived like that, and most importantly, that he would not be 'bothered' there by anyone.[5] He wrote: 'I like London best of all, though there are more beautiful cities (Rome, Hong Kong, Mexico, Rio de Janeiro). But I could never feel at home in any of them, and I'd go mad within a week in America [...].' He liked the English, who 'are calm, discrete, they don't reveal much of themselves, and that's why you can rely on them (inasmuch as you can "rely" on anyone, which I suspect you can't)' (Janowska 2014, p. 50).

The hundreds of letters he left behind show exactly how at ease was Tchaikowsky with other cultures and languages – he wrote in idiomatic English, French, and, of course, Polish. A particularly colourful example is a letter sent in October 1957 to his close friend Jean-Pierre Marty, written in French, mostly probably while in the air, on American Airlines paper, and perforated with references to oriental cultures, and phrases in English and Russian.

The boy in the wardrobe

Perhaps a clue to Tchaikowsky's need for solitude and his lifelong search for personal safety is contained in a relatively short, but significant, episode of his life. He was born in Warsaw, just four years before the city's Jews were forced into the ghetto. The family's apartment was already in the ghetto area, and Tchaikowsky's miraculous survival was only possible because his grandmother Celina, a formidable woman, demonstratively moved out of the ghetto as a Christian, even though she was Jewish. At first ensuring his survival in the ghetto by bringing necessary provisions to her remaining family (which included Tchaikowsky's mother and her new husband; his parents separated even before he was born), she saved him two years later by leading him out dressed as a girl, with his eyelashes, eyebrows, and hair dyed blonde with peroxide. Here the story takes another turn: leading him out through the gates past the Nazis as her granddaughter, Tchaikowsky's grandmother had in her pocket new papers for her grandson, who in them was named as Andrzej Czajkowski. In a split moment, he left behind his birth name of Robert Andrzej Krauthammer and adopted one of the most famous names in music history, which would later add another layer of subliminal confusion to an already confused and tormented mind.

Thus, the survival of six-year-old Tchaikowsky began with the need to conceal his true identity and adopt someone else's. What followed were three long years during which he was hidden in at least a dozen places, and with each move he had to learn a new identity: a new name, a new set of parents, a new place of birth, and a new, Christian, religion. One of these hiding places was a single young woman's wardrobe. Tchaikowsky describes one of his hiding places, a wardrobe, in his unpublished autobiography:

> How long had I been in this wardrobe? Seven weeks, two years? I had meant to count the days, but I'd forgotten. Anyway, there weren't any days in the wardrobe, or any hours: the dark was always equally complete, and the

chamber-pot in one of its corners had to be located by touch. I had now learnt to do that, as I had learnt to use it silently.

(Belina-Johnson 2013, p. 28)

It is easy to see what impact this would have on a young impressionable mind, who learnt that he must exist in darkness and silence, because his very own life was not worth anything. The new identities, adopted frequently, could not pass without leaving a deep emotional furrow. But the young boy had to deal with a tragedy that had affected his life the most: two weeks after he left the ghetto, his mother was deported to Treblinka and murdered there. For decades he believed that she refused to leave the ghetto with him because she cared more about the man she lived with; only in 1980 did he realise that she remained in order to give him a better chance of escape and survival.

Another trauma caused by erasing his origins was physical: his grandmother made him undergo three operations to reverse circumcision, which had to be done without anaesthetic. So, a boy who was born into a family who identified clearly with a particular culture, then had to suffer under the knife because that identity was deadly.

Jews had no right to exist, and even if they managed to survive in hiding, that existence unfolded in dark corners, tight places, closets, where they had to be concealed from the world but could not run away from themselves. This damaged the young Tchaikowsky beyond repair, and although the world was open to him and welcomed him with open arms, he could reciprocate only with distrust, and hide his innermost self – this, to him, probably meant survival even when his life was no longer in danger.

The man behind the skull

As he sought and found attention wherever he went in life, so he did in death, making headlines in 1982, when the donation of his head to the Royal Shakespeare Company (RSC) was announced. Even today, if his name seems familiar, it is most likely because of his bequest, and not because of the compositions or recordings he left behind. Apparently, he left his skull to the RSC in his will, and there were at least two reasons for it: first, he loved Shakespeare and wanted to be an actor but knew that the only way to the dramatic stage for him was as Yorik. The second comes from an apocryphal story, in which Tchaikowsky comments that if Shakespeare were indeed an anti-Semite, then it would give him great pleasure to know that there is a Jewish skull rolling around in his *Hamlet*. To the general public, who read about this event in the press, this was an outrageous move by an eccentric artist, but to Tchaikowsky's friends it was nothing out of the ordinary.

But in 1982, behind the skull was a man who finally started to come to terms with who he was at his birth: a Jewish Pole born in Warsaw. This process began when he visited Israel for the first time in January 1980, which he called 'a case of self-discovery and the corresponding joys':

> I could never say that I am *proud* of being a Jew, for what have I done to become one? But for the first time in my life I actively *enjoy* being a Jew: the word has lost its ghetto connotations. Always and everywhere, I have felt myself to be different. I felt equally out of it among Jews and among Gentiles, among homosexuals and family men, in all communities and with most individuals.
>
> (Belina-Johnson 2013, p. 269)

Visiting Israel with his friends and colleagues, who led him to a place where he could experience a sense of belonging for the first time in his life was a catalyst. He finally started to reflect about breaking away from self-imposed isolation, and understood its cause:

> I had never realised to what extent my crippling insecurities were not social or even sexual, but racial. In the last two weeks they had simply left me – I did not notice them. At some point I realised that I've been saying just what I meant to people, doing largely what I wanted, without asking myself what they expected of me and whether I was acceptable to them. If I wasn't, it was their problem: I had just as much right to be there as they did.
>
> (Belina-Johnson 2103, p. 273)

He understood how little he knew about his own past and even about his own survival, how sheltered he had been by his grandmother, and how egocentric he was himself. He started having dreams about the Warsaw Ghetto, about buried dangerous things and items, and saw how insidiously he was caught up in his own mind. Some years prior to his visit to Israel, on a recommendation of either his doctor or a friend, he started writing an autobiography, starting with what he remembered about his childhood in Poland. But meeting other Jews who survived the Holocaust and who experienced horrors more terrible than his own and who still went on living, he realised that he no longer needed this form of self-therapy:

> For some time now I've felt disinclined to continue the work on my book. The bitterness that impelled me to write it had worked itself out: the therapy had been so successful as to make itself obsolete. Each time I murdered an old foe in the book (Grams, Father, Dorka) I'd find myself free of them and either forgive them or stop thinking of them. Still, it seemed a pity to abandon so much good writing, and I thought it possible to continue the book freely, not out of compulsion. But that bitterness was my fuel: once gone, it took the motivation to continue with it. No doubt it was the worst possible reason for writing a book, but such as it was it had been mine and I no longer had it. […]
>
> But the most instructive discovery is that of my own self-centredness. I've always known it of course, but never till now had I realised how much it made me miss in terms of perception, compassion, sheer humanity; never till now have I been so ashamed of it. Why, it's positively indecent to devote a whole book to petty personal vendettas while ignoring the appalling catastrophe

that went on all around me! It's like quarrelling at a funeral. One could write a good book about a neurotic grandmother and a nasty aunt, but NOT in the context of the Warsaw ghetto. Some of the people who contributed to the Ringelblum archives were just as interesting as me, and led equally complex personal lives; but they chose to describe the *common* fate, and a footnote in small print invariably informs one that they came to share it. However special they were (and some of the writing and perception is astonishing) they all became part of that same heap. And in the middle of that universal waste I stand complaining *of a nasty aunt!!*

(Belina-Johnson 2013, pp. 309–310)

Finally, one of the core cosmopolitan values emerged with clarity: the 'absolute necessity to learn how to relate to *people* and not just their reflections in my mind.' (Belina-Johnson 2013, p. 280). Finally, Tchaikowsky started to reflect on connections that are true and not imagined, despite the differences, perceived or real.

In the opening of *Rebel of the Keys* (2016), the pianist Fou Ts'ong, who knew Tchaikowsky well, reflected how poignant it was that his friend died just as he started to find real peace within himself. Diagnosed with cancer, Tchaikowsky went through a reappraisal of his life as a human being and as an artist. He made a decision to stay true to what he wanted to do all along: compose, and promised himself that should he survive, he would dedicate his life to his true calling:

I already realised that I should have to live differently, indeed *be* different, if I recovered. [...] Perhaps I'd now find the guts to brave poverty, give up the piano and devote myself entirely to composition? I had a very strong suspicion that my organism had produced the disease to force on me that very decision, to turn me back into the person I was born to be, doing the thing I was born to do. My career as a pianist, pleasant as it often was, was like having married for money; the wife was nice as well as rich and deserved to be lived for herself, but I did not love her, and in choosing her I had turned my back on my very identity. I still remember my grandmother's words: 'If you are a composer, you'll be famous after you're dead! What good will that do you?' I knew myself too little to realise that my first wish, or rather need, was not to be famous: it was merely to be myself. It takes the whole of one's life to acquire self-knowledge, and it often needs a collapse like my present one to bring it about.

(Belina-Johnson 2013, p. 342)

Perhaps it does not matter that Tchaikowsky never got to make the crucial decision: he died in June 1982. What matters is that he finally had a glimpse into his own world, the world that only began to open up as its light was extinguished.

The humiliated Jew

Shakespeare was Tchaikowsky's favourite author. Fou Ts'ong remembers the game Tchaikowsky liked to play with him, where he would hold out a volume of the complete works of Shakespeare, ask him to open it randomly, read him a line, and he would name the work, chapter, or section, always correctly, often continuing to recite the quote.

In recent years, Tchaikowsky has had something of a revival, and it began with *The Merchant of Venice*, which finally received its world premiere in Bregenz in 2012. *The Merchant of Venice* was Tchaikowsky's last completed work. Although he began it in full health, he finished it on his deathbed, even refusing morphine injections so his mind would stay clear.[6] Interestingly, the opera is not 'about' being Jewish, nor is it about anti-Semitism. It is about alienation from society, from self. Shylock and Antonio are alienated for different reasons, but the result is the same – loneliness, sadness, not being understood. The opera ends with a seemingly happy resolution, with all lovers united, and with Antonio's flesh intact, but the intense melancholy in the ending reminds the audience about one man who was humiliated in his last hours in society and another who will always be alone even among friends.

Not surprisingly, this opera is about an outcast, about alienation, which is multifaceted: it is alienation from society, from family, from friends, but above all, from oneself. It is also about humiliation. Halina Janowska believes that Tchaikowsky's tragedy was that for almost as long as he lived, he saw himself not as a Jew, but as a humiliated Jew.[7] But having spent his life as an outcast who knows the full extent of being one, who is better to write an opera about Shylock than such a person? The final opus of Tchaikowsky brings him finally to 'universality plus difference': he shows universal themes in Shakespeare's work through the lens of personal, local, experience that can still be shared and understood by those who live.

Concluding thoughts

To understand Tchaikowsky, one must understand the first lesson he learned in his childhood: he had no right to live, he belonged to a people who were exiled, persecuted, and exterminated, and his survival was as traumatic as the death of his mother at the hands of Nazis. It is not surprising, then, that he would spend the rest of his life seeking a safe place in the world of strangers, both in a physical, and emotional sense. It is also not surprising that he would seek acknowledgement of any kind, positive or negative, after years of oblivion, and 'as long as I was noticed' was the point, while, at the same time, protecting himself ferociously from the gaze of others. Pessoa's self-description seems to be made for Tchaikowsky too: 'To mark the boundaries of the garden of my being I put up high railing, more daunting than any wall, so that whilst I can see others quite clearly, at the same time I exclude them and keep them other' (2010, p. 152). Perhaps the famous skull donation shows that Tchaikowsky never really made peace with himself, and never recovered from the trauma related to his survival. In a life that offered him so many opportunities to embrace cosmopolitan values and to become a cosmopolitan who could share the journey with his fellow travellers, he still chose to hide his innermost self among many acts of outrageous attention-seeking and self-destruction.

Notes

1 For further biographical details on Tchaikowsky and for his selected diaries, see Belina-Johnson (2013).
2 Manuscript of the autobiography is held in a private collection (Eve Harrison, London). Parts are quoted in Belina-Johnson (2013). Various letters are held in the Warsaw University Library, in the André Tchaikowsky archive, and many still remain in private possession.
3 This seems to be a reference to William Blake's image of 'mind-forged manacles', or mental handcuffs, in his poem 'London' (1794):
    In every cry of every Man,
    In every Infant's cry of fear,
    In every voice, in every ban,
    The mind-forg'd manacles I hear.
    Thank you to Derek Scott for pointing this out.
4 Peter Frankl, interviewed by David Ferré, 3 July 1985, London.
5 In a letter to Halina Janowska dated 27 October 1968 he describes England and London as a place where nobody bothers you. See Janowska (2014).
6 For history of composition, see Belina-Johnson (2013, pp. 384–400).
7 Private conversation, Warsaw, 2016.

References

Appiah, Kwame Anthony, 2006. *Cosmopolitanism: Ethics in a World of Strangers*. London: Penguin Books.
Belina-Johnson, Anastasia, 2013. *A Musician Divided: André Tchaikowsky in His Own Words*. London: Toccata Classics.
Frith, Simon, 2004. *Music and Identity*. London and New York: Routledge.
Janowska, Anita Halina, 2014. *My Guardian Demon: Letters of André Tchaikowsky and Halina Janowska 1956–1982*. London: Smith Gordon.
Komisarjevsky, Theodore, 1929. *Myself and the Theatre*. London: Heinemann.
Pessoa, Fernando, 2010. *The Book of Disquiet*. London: Serpent's Tail.
Rebel of the Keys, 2016. Documentary film, directed by Mark Charles. United Kingdom: Entertaining TV. See https://rebelofthekeys.com/ (accessed 13 May 2019).
Shore, Marci, 2006. *Caviar and Ashes: A Warsaw Generation's Life and Death in Marxism, 1918–1968*. New Haven and London: Yale University Press.
Tchaikowsky, André. Unpublished autobiography, private archives, London.

8 The elision of difference, newness and participation

Edward J. Dent's cosmopolitan ethics of opera performance

Sarah Collins

> Ultimately the alternative to politics turns out to be aestheticization, viewed as the constitution of a new collective ethos.
>
> (Rancière 2002, p. 137)

Histories of the development of an 'English National Opera' in the late nineteenth and early twentieth century typically emphasize the origins of the movement in ideas about social reform. The story of the Old Vic and Sadler's Wells theatres in particular – such as Edward J. Dent's *A Theatre for Everybody* (1945) and Susie Gilbert's *Opera for Everybody* (2009) – brings together themes of democratic accessibility and national cultural renewal in a way that makes these agendas seem inextricably linked, relying on the logic that opera made available *to* the people can result in the development of an opera culture *of* the people. With national culture in mind, the emancipatory 'everybody' in both titles referred to a broadening of the audience for an elite art form along class lines. While the historical existence of this rhetorical link is indisputable, what follows will seek to reposition ideas about opera and democracy in relation to an 'everybody' that extends beyond – and often runs counter to – the version of community bounded by national identity; and indeed against identity as such. This involves reading Edward J. Dent's work on topics such as libretto translation, amateur opera productions, and the history and aesthetics of opera performance as an echo of the cosmopolitan attitude of 'friendship' that has been attributed to some of his Cambridge associates – an attitude that had both political and aesthetic implications.

Newness and difference

This denouncer of veneration and moral fervour declared that Gluck 'could only be venerated as the expression of a moral ideal; and for that he still stands even now.' He was an aristocrat who resented his upbringing and a socialist who despised public taste: 'what the general public has always wanted was to hear the greatest singers in the most trivial music.' The sensitive appreciator of the roles of Mozart's Pamina and Beethoven's Leonore indulged in bouts of rabid anti-feminism, especially if his friends showed signs of getting married. A lover of all things new and experimental, he rejected the radio and the gramophone, which 'make all orchestras sound more or less like a harmonium' (this was in 1940, not 1910). He sang the praises of modern British music in foreign periodicals, and modern Continental music in British periodicals. He was said (not without reason) to have the kindest heart and the bitterest tongue in Cambridge.

(Dean 1976, p. 360)

Edward Dent's activities and outlook are often seen as oppositional in nature, as we see here from Winton Dean's tribute to mark the centenary of Dent's birth. On the one hand, Dent was an avid supporter of the music of continental modernism in Britain during the early decades of the twentieth century. He was one of the founders of the International Society for Contemporary Music (ISCM), and its president from 1922 to 1938. He counted among his personal friends a range of figures at the forefront of the literary and musical avant-garde. He maintained a large international network of correspondents from a broad range of musical traditions, including Berg, Webern, Schoenberg, Sibelius, Adorno, Busoni, Bartók, de Falla, Honegger, Ibert and Krenek, among others; and he supported and fostered the performance of new music through the ISCM festivals. In addition, Dent was deeply embedded in the early twentieth-century Cambridge milieu that involved E. M. Forster, John Maynard Keynes and other Bloomsbury figures; and the ultra-modern Sitwells thought of him as family. Dent aimed to encourage a sympathetic audience for new music by emphasizing the intellectual, as well as physical, vitality produced by unfamiliar experiences of the new:

So much listening to familiar music is time wasted. As soon as the sonata begins he knows what is coming or what is likely to come, why waste the afternoon over it when one might be gaining some entirely new experience? The only experience worth recapturing is the experience of hearing a work for the first time. [...] The average concert-goer is content to waste his time rather than make the mental effort of trying to understand something unfamiliar.

(Dent 1926, *GB-Ckc*, EJD/1/1/2/1)

At first glance, Dent's modernist associates, his international networks, his scepticism towards habits of passive consumption, and his advocacy of the unfamiliar, could easily call to mind the type of elitist withdrawal and championing of abstraction that is associated with cosmopolitan modernism. Or equally, Dent's elevated social position and privileged educational context might have rendered him detached in a different way (Philip Brett once described him as 'something of a snob', but never 'pompous or self-important' (Brett 2000, p. 423)), at least in the wider public perception. Yet Dent was committed to supporting amateur theatre productions, such as by school boys and Cambridge undergraduates (albeit extremely talented ones); he translated operas by Mozart into English to enhance accessibility; he wrote popular introductory books on musical appreciation of opera and general music history; and he advocated vehemently for the establishment of an English National Opera. In other words, he clearly attributed to music an ethical function and saw musical participation as a vital form of self-cultivation, describing his activities in promoting this kind of access as 'welfare' and 'philanthropy' (Dent 1947, *GB-Ckc*, EJD/1/1/2/18). And this, despite his distaste for music with an overt programme, moral message or 'ethical passion' (Dent 1927, p. 51).

There are some who have suggested that the oppositional character of Dent's work and outlook was consistent enough to point towards a more deeply ingrained existential project. Along these lines, Philip Brett has argued that Dent's shifting opinions, nonconformist writing style and conflicting agenda were an expression of his homosexual identity. The necessarily closeted nature of Dent's homosexuality and his association with a brilliant group of homosexual intellectuals at Cambridge at the turn of the century allowed him to fashion a form of scholarship that remained both nimble and subversive – an approach that was not available to the mid-century generation of musicologists whose more openly expressed homosexuality led them to insist upon the separation of their work from their personal outlooks, according to Brett (2000).

This type of reading has been extended within the area of cosmopolitan studies to show how homosexual identification at the turn of the century enabled non-normative forms of kinship, or in Leela Gandhi's terms, 'affective communities' (2006). Gandhi has described how a collection of figures – with some of whom, incidentally, Dent had direct associations (including Edward Carpenter and E. M. Forster) – practised a distinctive form of homosexual politics that involved a 'radical reconfiguration of association, alliance, relationality, community' (p. 36). Positioned alongside contemporaneous practices in vegetarianism, spiritualism, and anti-colonialism, what this amounts to is a recognition of the ethico-political nature of friendship. In Gandhi's formulation, friendship is a form of relation that emphasizes the non-instrumentalist, spontaneous, unofficial, and non-institutional. It pays attention to the local and particular in associations, rather than the universal, procedural, and systematic. Fundamentally (and here Gandhi draws from Derrida's noted text on the politics of friendship) it is open-ended and improvisational, opposing forms of community defined by exclusion, and preferring the constant deferral of its end. In never closing the loop around a defined community, as it were, friendship circumvents the logic of sameness involved in communitarianism, and remains open to difference. Even more radically, it views the individual as constituted by the very act of relating to different and unfamiliar others – a notion that subverts the reductive forces of collective identity, and its tendency towards sameness.

As we continue to extrapolate these themes with respect to Dent's work below, it is important to recall the very specific local context for the initial formulation of Dent's ideas in Cambridge at the turn of the century, and in English intellectual circles more generally. So while, for example, spontaneity and open-endedness may be said to characterize alternative forms of community that remain open to difference per se, these attributes held specific meanings with respect to perceptions about the English national character in the early twentieth century, a point that becomes important when considering the shifting valences surrounding the notions of 'refinement', 'vulgarity', and the 'amateur' in Dent's thinking (Collins 2018). Even more locally, the forms of relation and the practices attributed to them under a Gandhian reading of 'friendship', when viewed in the Cambridge context specifically, clearly reflected the ongoing influence of the intuitionist ethics of George Moore on Dent's Bloomsbury colleagues, even after the First World War. Equally, while the translation of opera librettos into the vernacular was a common practice throughout Europe, what will interest us here is the particular implications attached to 'opera in English' and the operatic activities of specific suburban theatres in London that were established as part of a philanthropic venture and whose audiences were drawn from the local area, at least initially. Dent's personal involvement in the story of Sadler's Wells and the Old Vic, and his experiences in opera production in a range of settings, meant that his views regarding the accessibility of culture and the importance of participation in the production of cultural products cannot be aligned along either commercial lines or democratically reformist (and potentially paternalistic) lines alone.

It is also worth noting that our sense of the oppositions within Dent's agenda is surely compounded by the prevailing framework of understanding that aligns modernist artistic sensibility with transnational, elite, and progressive impulses, and that attributes a contrasting characterization to nationalist agendas, political gestures advocating the democratization of art, and historical narratives that emphasize continuity over rupture. The influential notion of autonomy played a crucial role in shaping this framework and the form of modernist detachment that it implies. For example, an aspiration towards autonomy underpinned positions such as the privileging of aesthetic form over representation in modernist art, the distancing of art and artist from political and social engagement, and a refusal to view art as historically located, among others. These types of position can be mapped directly onto the conventional alignments just mentioned, such that the appearance of opposition in Dent's activities can be seen as being predicated upon a particular understanding of autonomy – namely one opposed to communal engagement at the level of the artwork or artist.

In addition, part of what allowed Dent to hold these seemingly conflicting views in balance was that he maintained a distinction between aesthetic qualities and their effects. For example, a work need not be chronologically recent or technically progressive in order to have the positive effects that Dent attributes to newness and unfamiliarity. Indeed, Dent's view of music history was aptly suited to this approach, as Annegret Fauser observed when she wrote that Dent 'locates musical developments in their historical contexts on the principle that different contexts might nevertheless produce the same aesthetic principles through the ages' (Fauser 2014, p. 246). Dent shared with other interwar modern classicists the notion that modern music had more in common with early music than music of a more recent age. As a consequence of this view of musical history, Dent's conception of musical newness was not related in any way to chronological proximity. 'There is old music and there is new music', Dent wrote in 1926,

Edward J. Dent's cosmopolitan ethics of opera performance 121

old music is music which one has heard before, new music is music which one has not heard before. The actual period of its composition does not matter. A work may have been written yesterday and still give us the impression that we have heard it all before, some time or other. In that case it must be classed as old music, and it is waste of time to listen to it.

(Dent 1926, *GB-Ckc*, EJD/1/1/2/1)

While this synchronic principle did not adequately allow for the possibility of new interpretations of familiar works—an omission that was surely more related to the polemical mode of Dent's address in this essay, rather than reflecting a systematic position—it did nevertheless allow Dent to view Mozart as the consummate modern composer of his time, concurring with his friend Ferruccio Busoni when he described Mozart as 'never out of date and never modern' (Busoni 1921). Dent's adoration of Mozart then, was not in tension with his derision of 'old music':

How is it possible [the older generation] ask, for people who admire Stravinsky to admire Mozart, too? One of these admirations, they feel sure, must be purely hypocritical. There is no reason why we should doubt the honesty of the young people. It is often alleged that the young are foolish and ignorant but aesthetic receptivity is certainly much keener in the young than in the middle-aged, and intellectual honesty is often emphasized by the young to an extent which the more tactful elderly regard as a positive nuisance. The admirers of Stravinsky find no difficulty in admiring Mozart, too, for their admiration is of an entirely different type. The younger generation have acquired, subconsciously it may be, a more historical outlook than their elders.

(Dent 1926, *GB-Ckc*, EJD/1/1/2/1)[1]

For Dent, Mozart was modern because he successfully combined technical and structural perfection with human feeling, in contrast to the descriptiveness and the impasse of Beethoven's music, which according to Dent was 'always struggling to express the infinite'. Beethoven was too fond of idealism and description, which Dent felt was sure to date, whereas he preferred the human feeling and formalism of Mozart.

There is a sense in which Dent's activities seem to move along an alternative axis to the general bifurcation of autonomy and participation. Examining this alternative axis involves reflecting upon what construct of autonomy could feasibly support Dent's range of agendas as a coherent programme, rather than as one that was riddled with paradox and contradiction. In examining this possibility, it may be productive to consider how, as Andrew Goldstone has argued, practices of autonomy 'change according to what they seek to be autonomous from' (p. 15). Goldstone characterizes autonomy in terms of the type of constraint to which it stands in relation. He discusses four versions of autonomy in the early twentieth-century literary field – autonomy from labour, personality, political community, and external reference. Focusing on a different type of constraint, I would suggest that Dent's activities may be understood specifically in terms of seeking autonomy from the consumer market, and that this particular version of autonomy in fact supported practices of social engagement, contrary to the usual association between autonomy and withdrawal or non-participation. In rejecting the self-interested ethos of market-driven modernization – or what Dent's Cambridge colleague Keynes called the 'decadent international but individualistic capitalism' (Keynes 1933, pp. 760–761) – modernists such as Dent sought to propose an alternative communal sphere in the form of aesthetics. They sought a *new collective form of life*, but one that was an alternative to the sphere of the market and outside the authority of the state and religion. They proposed a way to be individual but not merely self-interested; a way to empower the populace without succumbing to mass commodification, treading that fine line between promoting a musical idiom 'of the people', that did not involve pandering to the popular whim.

With this frame in mind, Dent's seemingly oppositional activities appear as part of a coherent project, each activity being an expression of a desire to withdraw from the individualism of the international market economy – the emblem and aim of the very processes of modernization and homogenization against which many modernists positioned themselves. Further, this realignment of the relationship between autonomy and participation helps us comprehend the three other aspects of the conventional framework of understanding outlined above – namely the relationship between the national and international, elite and egalitarian, and between 'old' and 'new' music, or tradition and innovation. Construing Dent's central organizing agenda as seeking autonomy from market forces realigns our understanding of these conventional oppositions, and suggests how nationalism, the democratization of culture, and an engagement with tradition were not antithetical to the modernist paradigm of autonomy.

National character and the 'consciousness of modernity'

Dent is often celebrated as an egalitarian internationalist, whose enlightened humanitarian sensibilities saw him assisting musicians from a range of national backgrounds during the First World War and between the wars (Arrandale 2011). Dent's magnanimousness in this regard is recorded in the letters organizing these activities, such as one to W. Hill in 1914:

> We shall have hard work this winter to keep music and musicians alive but I hope we shall be successful. There will no doubt be organizations of relief for destitute musicians, but I hope we shall be able to give them, which is better for them and for all of us, the chance of earning their living in something like their normal way. [...] Charity begins at home but the French are in greater straights than we are, and I don't think we can make much distinction between French and English at this moment. And M. Prunières tells me that they are trying to help musicians of all the allied nations.
>
> (Dent 1914, *GB-Cu*, Add MS 8856/108)

Dent's linguistic and diplomatic abilities were recognized in his lengthy term as president of the ISCM, and he was lauded for his dedication to fostering good relations and mutual understanding between warring countries through the vehicle of international music festivals, which, as Egon Wellesz described, sought to foster a communal progressive transnational ethos by 'spread[ing] the idea of modern music' (Wellesz 1946, p. 206). Dent rallied against national factions in the musical sphere, writing of the opposition he faced from local authorities in holding international musical festivals during his presidency of the ISCM – 'Our detractors', he wrote, 'went about saying (if not writing too) that we were all of us Bolshevists and Jews', for being international in their aims and outlooks (Dent 1943, *GB-Ckc*, EJD/1/1/1/2). Dent described the infighting among regional chapters of the ISCM, and the difficulty in finding jury members 'cosmopolitan' enough to refrain from making selections on the basis of national bias (Dent 1943, *GB-Ckc*, EJD/1/1/1/2).

On the other hand, Dent is undoubtedly considered to be a paradigmatically British (or, more accurately perhaps, English) musicologist, not only by breeding but by temperament, and by his historical and contextual approach to music research. Indeed, as Fauser noted, Dent 'defined [his] methodological choice in nationalist terms' (2014, p. 249). Throughout his scholarly oeuvre and personal letters, Dent consistently demonstrated a preoccupation with how differences in national character were manifest in approaches to writing music history, in music composition and appreciation, and in general habits of mind.

As a further expression of his awareness of national differences and sympathy for the idea of national identification, Dent was also a tireless advocate for the establishment of an English National Opera, and for the performance of operas in the English language, by English singers:

> I need hardly say that I take it for granted that this one opera house must be a truly national opera, with all performances in our own language, except for occasional visits from foreign ensembles. We must have no more of the old Covent Garden system of engaging the stars from a dozen different foreign countries and allowing them to sing, without any sort of serious rehearsal or stage-production, in which they may be pleased to call Italian, or even, as I have heard in the past, to sing French operas in German, and German operas perhaps in a mixture of Italian and French. Anything, in fact, as long as it is not English! And if foreign singers are invited to join [...] it must be on a long-term contract, and on the clear understanding that they sing in English and rehearse regularly like their English colleagues.
> (Dent 1945, *GB-Ckc*, EJD/1/1/1/5)

Dent was committed to making opera accessible and intelligible to a popular English audience, which involved facilitating amateur performances and taking heed of what he called 'our duty to provincial audiences' (Dent 1945, *GB-Ckc*, EJD/1/1/1/5).

In approaching the apparent polarity between Dent's international modernist networks and his dedication to opera in the vernacular and to fostering national institutions to support it, we might consider two possibilities for revision. The first revision involves recognizing the way in which discussions of national temperament in England were aligned with, rather than opposed to, the progressive impulses of modernity; or in other words, the possibility that 'turning inward [did] not necessarily mean turning backward' (Mandler 2001, p. 134). The second revision involves reorienting our view of English particularism, construing it not as a withdrawal from a universal conception of humanity, but rather as a reaction against the individualistic and self-interested logic of the consumer market. Autonomy was central to modernism, but the Anglocentric turn inwards and the related support for the democratization of culture need not be seen as antithetical to autonomy. Instead, while those transnational figures of high modernism sought autonomy *from* national affiliations and *from* the notion of socially committed art, others sought a recuperation of national culture – a turn back to the centre – in order to gain autonomy *from* the cosmopolitan market of consumers, who threatened art's independence. The Anglocentric turn can thereby be seen as being not so much anti-modern, but anti-market, and Dent's agenda might be viewed in a similar way.

Viewing the interwar turn inwards as part of a modernist desire to maintain autonomy from transnational market forces is suggested in part by the way in which discussions of English national character had become bound up in what Mandler has described as the 'consciousness of modernity'. As Mandler has noted, since the mid-nineteenth century these types of discussions remained separate from racially and biologically deterministic premises, and equally they did not seek to explain national temperament with reference to climate or geography. Instead, English national character was viewed as being predicated on shared political and legal structures, moral traditions, religion, and literary and historical traditions. In other words, discussions of national character were not conservatively oriented as a bulwark against change (as biological conceptions were), but rather were used to 'explain change by reference to national, popular characteristics' – giving the English national character an explicitly progressive edge (p. 126). In addition, central to liberal conceptions of national character was the idea that the English were predisposed to valuing liberty, and were the primary practitioners of liberty's modern political institutionalization in the form of democracy. Indeed, Mandler argues that these discussions were predominately liberal right up until the interwar period, as the conservatives were more aligned with talking of patriotism, construed as involving self-sacrifice to flag and leader. It was felt that 'the failure of democracy on the Continent [over the course of the nineteenth century] could be explained […] by the lack of national traditions of discussion, tolerance and association' (p. 127).

For Dent, it was this conception of the English temperament as being committed to collective exchange and freedom of communication that should characterize the activity of opera in Britain, meaning opera by British composers in addition to opera by foreign composers translated into English for local audiences:

The great achievement of Sadler's Wells is to have developed a style, a really English style of singing opera – not just a bad imitation of Italian or German. It is based first and foremost on Team-work, a method of organization essentially British. There are no stars but a fine all-round cast, all of whom work for the show itself and not for their individual glory; and it is an opera house where you can always hear the words, as the ripple of laughter in the house often proves.

(Dent 1932–1957, *GB-Ckc*, EJD/1/1/2/3)

Importantly, a key feature of Dent's advocacy for the democratization of the opera sphere was the fact that it was not driven by commercial imperatives. 'Whatever of real cultural value the Old Vic and Sadler's Wells have so far achieved between them', Dent wrote, 'has been the result not of commercial routine but of the enthusiasms of idealists and visionaries. It is in their hands that the future of the British theatre lies' (Dent 1945, *GB-Ckc*, EJD/1/1/1/5).

The theme of teamwork, and the self-sacrifice of individual interests to the cause of the whole as being a distinctly English trait, similarly played into Dent's view of the historical development of harmony:

The early history of harmonic experiment is still a matter of controversy; but whether it came from the Netherlands, from England or from Scandinavia, it undoubtedly originated in the North of Europe. [...] Melodic music is individualistic, harmony is co-operative. When two voices sing different notes simultaneously in a piece of music, they are obliged to show a certain consideration for one another. In the first place they must not try to shout each other down. Secondly, they must agree to accept some common system of rhythm and pace if there is to be ordered principle of consonance between them. And if their music is to be pleasing in its general effect, they must accommodate their voices one to the other so that they blend agreeably. Each of these points involves a certain self-sacrifice and subordination of the individual to the community which is fundamentally irksome to the Mediterranean temperament.

(Dent 1927, p. 38)

Here we see Dent locating the impetus towards musical modernization in the Northern temperament, which he explicitly associated with a cooperative mindset. For him, musical modernization seemed to go hand-in-hand with a more communal spirit. This was also no doubt aimed against the prevailing elite market for Italian opera, which was an explicitly commercial and transnational enterprise, often held to ransom by the individual careerism of the leading prima donnas. In this context, Dent's plea to recuperate a national tradition in opera was less a rejection of his international modernist outlook, and more a proclamation of independence from the individualistic forces at play in the commercial sphere. In other words, Dent's advocacy for 'opera in English' was a vehicle for the democratization of culture, and in turn, his advocacy for the democratization of culture was explicitly tied to his rejection of the commodification of music.

For Dent, opera in this vein could be new and distinct because it was not defined by self-interested, 'individual glory', but rather by a collective commitment to the art itself. This idea links the belief that music performance could facilitate the development of a communal sphere beyond the individualism of the market as an international phenomenon, to the notion that this sphere would be best achieved within a national framework, given that the English temperament was particularly predisposed to teamwork and cooperation.

This reading of the turn towards national cultural recuperation as a foil to the international market – rather than it being an anti-modern development – could also be seen in the work of Dent's friend and Cambridge colleague, the economist John Maynard Keynes. In 1933, Keynes declared in an article in the *Yale Review* that

> the decadent international but individualistic capitalism, in the hands of which we found ourselves after the war, is not a success. It is not intelligent, it is not beautiful, it is not just, it is not virtuous – and it doesn't deliver the goods.
> (Keynes 1933, pp. 760–761)

While Keynes admitted he himself, 'like most Englishmen', had believed that 'free trade was based on fundamental truths', he conceded that habits of mind had changed in the early twentieth century, such that these 'truths' needed revising. Though formerly an ardent cosmopolitan, committed to the Moorean individualism of his early twentieth-century Cambridge milieu, during the interwar years Keynes began to argue for the virtues of national self-sufficiency. He proposed conceiving of the economy in national terms, contrary to the free-trade belief in the international division of labour.

After the significant financial crashes of the 1930s, Keynes produced his *General Theory of Employment, Interest and Money* (1936), offering what Jed Esty has described as a 'middle way between raw capitalist individualism and the new authoritarian collectivism' or a 'state-smoothed capitalist equilibrium' (Esty 2004, p. 172). As Esty suggests, Keynes' *General Theory* was not a complete disavowal of individualism in favour of collectivism, especially as Keynes' classical liberalism meant that he had a fundamental mistrust of centralized authority. Crucially, Keynes was not empowering the state in the sense of centralized political power, but rather a combination of nation and state, with nation understood as the 'mainstream tradition of civil nationalism' drawn from Burke and Coleridge. Keynes' vision for a managed capitalism relied on a liberal notion of English statehood with the capacity to conceive of the 'national interest'. Under Keynes' *General Theory* 'dynamism would be measured not by the expansion of political boundaries but by the evolution and refinement of civilization *within* them' (p. 178). This indicates a key shift in conceptions of value, that was enabled by viewing the national economic system as a closed object that could be formed under the guidance of the nation-state, facilitating a new idea about economic growth 'not as material and spatial extension, but as the internal intensification of the totality of relations [defining] the economy as an object'.

Keynes' new commitment to this 'internal intensification' was not a retreat from internationalism, but rather a means to foster international peace in light of the inability of the nineteenth-century habits of mind associated with the free-trade market to do so. His conception of the nation-state was in this sense a mechanism to foster a 'common sense' based on egalitarian ideas. It was not an exclusivist commitment to Englishness, as it was for some, but rather a means to an end of offering an aesthetic sphere for citizens to remain outside the market of consumers.

Participation, or the 'self-dedication to an idea'

A key event in Dent's career was his involvement in the production of an amateur performance of Mozart's *The Magic Flute* in Cambridge in 1911. The event was not without its challenges – Pamina caught a cold and lost her voice for the second performance, and her part had to be sung from off-stage by Papagena. Neither the conductor of the orchestra nor the stage manager had any experience in those roles in opera; and they were working on a shoestring budget (Carey 2009, p. 58). In an article in the *Athenaeum* it was recounted that the performance included 'gorgeous gilded helmets' that were 'fashioned out of biscuit boxes', and that the 'cloaks worn by the central figures in the chorus were proportionately cheap, but the effect, aided by skillful grouping, was wonderful'; and 'The Magic Flute was an artistic success'. 'My only misgivings about the music', wrote the anonymous contributor 'J', 'are that I, a most unmusical Philistine, enjoyed myself throughout' (J 1911, p. 794). For the Cambridge performance, the German libretto had been translated into English in its entirety by Dent, and Dent went on to write instructional essays on the translation of opera librettos (see for example 'The Translation of Operas' and 'Verdi in English', both reproduced in Dent 1979).

After the performance, Dent wrote a letter to Clive Carey, one of the only professionals involved with the production, who had played Papageno, noting that beyond the difficulties and 'quarrelling over bouquets etc.', the 'real results achieved' were that 'a lot of people came to the theatre thinking themselves unmusical Philistine[s], and found that their ears really were opened to them, by Mozart' (quoted in Carey 2009, p. 61). Dent later wrote:

> There are several old plays and operas which can always be produced much more intelligently and convincingly by amateurs than on the professional stage, and *The Magic Flute* is one of them. [...]
>
> The critics who went to Cambridge in 1911 seem, judging by their notices, which I have just re-read, to have heard for the first time that *The Magic Flute* was not a silly pantomime with some famous songs for exceptional singers, but a serious allegory of human life like *Everyman*. I took an experienced opera-singer to see the [schoolboy] performance in the Isle of Dogs; she said to me, 'I have sung in this opera dozens of times, but this is the first time that I have really understood it'.
>
> (Dent 1947, *GB-Ckc*, EJD/1/1/2/18)

Dent's translation of opera librettos for English audiences was expressly designed to challenge the dual barriers of class and nationality, with his view of the translator's function being to 'translat[e] the work for the man in the audience who is seeing it for the first time' (Dent 1934/1935, p. 1). He also wrote popular books on opera, such as the best-selling *Opera* (1940). Dent's commitment to musical appreciation might be viewed as an expression of a belief in the purportedly elevating powers of music. With reference to the 1911 Cambridge performance, this reading also implies that it was the enterprise itself that was Dent's concern – the labour of producing the opera and thereby producing the autonomous selves through that production – rather than a concern for the aesthetic character of the music, and therefore entirely separate from Dent's support of unfamiliar and new music more generally. The performances were not intended to carry political import in the manner of cultural philanthropy, in fact – which would be contrary to his belief in the autonomy of art – but they *did* partake of 'the political', in the sense of being a practice or process intended to have an impact on social relations. On this point, Dent wrote:

> The main moral of the allegory of *The Magic Flute* is self-dedication to an idea. This may sound rather like going into a monastery; but what religious people call self-dedication is just the same thing as the spirit of team work which is taken for granted in every game of football. Consequently what *The Magic Flute* wants more than anything else is team work and devotion to the work of art itself.
>
> (Dent 1947, *GB-Ckc*, EJD/1/1/2/18)

Dent's use of the language of spiritual sentiment in describing the communal act of performance is significant in that it positions his views squarely in relation to the ethos of Aestheticism, which invested art with an explicitly transcendental function, and artists with a priestly significance. Holding fast to the separation of art from heteronomy, which was so central to that ethos, Dent nonetheless viewed this separation as being facilitated by a collective spirit of self-sacrifice and thus of friendship. His point was not that the artwork was socially embedded because it was a manifestation of community, but rather that art's autonomy could be preserved through a forfeit of self-interest to the open-ended purpose of art.

The participatory form of this act of self-sacrifice was also significant in that it shielded the artwork from becoming merely an object of passive consumption. Indeed, for Dent, the very act of participation that enabled art's autonomy to be preserved was only possible because of music's inherent accessibility to non-professionals. Music was accessible, according to Dent, because it was a sounding art – something that exists only in performance, in interpretation, and which is an open form – rather than a completed, material work of art:

> The owner of a picture by Titian possesses property which is his and his alone. He might say the same of an autograph manuscript by Beethoven; but he cannot possess the symphony itself – that belongs to the world at large.

The autograph may fetch a thousand pounds at auction, but it is no more than a piece of dirty paper. You can hear the symphony played for a shilling.

(Dent 1927, p. 23)

Dent's dedication to amateur performance of Mozart then, was underwritten by a belief in the notion of music as a sounding or performance art, rather than a textual phenomenon, from which issued its egalitarian potential and accessibility. The sounding performance enabled music to escape commodification – to escape the self-interested imperatives of the market – just as the collective production of an opera thwarted the individualistic tendencies of foreign opera, which itself had fallen prey to the market for sensation, novelty, and virtuosic prima donnas.

Dent was clearly committed to international cooperation, and saw music as a means to promoting this end, yet he was also committed to the autonomy of art from social concerns or descriptive attachments; the utmost importance of newness in art; and the freedom of the artist from ethical considerations. The coherence of Dent's programme – when viewed as non-paradoxical – suggests how aesthetic autonomy was not necessarily set against commitment in modernism, but rather that it facilitated the withdrawal from the market of mainstream tastes, by promoting a communal, more humane sphere of purely aesthetic ideas that could be collectively produced and experienced.

Note

1 Dent set this desirable 'historical outlook' against what he termed the 'religious outlook on music', which he saw as the cause of the 'reverence for the classics' (see his essay 'The Historical Approach to Music', reprinted in Dent 1979, pp. 189–206, p. 193).

References

Archival materials

Dent, Edward J., 1914. Letter to W. Hill. 26 August. *GB-Cu*, Add MS 8856/108.
Dent, Edward J., 1926. 'Beethoven and a Younger Generation'. Typescript. 12 February. *GB-Ckc*, EJD/1/1/2/1.
Dent, Edward J., 1932–1957. 'Sadler's Wells – Our National Opera'. Typescript. *GB-Ckc*, EJD/1/1/2/3.
Dent, Edward J., 1943. 'Introduction'. Typescript introduction to *Music between Two Wars* to celebrate the 21st anniversary of the foundation of the International Society for Contemporary Music. *GB-Ckc*, EJD/1/1/1/2.
Dent, Edward J., 1945. 'A Theatre for Everybody'. Typescript. *GB-Ckc*, EJD/1/1/1/5.
Dent, Edward J., 1947. 'The Magic Flute'. Typescript prepared for *The Gazette of the John Lewis Partnership*. *GB-Ckc*, EJD/1/1/2/18.

Books and articles

Arrandale, Karen, 2011. 'Artists' Rifles and Artistic Licence: Edward Dent's War', *First World War Studies*, vol. 2, no. 1, pp. 7–16.

Brett, Philip, 2000. 'Musicology and Sexuality: The Example of Edward J. Dent', in David Greer, Ian Rumbold, and Jonathan King (eds.), *Musicology and Sister Disciplines: Past, Present, Future*, pp. 418–427. Oxford and New York: Oxford University Press.

Busoni, Ferruccio, 1921. 'Sketches and Leaves from a Diary', *The Sackbut*, vol. 2, no. 1, pp. 33–37.

Carey, Hugh, 2009. *Duet for Two Voices: An Informal Biography of Edward Dent Compiled From His Letters to Clive Carey*. Cambridge: Cambridge University Press.

Collins, Sarah, 2018. 'Anti-Intellectualism and the Rhetoric of "National Character" in Music: The "Vulgarity" of Over-Refinement', in Jeremy Dibble and Julian Horton (eds.), *British Musical Criticism and Intellectual Thought, 1850–1950*, pp. 199–234. Woodbridge, UK: Boydell.

Dean, Winton, 1976. 'Edward J. Dent: A Centenary Tribute', *Music & Letters*, vol. 57, no. 4, pp. 353–361.

Dent, Edward J., 1927. *Terpander: Or Music and the Future*. New York: E. P. Dutton.

Dent, Edward J., 1934/1935. 'The Translation of Operas', *Proceedings of the Musical Association*, vol. 56, pp. 81–104. Reprinted in Edward J. Dent, *Edward J. Dent: Selected Essays*, edited by Hugh Taylor, pp. 1–25. Cambridge: Cambridge University Press.

Dent, Edward J., 1940. *Opera*. Harmondsworth, UK: Penguin.

Dent, Edward J., 1945. *A Theatre for Everybody: The Story of The Old Vic and Sadler's Wells*. London and New York: Boardman.

Dent, Edward J., 1979. *Selected Essays*. edited by Hugh Taylor, Cambridge: Cambridge University Press.

Esty, Jed, 2004. *A Shrinking Island: Modernism and National Culture in England*. Princeton, NJ: Princeton University Press.

Fauser, Annegret, 2014. 'The Scholar behind the Medal: Edward J. Dent (1876–1957) and the Politics of Music History', *Journal of the Royal Musical Association*, vol. 139, no. 2, pp. 235–260.

Gandhi, Leela, 2006. *Affective Communities: Anticolonial Thought, Fin-de-Siècle Radicalism, and the Politics of Friendship*. Durham, NC: Duke University Press.

Gilbert, Susie, 2009. *Opera for Everybody*. London: Faber.

J, 1911. 'Notes from Cambridge', *The Athenaeum*, 23 December, p. 794.

Keynes, John Maynard, 1933. 'National Self-Sufficiency', *The Yale Review*, vol. 22, no. 4, pp. 755–769.

Mandler, Peter, 2001. 'The Consciousness of Modernity? Liberalism and the English National Character, 1870–1940', in Martin Dauton and Bernhard Rieger (eds), *Meanings of Modernity: Britain from the Late-Victorian Era to World War II*, pp. 119–144. London: Bloomsbury.

Rancière, Jacques, 2002. 'The Aesthetic Revolution: Emplotments of Autonomy and Heteronomy', *New Left Review*, vol. 14, pp. 133–151.

Wellesz, Egon, 1946. 'E.J. Dent and the International Society for Contemporary Music', *The Music Review*, vol. 7, pp. 205–208.

Part 3
Music and urban cosmopolitanism

9 Tip, *Trinkgeld, bakšiš*

Cosmopolitan and other strategies of touring music groups before the Great War in Sarajevo

Risto Pekka Pennanen

How best to compete in the restaurant music business in a highly aggressive market before the First World War was a tough challenge for restaurant owners and touring artistes in Germany and Austria-Hungary. To solve this problem, touring music and dance groups utilized several business strategies for maximizing their audiences and earnings. The underlying reason for this was the great diversity of audience and repertoire.

In essence, strategies had to negotiate what we may term 'cosmopolitanism'. The Sarajevo German-language press did not explicitly refer to cosmopolitanism in the city; instead, from the late 1900s, the closely related term was metropolitan (*großstädtisch*), by which the writers described the atmosphere of, for instance, the modern Winter Garden Café in the first-class Hotel Europe, the temporary variety theatre Imperial-Orpheum and the indoor promenade concerts in the Vereinshaus (Community Centre).

This chapter analyses the business strategies of three touring bands, namely: the Viennese Ladies' Orchestra (*Wiener Damenkapelle*) Portugal; the south Slavic folk costume band (*Trachtenkapelle*) Graničar of long-necked *tamburica* lutes; and the Serbian Roma band of the folk violin virtuoso and singer Andolija as examples. The business strategies, repertoires, performing venues, audiences and sources of income of the groups differed to varying extents from each other.

The primary sources here are the surviving music licence documents of the Provincial government in Sarajevo, kept in the collections of the Archive of Bosnia and Herzegovina (Arhiv Bosne i Hercegovine), which forms a part of the Bosnian-Herzegovinian State Archive (Arhiv Federacije Bosne i Hercegovine) in Sarajevo, the Austro-Hungarian press, the widely distributed Central European weekly trade journal for music and show business *Der Artist* and, finally, picture postcards of the bands. The Düsseldorf-based *Der Artist* was crucial in marketing because the venue owners could contact the artistes through the office of the journal and, on the other hand, the artistes could have their current place of work or home address and description of their ensemble and repertoire printed in the paper.

Staged representation of the mainstream: Viennese ladies' orchestra

A typical Viennese ladies' salon orchestra, which often included non-German members from other parts of Austria-Hungary, concentrated on Viennese salon and popular music and Western classical music. Besides the city of origin, 'Viennese' referred to the repertoire typical of such groups and, especially, to the instrumentation. The Viennese instrumentation (*Wiener Besetzung*) – at its largest consisting of piano, harmonium, flute, obbligato violin, violin, viola, cello or double bass and percussion – was one of the nine types of basic salon line-ups in Friedrich Hofmeister's catalogue (Kaufmann 1997, p. 193, n. 170; Saary 2018). Small ensembles could lack harmonium, viola and percussion, but the flute was more or less essential to the Viennese sound.

The first ensemble analysed in this chapter is the Wiener Damenkapelle Portugal, a typical Viennese ladies' orchestra. The earliest newspaper sources on the band are from 1908, when the seven-piece line-up of the band consisted of three violins (including obbligato violin), viola, flute, piano and harmonium (*Grazer Tagblatt* 1908). The next year, a journalist in the South Tyrolean town of Bozen (now Bolzano in Italy) particularly praised the band's decision to exclude percussion from the line-up (*Bozner Nachrichten* 1909a). Subsequently, the band consisted of five members: bandleader, solo violinist Maria Portugal (b. 1858), her daughter Marie (b. 1878), Emma Mertahaus and Rosa Maxner – all from Vienna – and Jaroslav Pilňáček from Lochenice (Ger. Lochnitz) near Hradec Králové (Ger. Königgrätz) in north-eastern Bohemia (Portugal 1913). Judging from a picture postcard of the band, the Czech young man from Bohemia may have been a harmonium player.

The tours of the Viennese Ladies' Orchestra Portugal remain shrouded in mystery as Maria Portugal did not advertise her orchestra in *Der Artist*, nor is she known to have published any job advertisements in newspapers; the marketing strategy of the band is thus unclear. Nevertheless, the Orchestra Portugal had engagements at high-quality cafés and restaurants, such as Biffi Caffè in Milan and Meraner Weinstube in Meran (It. Merano) in South Tyrol (*Bozner Nachrichten* 1909a; *Maiser Wochenblatt* 1910). In Bosnia, the orchestra worked, possibly, in Mostar in spring 1913 and certainly in the restaurant of the Sarajevo Vereinshaus a year later (Portugal 1913; *Bosnische Post* 1914). Between these two engagements the band worked in the wine house Palmengarten in Salzburg (*Salzburger Volksblatt* 1913; *Salzburger Wacht* 1913).

The Sarajevo press did not write about the Orchestra Portugal, but we can nevertheless find sources about its repertoire. Usually, ladies' orchestras had a set programme for each concert; the possibility of music requests from the audience seems somewhat improbable because the musicians were dependent on written arrangements. Fortunately, the press outside Bosnia described the repertoire of the Orchestra Portugal. According to the newspaper *Bozner Nachrichten* (1909a), during the engagement in autumn 1909 in the restaurant of Hotel Walther von der Vogelweide in Bozen, the band's programme included a technically very demanding violin solo from *Orpheus in the Underworld* by Jacques Offenbach and potpourris on *Carmen* by Georges Bizet, *Cavalleria rusticana* by Pietro Mascagni and *Pagliacci* by Ruggero Leoncavallo. Possibly, the writer was mistaken; fantasias on such operas were more common in the repertoires of Viennese ladies' orchestras than potpourris. In addition, the standard programme was comprised of marches, waltzes, polkas and other dances, character pieces, latest hit tunes, operetta pieces, overtures, and vocal sections from operas (arias, quartets and sextets), which were usually performed instrumentally.

In an advertorial on the farewell concert of the band in January 1910, *Bozner Nachrichten* (1910) reveals the lighter side of the repertoire as the band planned to perform operetta music and *Wienerlieder* (Viennese songs). The concert of *Wiener Heiterkeit* (Viennese cheerfulness) underlined the Viennese origins of the band. The operetta pieces were very probably Viennese or at least Austro-Hungarian, and the *Wienerlieder* were sung in the Viennese dialect and associated with inns, restaurants and wine taverns of Vienna. The writer does not mention whether the band performed the pieces with vocals, but usually ladies' orchestras played operetta numbers instrumentally. The *Wienerlieder* could be performed either vocally with an instrumental accompaniment, or purely instrumentally. The advertorial lacks any information about the instruments the band used for the songs. One possibility is Viennese *Schrammel* instruments, including a double-necked contra guitar (*Schrammelgitarre*) and a button accordion (*Schrammelharmonika*), but possibly the band made a compromise and used the standard instrumentation.

Lastly, touring ladies' orchestras were supposed to include something local in their repertoire. Therefore, in Bozen in 1909, the Orchestra Portugal played 'Kamposch Marsch' in honour of Anton Kamposch, the owner of the Hotel Walther von der Vogelweide, by Czech military bandmaster Vojta Mádlo (1872–1951) of the Imperial and Royal Infantry Regiment Archduke Leopold Salvator No. 18 stationed in Bruneck (It. Brunico) (*Bozner Nachrichten* 1909b). Performing such homage and other pieces by local composers seem to have been common in the repertoires of ladies' orchestras (cf. Pennanen 2015, pp. 110, 117).

The women musicians of Viennese ladies' orchestras tended to dress uniformly in evening dress, often white (Myers 1993, pp. 143, 178–179), while the male members favoured a black suit. In Bozen, the Orchestra Portugal appeared in simple black dresses with white shirts, 'thus yielding the impression of a family' (*Bozner Nachrichten* 1909b). A later picture postcard of the band, however, consists of separate portraits, and because of the lack of uniformity, the musicians are presumably not in their stage clothes (see Figure 9.1). Bandleader Maria Portugal is wearing a black shirt with a white lace collar, the female members have mostly white clothing while Jaroslav Pilňáček is in a black suit, white shirt and black bow tie.

The income of the members of ladies' and other touring orchestras could consist of fees from the venue owners, ticket fees, tips (*Trinkgeld*), and a collection (*Sammeln*), but the sale of picture postcards of the band provided another possible means of income (Kaufmann 1997, pp. 131–134). According to Dorothea Kaufmann (1997, pp. 134–135), the contracts of ladies' orchestras, especially in

Figure 9.1 Postcard of Wiener Damenorchester Portugal with bandleader Maria Portugal in the centre.

Germany, almost always included the duty of encouraging the members of the male audience to order alcoholic drinks (Ger. *Animierung*) during the intervals and after the concert. With a few exceptions (e.g. *Österreichische Land-Zeitung* 1904; *Deutsches Volksblatt* 1906), the Austro-Hungarian press tended to write about *Animierung* in Germany, whereas the Bosnian press very rarely mentioned it at all (but see *Bosnische Post* 1913b), and such a habit may have been uncommon in Bosnia. As for the Orchestra Portugal, the main source of income seems to have been the fees with the addition of the proceeds from the sale of the band's picture postcards. No sources on the orchestra mention tips or a collection, which does not exclude the existence of this form of payment. Possibly, tipping was such a natural part of the performances that writers living in the same culture as the audiences did not see the need to mention it.

The business strategy of the Orchestra Portugal strived for maximal artistic specialization and maximal attraction of specific audiences, particularly educated classes and, to a lesser extent in the case of instrumental performances, German-speakers. Through its salon, operetta and opera music in Viennese-style arrangements, the orchestra represented the Central European mainstream and Vienna – irrespective of the fact that one of the members was a Czech. The repertoire made only minor concessions to the local music of each stop in the tour.

Performances in folk costumes: Graničar

Performing in traditional or folk-like fantasy costumes, the *tamburica* band Graničar was a typical *Trachtenkapelle* band, which worked in Sarajevo for several occasions before and during the Great War. The name of the group referred to a border guard or a frontiersman, especially an inhabitant of the historical Military Frontier against the Ottoman Empire in the southern borderland of the Habsburg Monarchy.

The bandleader of Graničar was Croatian *tamburica* player Milan Biro, and he and his wife constituted the core of the group. The rest of the line-up, whose majority was always female, tended to change according to the requirements of each touring area. For example, in Café Wettin in Hamburg in January 1909, the group comprised five or six young women and three men, whereas for his engagements in Mostar and Sarajevo in 1914, Biro organized a line-up consisting of himself, his wife, his 18-year-old relative Gustav Biro from Sarajevo and four female members (*Der Artist* 1909; Biro 1913a, 1913b). Such an inclusion of family members was common in ladies' and other travelling orchestras. Graničar appeared for the first time in the listings of *Der Artist* in 1908 when the group was touring in Germany (*Der Artist* 1908). In Germany, they had engagements for high-quality locales, such as Thüringer Grottenhalle in Breslau, Silesia (now Wrocław in Poland), the restaurant of Hotel König in Diedenhofen, Lothringen (now Thionville in Lorraine, France) and Café Germania in Völklingen, Saar. The group toured also in the Austrian Littoral (Österreichisches Küstenland, now split between Slovenia, Croatia and Italy), Dalmatia and Bosnia-Herzegovina.

The group worked on several occasions in Bosnia. In Sarajevo, Graničar played long engagements in the Hotel Continental in 1911, Café Marienhof in 1914, the restaurant of the Vereinshaus in 1916 and 1918, and Café-Restaurant Grüner Hof in 1916 to 1917, which were among the finest locales in the city (*Bosnische Post* 1911, *Sarajevoer Tagblatt* 1914; *Bosnische Post* 1916a, 1916b, 1917a, 1918). In addition, with the permission of Josef Tábory, the owner of Grüner Hof, Graničar performed in a charity concert for the Red Crescent in Sarajevo on 4 October 1916 (Vancaš 1916). Such charitable events were common during the Great War, and artistes for these occasions were chosen carefully. Outside Sarajevo, the group had further engagements in Trebinje in late September 1912 and Mostar in Café Hercegovina in spring 1914 (Biro 1912; *Der Artist* 1914). I know of no sources that mention the band after July 1918.

Although Graničar was de facto a ladies' orchestra in traditional costume, Biro preferred to place his band in the category *Diverse Kapellen und Ensembles* rather than *Damenkapellen* in the listings of *Der Artist*. Other similar bands appeared in either category. The advertisements in *Der Artist* mention that Graničar 'change their beautiful national costumes four times'. Since the band had a Croato-Serbian image, periodically with additional Roma components, some of the costume sets referred to Croatian traditions and others to Serbian ones. The Roma clothing may have been of fantasy design. It remains unclear whether the band actually changed costumes during a single performance; Kaufmann (1997, p. 123) questions the frequent change of costumes as impractical, speculating that a costume band would have worn different stage dresses on successive days.

Biro often published advertisements in *Der Artist,* with some information on the line-up, repertoire and appearance of the band. The basic instrumentation of the band consisted of *tambura* lutes of various sizes and piano. In 1910 and 1911, the band had a xylophone virtuoso, probably female (*Der Artist* 1910, 1911). The xylophone was relatively common in ladies' orchestras and, because of its bright sound and suitability for technically impressive performances, it also belonged to variety shows. Thus, in his 1898 article on the repertoires of ladies' orchestras, a German writer named Franzel (1898) suggests that a concert should include 'a concert polka, preferably on piccolo, trumpet, xylophone, etc.'.[1] Here Franzel refers to female virtuosic multi-instrumentalists who performed in salon orchestras and variety shows on standard or novelty instruments and who were listed in the *Imitatoren und Instrumentalisten* section of *Der Artist*. Novelty instruments included, for instance, hand bells, sleigh bells, tuned drums, tuned flowerpots and xylophone, and they were instrumental in arousing the interest of the audience through introducing sensational and unusual elements to the show (Kaufmann 1997, pp. 78–79; Myers 1993, p. 178). By contrast, Tyrolean *Trachtenkapellen* could use the Alpine folk xylophone *hölzernes Glachter* as a substitute for hammered dulcimer (Ger. *Hackbrett*).

No sources describe the repertoire of Graničar in detail, but its general characteristics during the group's German years are traceable. In 1910 and 1911, Graničar advertised 'first-rate music, soli and choir singing in German and Croatian, dances, xylophone pieces and large modern, classical and national repertoires' (*Der Artist*

1910, 1911). The songs in German must have been popular songs from operettas and other popular songs and instrumental pieces of the day. Whether they sang some south Slavic songs in German translations remains an open question. Furthermore, the repertoire certainly contained arranged Croatian, Slavonian, Serbian and even Bosnian folk and folk-like pieces. A unique source illustrates how Biro strived to find new 'folk' compositions. In the only picture postcard of Graničar to have surfaced, sent by Biro personally from Dubrovnik in mid-May 1914, Biro wished to order 'new Serbian *Sardalinski* songs for *tamburica* or piano with lyrics' (Biro 1914b). By '*Sardalinski*' Biro meant Bosnian *sevdalinka*-style compositions. Biro addressed the postcard to instrument maker Béla Truppel in Novi Sad, southern Hungary, but Truppel struck through the name and forwarded the postcard to famous composer and *tamburica* musician Marko Nešić (1873–1938), who lived in the same town.

Biro's advertisements in *Der Artist* contain standard abbreviations such as '5 j., h. D., 2 H.' which means '5 junge, hübsche Damen, 2 Herren' (five young pretty ladies and two gentlemen) (*Der Artist* 1911). Biro's job advertisements contain similar characterizations of women. In an advertisement in *Bosnische Post,* a Sarajevo German-language newspaper, in October 1908, Biro (1908) was looking for two young women to expand his group for a tour in Germany; they should already play some *tamburica* and should, if possible, have a beautiful voice. Subsequently, in Mostar in March and April 1914, Biro (1914a) was looking for a female singer with a good soprano voice and asked the candidates to write to him with a photograph. The girls may have had the status of trainees, which was common in such bands, but, just as probably, they may have played a central role in *Animierung* during German engagements. By contrast, when Biro (1914c) was looking for a male player of the first *brač tambura* when in Dubrovnik in May 1914, his main concerns were the good sight-reading and bass or baritone vocal skills of the applicants; the advertisements do not mention a photograph. The emphasis on the aesthetic qualities of the female members seems to imply that the main target audience of the band especially in Germany was male. Moreover, the importance of good sight-reading skills implies that the band played and sang from written arrangements. That procedure must have been normal in rehearsals but unlikely on stage.

Table 9.1 summarises the logic behind Graničar's marketing strategy. In Germany, Graničar always employed a Croato-Serbian image, although in autumn 1908 Biro labelled his band as, in addition to the customary 'Croato-Serbian *tamburica*, music [i.e. instrumental] and vocal ensemble', a 'Gipsy group' (*Der Artist* 1908). To judge from various advertisements in *Der Artist*, Roma exoticism was a gimmick that sold well in Germany. Unfortunately, no sources describe the 'Gipsy shows' of Graničar. Another interesting deviation from the group's standard labelling is the inclusion of folk dance performances in 1910 and 1911, which certainly attracted the German public (*Der Artist* 1911).

However, when working in the Hotel Continental in Sarajevo in March 1911, the band represented itself as solely Croatian, playing and singing in Croatian national costumes (*Bosnische Post* 1911). Apparently, the Serbian repertoire

Table 9.1 Some epithets which Biro himself and the venues used for describing Graničar

---

November 1908, Breslau: kroatisch-serbisches Zigeuner-, Tamburitza-, Musik- und Gesangs-Ensemble Graničar
December 1908, Magdeburg: kroatisch-serbisches Tamburitza-Ensemble Graničar
February 1911, Völklingen (Saar): kroatisch-serbisches Tamburitza-, Musik-, Gesang- und Tanz-Ensemble Graničar
March 1911, Sarajevo: kroatische Tamburica-Kapelle Graničar
May 1911, Zwickau: kroatisch-serbisches Tamburitza-, Musik- und Gesang-Ensemble Graničar
May 1914, Dubrovnik: Hrvatsko tamburaško i pjevačko društvo Graničar
December 1914, Sarajevo: beliebtes Damen-Tamburica-Orchester Graničar
January 1916, Sarajevo: bekannte Kapelle Graničar
January 1917, Sarajevo: beliebte Tamburašen-Damen-Kapelle Biró

– let alone the Roma component – yielded no extra value in Sarajevo. Back in Germany in May 1911, Graničar restored its usual Croato-Serbian image for the engagement in Gasthaus Bratwurstglöck'l in Zwickau. From late 1913, however, Biro avoided using any national epithets, and after the break of the Great War, 'Serbian' would have carried negative, even antagonist connotations. Throughout the year 1917, Graničar worked under the name Tamburašen-Damen-Kapelle Biró in Café-Restaurant Grüner Hof in Sarajevo (*Bosnische Post* 1917a, 1917b). The acute accent above the letter o in Biró's name refers to the Hungarian origin of the name; biró means 'judge', and it is a common surname in Hungary as well as in Eastern Slavonia. Interestingly, Milan Biro never used the accent in his surviving music licence applications nor in the pre-1917 advertisements, and therefore the change in spelling must have been a marketing trick that was useful during the war.

Salaries constituted the main source of income for the musicians, and the sale of band picture postcards provided additional income. Furthermore, *Animierung* yielded profit in Germany. As a rule, a collection was avoided in the finer cafés and restaurants of Sarajevo, but tipping was still possible.

Graničar exploited wide artistic diversity that combined a large multilingual repertoire of various styles in German and Croatian, opera, operetta and hit tunes, novelty instruments and periodically folk dancing and even 'Gipsy music'. The band was able to adapt itself to the demands of each touring area, various audiences and the conditions of wartime life. Therefore, Milan Biro emphasized exoticism and Orientalism in Germany and local national music in Dalmatia and Bosnia. The range of the repertoire stretched from Central European mainstream to exotic and even local.

Serbian Roma virtuoso: Andolija

Vaso (or Vasa) Stanković (1852–1934) – stage name Andolija – was an illustrious Serbian Roma folk violinist and singer who was born in the border town

Šabac (R. M. 1937, p. 1) or possibly in the village of Drenovac near Šabac in the Mačva district, at that time in north-western Serbia. He seems to have lived mostly in Šabac.[2] The earliest known printed source on Andolija's growing fame in Bosnia as a musician stems from summer 1896 when he and his Roma band were performing in the fashionable Topčider Park in Belgrade (Matoš 1896, p. 296). He worked in the taverns of Belgrade and toured extensively in Bosnia between 1899 and 1912. Branko Šašić, in his notoriously unreliable biography of Andolija, which relies heavily on newspaper journalism and an interview with Andolija's granddaughter, claims that alongside Bosnia, Andolija toured also in Szabadka (now Subotica), Budapest, Bucharest, Sofia, Plovdiv and Zagreb (2007, p. 28). No known archive or printed sources, however, support the often fantastical stories of Šašić.

According to the surviving music licences, Andolija first toured in Bosnia as a bandleader from December 1899 onwards with his ten-piece all-male band, consisting mostly of his relatives, and at that time the band worked in Sarajevo (Stanković 1899). In September 1904, in Sarajevo, Andolija's remarkably large 14-piece band consisted of himself and musicians from the Stanković family (Ilija, Jefto, Jovan, Jovo, Marinko, Milan, Nikola, Paun and Simo), the Radosavljević family (Miloš, Pajo and Vaso) and the Stojković family (Stanko); the core of this line-up remained unchanged for an unusually long period. Another long-term line-up included members of the Stanković family (Dimitrije, Ilija, Jefto, Marinko, Milorad and Nikola) and the Radosavljević family (Mito, Pajo, Paun, Pavle and Vaso) (Stanković 1905, 1910). In principle, Andolija did not advertise for vacancies in *Der Artist* or newspapers. Instead, preferring his male relatives, he engaged male Roma from the Mačva district as musicians through his personal contacts.

Restaurant owners commonly used Andolija and his band as an attraction for launching new taverns and garden restaurants. Good examples of such business in Sarajevo are the opening campaigns of Stanko Mimić's café and inn in the riverside neighbourhood Bendbaša in the outskirts of the city on the first day of Orthodox Easter 1904, a garden café in Ćemaluša Street in May 1905, and Marko Katić's garden restaurant Mostarska bašta in Franz Josef Street in May 1910 (*Sarajevski list* 1904; *Bošnjak* 1905; Katić 1910). Andolija's band also performed in the Dariva Inn by the river Miljacka a few kilometres from Bendbaša and in the relatively central second-class locale Café Abbazia (or Abacija) in Ćemaluša Street in May and June 1907. In June 1911, they performed in the Knežević Garden in Koševo on the periphery of the city during the excursion of the Serbian Orthodox Church Choir Society Sloga (*Srpska riječ* 1907a, 1907c; *Sarajevski list* 1911). Considering his background, among Andolija's many exceptional performances the most remarkable took place at the imperial charitable feast for the recreation of disabled soldiers by the White Cross Society (Die Österreichische Gesellschaft vom Weißen Kreuze) in the spa resort Ilidža near Sarajevo in late August 1910 (*Musavat* 1910). However, in the reportage on the feast, *Sarajevoer Tagblatt* (1910) failed to mention Andolija, which may indicate either the postponement of the performance or the anti-Serb policy of the newspaper.

As is evident from his engagements in Sarajevo, Andolija's status as a musician was far from unambiguous. He enjoyed great fame as a technically superior violinist, excellent tenor singer and charismatic showman who knew how to please his audiences with his band. Indeed, the Sarajevo Serb newspaper *Srpska riječ* (1907b) mentioned that Andolija was one of the few musicians whose performances could excite and touch the usually emotionless Sarajevo audiences. Furthermore, the line-up of his group remained almost the same throughout the years, which certainly contributed to achieving an extraordinarily smooth cooperation between the members and a large repertoire. Finally, Marko Katić (1910) mentioned that the group could perform in Serbo-Croatian, Hungarian and German, which was rare in Sarajevo. On the other hand, as a Serbian Roma, Andolija's position was suspicious in the eyes of the Austro-Hungarian authorities, the educated classes and many non-Serbs in Bosnia. Hence, in contrast to Hungarian Roma bands, Andolija seems never to have played engagements in the first-class cafés and restaurants of Sarajevo. For instance, the five-piece Hungarian band of *primas* Miklós Lakatos played in December 1913 in the Winter Garden of Hotel Europe, as did the eleven-piece band of *primas* Lajos Horváth in January 1914 (*Bosnische Post* 1913a, 1913c).

According to the anti-Roma claims and opinions, Serbian Roma musicians corrupted the youth with their low-quality music, and, besides, they performed irredentist propaganda songs for Greater Serbia. Therefore, after 1907, heightened political tension between Serbia and Austria-Hungary diminished the number of licences for Serbian musicians in Bosnia (see Pennanen 2017, pp. 174–175). Consequently, the Provincial government seems to have granted Andolija's last music licence for Sarajevo in August 1911, and after that, the surviving archive documents show growing difficulties of renewing the licence in Bosnia (Pennanen 2007, pp. 122–123). Much of Andolija's later life remains in shadow; he may have spent the war years in internment camps in Hungary, and although highly esteemed and even decorated with a medal by King Alexander after the war, he died in poverty in Šabac in 1934 (R. M. 1937, p. 2).

Andolija's group is the only band in this chapter that recorded commercially, namely 27 sides for Deutsche Grammophon-Aktiengesellschaft, the German branch of the Gramophone Company of London. The recording sessions took place in Sarajevo in May 1907 and, judging from the few available sound examples, the line-up in the recording sessions consisted of several violins, one or more *tamburice* and possibly a double bass. The band did not use written arrangements; the music was memory-based. Releasing the recordings in the Orient catalogue number series of the low-price label Zonophone, the Gramophone Company cross-marketed them in Bosnia, Serbia, Croatia-Slavonia and southern Hungary. The titles are in the Latin alphabet in the 1909 Bosnian catalogue, while in the Serbian catalogue they are in Cyrillic (see Pennanen 2007, pp. 123–124). The recorded repertoire consists of south Slavic urban songs from the south Slavic counties of southern Hungary (now forming Vojvodina in Serbia), Vranje and Serbia and a few Bosnian *sevdalinka* songs. The pieces present only a small, south Slavic fraction of the band's repertoire because the records were targeted at the south Slavic market rather than Hungarian- or German-speakers.

The press seems never to have described the performances of Andolija's band, their repertoire or their stage costumes. The only known photograph of Andolija, by Jovan Erić from 1927, shows the bald, Van Dyke-bearded 75-year-old musician holding a violin and bow and wearing an overcoat, a jacket, a shirt with tie and grey-black pinstripe trousers (*Ilustrovani list* 1927). Although the jacket is barely visible, it should have logically been from the same fabric as the trousers. The overall impression is of a refined individual. That said, the photograph does not necessarily depict the style of Andolija's stage costume before the Great War.

Andolija's business strategy utilized the staged representation of the virtuosic, exotic Roma professional musician, which was not as planned as the other two business strategies that have been discussed. The lack of picture postcards reflects the down-to-earth approach to business of Andolija and most Roma professional musicians. There was little demand for 'merchandise' as we now know it today, because the large multilingual repertoire and wide musical versatility guaranteed the interest of ethnically and socially diverse audiences.

Unlike Graničar, Andolija's Roma band retained their basic stage image when switching between repertoires of various ethnic origin. The band had no set programmes, which the audience would be aware of beforehand. Instead, the band played suitable pieces ad hoc for the given context. After this section, the listeners could ask for their favourite songs, and thus, instead of fees from venue owners, the main income of Andolija's band certainly consisted of *bakšiš* (tipping; from Turkish *bahşiş*) after each requested piece. Originating apparently from the Middle East, the practice was, and still is, widespread in the Balkans; in Greek it is known as *hartoúra* (Torp 1993, pp. 29–30).[3] Andolija's ability to fulfil the musical requests was incomparable; the Belgrade pictorial magazine *Ilustrovani list* (1927) praised the immense repertoire of songs and tunes he knew.

Conclusion: three approaches to cosmopolitanism

As is evident from the above three case studies, the potentially most successful musicians touring across the borders of states and cultural areas understood the diversity of their audiences and were able to adapt themselves and their repertoire in accordance with the changing listeners and viewers and their requirements. At their best, such performers were able to transcend the local and national. Having said that, one should always bear in mind that rather than musicians being providers and their audiences customers at any event, the two parties are always joint protagonists, being mutual creators of the shared experience.

The transnational Viennese Ladies' Orchestra Portugal consisted of members from two distinctive ethnicities but made use of one mainstream representation – that of the Viennese salon orchestra – and they were supposed to perform exclusively in German. However, since the repertoire consisted of instrumental music, the language issue played no role in the performances. This ladies' orchestra was dependent on the pervasive influence of the styles of Central and

Western European music, which the great majority of their audiences regarded as 'cosmopolitan'.

The *tamburica* band Graničar was comprised of several very closely related ethnicities that were able to unite in a single Croat representation on the one hand but divide into many representations on the other and, furthermore, employ several languages. Graničar displayed considerable adaptability according to the variation in audiences, performing venues and even political situation. Seemingly, the relationship of the band to cosmopolitanism was calculated and, in consequence, Milan Biro preferred a prearranged plan for each tour.

The strategy of Andolija and his band contrasts with the two other groups. Although performing in several languages and mastering several musical styles, they relied on their Roma ethnicity and one representation. The ability to perform all sorts of popular and folk music from memory when it was requested was their unbeatable characteristic. It is this spontaneity in cosmopolitan sensibility that informs a unique business strategy.

Abbreviations

ABiH   Arhiv Bosne i Hercegovine (Archive of Bosnia and Herzegovina), Sarajevo
ZVS   Zemaljska vlada Sarajevo (Provincial Government, Sarajevo)

Notes

1 Fantasia on *Wilhelm Tell* by Franz Krüger and the galop 'Souvenir de Cirque Renz' by Gustav Peter seem to have been among the most popular pre-Great War xylophone pieces; local orchestras performed them occasionally in Sarajevo (*Sarajevoer Tagblatt* 1908, 1911).
2 Depending on his respective dwelling place, Andolija yielded either Drenovac, Dvorište or Šabac as his place of origin in his music licence application for Bosnia.
3 For a description of *bakšiš* for musicians in the Sarajevo restaurant Zelena bašća (Grüner Garten) in the early 1900s, see the short story *Za pôke rakije* (For a Half *Oka* of Brandy) by the pen name Osman (1905, pp. 56–57).

Bibliography

Biro, Milan. 1908. 'Zur Vergrösserung meines Tamburašen-Ensemble für Deutschland', *Bosnische Post*, 21 October, p. 6.
Biro, Milan. 1912. Telegram. ABiH, ZVS, 21-21/537/1913, Trebinje, 29 September.
Biro, Milan. 1913a. Music licence application. ABiH, ZVS, 21-21/537/1913, Šibenik, November.
Biro, Milan. 1913b. Music licence application. ABiH, ZVS, 21-21/537/1913, Pula, 18 December.
Biro, Milan. 1914a. 'Tražim gospodjicu koja ima dobar glas (sopran)', *Novosti*, 5 March, p. 6.
Biro, Milan. 1914b. Postcard to Béla Truppel. Dubrovnik, 12 May.

Biro, Milan. 1914c. 'Tražim za moj bolji tamburaški zbor dobrog notalnog prvog bračistu', *Novosti*, 13 May, p. 6.
Bosnische Post. 1911. 'Tamburašenkonzert im Hotel Continental', *Bosnische Post*, 18 March, p. 5.
Bosnische Post. 1913a. 'Konzerte im Hotel Europe', *Bosnische Post*, 3 December, p. 5.
Bosnische Post. 1913b. 'Polenblut', *Bosnische Post*, 6 December, p. 4.
Bosnische Post. 1913c. 'Heute Sylvester-Feier und täglich bis 15. Jänner Zigeuner-Konzert im Wintergarten', *Bosnische Post*, 31 December, p. 8.
Bosnische Post. 1914. 'Restaurant Vereinshaus', *Bosnische Post*, 17 November, p. 11.
Bosnische Post. 1916a. 'Vereinshaus-Restaurant', *Bosnische Post*, 1 January, p. 19.
Bosnische Post. 1916b. 'Damenkapelle Biro im Grünen Hof', *Bosnische Post*, 30 September, p. 4.
Bosnische Post. 1917a. 'Café-Restaurant Grüner Hof', *Bosnische Post*, 13 January, p. 4.
Bosnische Post. 1917b. 'Café-Restaurant Grüner Hof', *Bosnische Post*, 15 December, p. 8.
Bosnische Post. 1918. 'Vereinshaus-Restaurant', *Bosnische Post*, 13 July, p. 6.
Bošnjak. 1905. 'Otvorenje nove bašće', *Bošnjak*, 11 May, p. 3.
Bozner Nachrichten. 1909a. 'Wiener Damenkapelle Portugal', *Bozner Nachrichten*, 24 October, p. 3.
Bozner Nachrichten. 1909b. 'Die Damenkapelle Portugal', *Bozner Nachrichten*, 15 December, p. 5.
Bozner Nachrichten. 1910. 'Die Damenkapelle Portugal im Hotel Walther von der Vogelweide', *Bozner Nachrichten*, 6 January, p. 8.
Der Artist. 1908. 'Diverse Kapellen und Ensembles', *Der Artist*, No. 1228, 23 August.
Der Artist. 1909. 'Kroat.-Serbisches Tambur.-Ens. "Granicar"', No. 1249, 17 January.
Der Artist. 1910. 'Diverse Kapellen und Ensembles', *Der Artist*, No. 1319, 22 May.
Der Artist. 1911. 'Diverse Kapellen und Ensembles', *Der Artist*, No. 1358, 19 February.
Der Artist. 1914. 'Diverse Kapellen und Ensembles', *Der Artist*, No. 1522, 12 April.
Deutsches Volksblatt. 1906. 'Eine Ministerialentscheidung gegen die "Animiermädchen"', *Deutsches Volksblatt*, 25 December, p. 10.
Franzel. 1898. 'Ueber Programme von Damen-Capellen', *Der Artist*, No. 717, 6 November.
Grazer Tagblatt. 1908. 'Damenkapelle', *Grazer Tagblatt*, 27 February, p. 10.
Ilustrovani list. 1927. 'Čika Vasa, zvani "Andolija"', *Ilustrovani list*, br. 15, 17 April, p. 15.
Katić, Marko. 1910. Letter to government commissioner for Sarajevo Franz Brodnik. ABiH, ZVS, 21-21/231/1910, 20 May.
Kaufmann, Dorothea. 1997. *'... routinierte Trommlerin gesucht': Musikerin in einer Damenkapelle. Zum Bild eines vergessenen Frauenberufes aus der Kaiserzeit*. Karben, Germany: Coda.
Maiser Wochenblatt. 1910. 'Am k. k. Hauptschießstande Meran', *Maiser Wochenblatt*, 26 January, pp. 4–5.
Matoš, Antun Gustav. 1896. 'Biograd, sredinom juna', *Nada*, br. 15, pp. 296–297.
Musavat. 1910. 'Carska svečanost na Ilidži u korist "Bijelog križa"', *Musavat*, 25 August, p. 3.
Myers, Margaret. 1993. *Blowing Her Own Trumpet: European Ladies' Orchestras and Other Women Musicians 1870–1950 in Sweden*. Gothenburg, Sweden: University of Gothenburg.
Osman. 1905. 'Za pôke rakije', *Bošnjak: kalendar za prostu godinu 1905*, pp. 48–57.
Österreichische Land-Zeitung. 1904. 'Küssen ist keine Sünd'!', *Österreichische Land-Zeitung*, 30 July, p. 9.

Pennanen, Risto Pekka. 2007. 'Immortalised on Wax: Professional Folk Musicians and Their Gramophone Recordings Made in Sarajevo, 1907 and 1908'. In Božidar Jezernik, Rajko Muršič and Alenka Bartulović (eds.), *Europe and Its Other: Notes on the Balkans*. Ljubljana, Slovenia: Filozofska fakulteta, pp. 107–148.

Pennanen, Risto Pekka. 2015. 'Colonial, Silenced, Forgotten: Exploring the Musical Life of German-Speaking Sarajevo in December 1913'. In Vesa Kurkela and Markus Mantere (eds.), *Critical Music Historiography: Probing Canons, Ideologies and Institutions*. Farnham, UK: Ashgate, pp. 107–121.

Pennanen, Risto Pekka. 2017. 'Materialising Invisible Musicians: Professionalism in Non-Classical Music in Habsburg Bosnia-Herzegovina, 1878–1918'. In Knut Holtsträter and Michael Fischer (eds.), *Musik und Professionalität*. Lied und populäre Kultur / Song and Popular Culture. Jahrbuch des Zentrums für Populäre Kultur und Musik, 62. Jahrgang. Münster, Germany: Waxmann, pp. 159–178.

Portugal, Maria. 1913. Music licence application documents. ABiH, ZVS, 21-21/117/1913, Mostar, 11 April.

R. M. [Radivoje Marković]. 1937. 'Vasa Andolija: načuveniji svirač preratne Srbije', *Šabački glasnik*, 13 May 1937, pp. 1–2.

Saary, Margareta. 2018. 'Salonorchester', *Oesterreichisches Musiklexikon Online*. https://www.musiklexikon.ac.at/ml/musik_S/Salonorchester.xml (Accessed on 4 July 2018).

Salzburger Wacht. 1913. 'Palmengarten', *Salzburger Wacht*, 11 October.

Salzburger Volksblatt. 1913. 'Palmengarten', *Salzburger Volksblatt*, 5 June, p. 12.

Sarajevoer Tagblatt. 1908. 'Die Kaiserfeier der Eisenbahnbeamten', *Sarajevoer Tagblatt*, 19 August, p. 3. xx

Sarajevoer Tagblatt. 1910. 'Die Kaiserfeier der k.k. Gesellschaft vom Weißen Kreuz', *Sarajevoer Tagblatt*, 30 August 1910, p. 3.

Sarajevoer Tagblatt. 1911. 'Militärkonzert in Ilidže', *Sarajevoer Tagblatt*, 13 July, p. 4.

Sarajevoer Tagblatt. 1914. 'Café Marienhof', *Sarajevoer Tagblatt*, 3 December, p. 8.

Sarajevski list. 1904. 'Kafana na Bentbaši', *Sarajevski list*, 8 April, p. 3.

Sarajevski list. 1911. 'Srpsko-pravoslavno crkv.-pjev. društvo Sloga', *Sarajevski list*, 28 June, p. 2.

Šašić, Branko. 2007. *Andolija*. Šabac, Serbia: IPK Zaslon and Turistička organizacija opštine Šabac.

Srpska riječ. 1907a. 'Gostionica Dariva', *Srpska riječ*, 12/25 May, p. 4.

Srpska riječ. 1907b. 'Koncerat "Balkana"', *Srpska riječ*, 15/28 May, p. 3.

Srpska riječ. 1907c. 'Kafana Abacija!', *Srpska riječ*, 6/19 June, p. 4.

Stanković, Vaso. 1899. Music licence documents of Vaso Stanković. ABiH, ZVS, 48/329/1899, Sarajevo, 2 December.

Stanković, Vaso. 1905. Music licence. ABiH, ZVS, 22-213/1/1905, Sarajevo, 6 September 1904.

Stanković, Vaso. 1910. Music licence application. ABiH, ZVS, 21-21/389/1910, Sarajevo, 30 August.

Torp, Lisbet. 1993. *Salonikiós: 'The Best Violin in the Balkans'*. Copenhagen, Denmark: Museum Tusculanum Press.

Vancaš, Josef von. 1916. 'Die Wohltätigkeitsakademie zugunsten des Roten Halbmond', *Bosnische Post*, 22 October, p. 5.

10 Musicians as cosmopolitan entrepreneurs

Orchestras in Finnish cities before the modern city orchestra institution

Olli Heikkinen and Saijaleena Rantanen

In the musical life of Western cities, the activities and maintenance of orchestras and bands have played a key role, because 'no other institution has been such a significant status symbol for the cultural well-being and national or regional visibility as a symphony orchestra' (Borris 1969, p. 7). Today, Finnish city orchestras are typically symphony orchestras funded for the most part by their home cities. Their primary duty is to play symphony concerts. In the field of Finnish music historiography, this was already considered to have been the main task of the city orchestras in the nineteenth century. This idea was certainly supported by the 'audience of serious music' (music professionals, critics, lovers of 'serious art music'), from whose vantage point music history has mainly been written. However, this approach gives a rather one-sided view of the function of the orchestras. In the nineteenth century, many orchestras were founded in Finnish cities, but playing symphony concerts was just a minor part of their activity. Moreover, some of the city-funded orchestras were not symphony orchestras at all; they were brass bands.[1]

The orchestral activities in the major cities of Finland in the nineteenth century have been studied extensively. Studies have been conducted, for example, on the former capital of Turku (Andersson 1952; Ringbom 1965; Tolvas 1990; Korhonen 2015), the current capital city of Helsinki (Marvia and Vainio 1993), and Vyborg (Viipuri), one of Finland's most significant music cities (Kuula 2006). As is the case with many other musical organizations, the emergence and history of these orchestras are often described through a heroic national or local narrative in which the creative contribution of national and local forces and the national character of the actions have been emphasized. For example, writing on the establishment of the Helsinki Philharmonic Orchestra in 1882, Erkki Salmenhaara states that 'the records of our history are not tired of repeating [Robert Kajanus's[2]] pioneering work' (Dahlström and Salmenhaara 1995, p. 493), although there had been an orchestra in the city since 1860 under the leadership of (mostly) foreign conductors.

To avoid the afore-described 'national gaze', we have selected two medium-sized coastal cities, Vaasa (3,966 inhabitants in 1860) and Pori (7,130) as the subjects of our research. Comparing two cities with each other and in relation to larger cities of national significance helps us to understand what was typical and what was exceptional in the musical life of Finnish cities after the mid-nineteenth century. We focus on the 1860s and 1870s, because in those decades significant changes were made to the orchestral activities in both cities. At the same time, newspapers began a lively public debate on the maintenance of orchestras and the need to promote urban musical life. The phenomenon was part of a wider European change in publicity, whereby the prosperous city bourgeoisie became increasingly responsible for musical activities (Habermas 2004 [1962]; Weber 1975). At the same time, the significant increase in instrument and sheet music trade, the emergence of the modern orchestral institution, and the itinerant foreign bands and musicians contributed to the development of musical activities in Finland as well.

As a theoretical frame, we will utilize discursive institutionalism (see Schmidt 2008 and Alasuutari 2015). Compared to other 'new institutionalisms' (rational choice institutionalism, historical institutionalism and sociological institutionalism), it considers the role of ideas and discourse in explaining institutional genesis and change more seriously. Institutions change, but not without agency, and agency implies discourse. There are two types of discourse involved: *coordinative* and *communicative*. The former consists of actors in the field (e.g. musicians, journalists, city officials), who among themselves try to find solutions to alleged institutional problems. The latter is directed at the general public by actors in the field in order to legitimize and find support for institutional changes (Schmidt 2008, pp. 304, 309–10).

Through discourse, ideas and institutions that circulate globally are *domesticated* to suit local resources and actors' own interests. In the nineteenth century, musicians trained in musical centres such as Leipzig and Berlin spread cosmopolitan musical ideas and models: in larger cities, such as Boston (see DiMaggio 1982a, 1982b), they were implemented as such, but in smaller cities, such as Pori and Vaasa, they were adapted to and domesticated for the fewer resources available. Therefore, in connection with the development of orchestral activities, we will pay special attention to the conductors: who they were, where they came from and where they went after their tenure in an orchestra ended. We will scrutinize the kinds of activities the work of orchestra conductors encompassed and consider their roles in domesticating the cosmopolitan orchestra institution and musical ideas in local environments.

Our core research material consists of newspapers published in Vaasa and Pori, where the concerts and other musical activities of the city were widely reported. Newspapers offered a forum – at the time the only one – for actors in the musical field to communicate with the wider audience and to persuade it to accept changes in institutional activities. In smaller cities, such as Pori and Vaasa, coordinative discourse happened in face-to-face meetings, both formal and informal. Fortunately, although the official minutes are mostly missing, the meetings were widely covered by newspapers. The material has also been supplemented with archival sources and histories of the cities.

Development of orchestral activities in Finland

The development of orchestral activities in Vaasa and Pori had much in common with the musical life of larger cities in Finland. More than predecessors of modern-day symphony orchestras, the orchestras in Finland in the middle of the nineteenth century – particularly as far as the prominence of their *Kapellmeisters* is concerned – seemed to have many similarities with the former cosmopolitan city musician (*Stadtmusikanten*) system in the Baltic Sea area (see Heikkinen and Rantanen 2018). The conductors were almost without exception itinerant musicians from abroad who brought many fashionable musical influences with them. Their main task, as with city musicians before, was to provide music to all the occasions where it was needed in the city, for instance, balls, musical evenings, promenade concerts, weddings and funerals.

In Finnish music historiography, however, this point has been downgraded. This is due, in addition to the musicians being foreigners, to the fact that these orchestras, which took care of music on a regular basis, were quite small by modern-day standards. For example, in his book on the orchestral history of Turku, Kimmo Korhonen refuses to call an orchestra of nine members in 1838 an 'orchestra' (Korhonen 2015, p. 115). However, the ensemble fulfilled the criteria of a contemporary city orchestra (see endnote 1): it was funded by the city and played dance and stage music indoors in the winter and brass music in the local spa in the summer (see ÅU 1 Jan. 1842; ÅT 16 Apr. 1845; and ÅU 6 Dec. 1847). Its leader was Wilhelm Friedrich Siber from Livonia, followed by the Vyborg-German Anton Rudolf Hausen (Korhonen 2015, pp. 115, 138). From 1868 onwards, a slightly larger orchestra (14 musicians) of the musical society in Turku (*Musikaliska Sällskapet i Åbo*) carried out the same tasks as Siber's and Hausen's orchestra earlier (Korhonen 2015, pp. 150–154).

In Vyborg, the situation was very similar to Turku. At public occasions, the music was mainly performed by an orchestra with seven musicians, led by the conductor Carl Spohr (Flodin and Ehrström 1934, p. 55). In 1867, a new 12-member orchestra was established, led by German-born Ernst Schnéevoigt (WT 11 May 1867, 31 Jul. 1867). As in Turku, the new orchestra mainly performed the same tasks as its predecessor (see, e.g. Ilm 20 Dec. 1867), except for brass music, which was performed by a brass band, especially in parks and elsewhere in the open air.

In Helsinki, the situation in the 1860s and 1870s was reminiscent of that in Vyborg, but there were also significant differences. A professional orchestra had been operating in the city since 1844, first under the leadership of Louis Lowe and then the German-born Carl Ganszauge. The orchestra's activities resembled both Siber/Hausen's and Spohr's orchestras. In 1860, a 20-member orchestra was set up in connection with the establishment of a new theatre. Unlike other cities, Helsinki did not support orchestral activities. The orchestra's position outside the theatre was also not as significant as in other cities. For example, in 1862, of the total of 189 performances, 145 were performances in the theatre (see Heikkinen, 2018, p. 23). Military bands took care of brass music.

In larger cities, the resources for musical activities were, of course, better. Larger resources enabled more effective and encompassing activities, such as organizing symphony concerts, much earlier than in Vaasa and Pori. However, the lack of resources did not reduce the need to set up an orchestra. On the contrary: an orchestra was a sign of the cultural awareness of the city and, in addition, a necessary maintainer of cultural life, especially in smaller cities.

Military musicians as town musicians

In Pori and Vaasa, the main difference compared to the larger cities was the role of military musicians. After the military reform following the Crimean War (1854–55), nine sharpshooter battalions were formed in Finland, one of which was placed in Vaasa and one in Pori. Each of the battalions was assigned 17 signalists, that is, bugle players. There were no separate bands appointed by the army, but the signalists assembled smaller groups to play in dances and other amusements in the cities (Vuolio 1985, pp. 62–63).

Professional musicians were hired as leaders of the bands. In Vaasa, the task was taken over by Bror Wilhelm Palin (1829–1904). He quickly became a key person in the music scene of the city. He was born in Stockholm, Sweden, and had received his music education at the Stockholm Royal Academy of Music. In its versatility, Palin's work resembled that of the former city musician's incumbent. He worked as a singing teacher in the local high school, taught the piano and several string instruments, played the organ and the clarinet, organized concerts and set up choirs. He was also trained as a piano tuner and promoted his services in local newspapers. In addition, he was responsible for the music school, which functioned in connection with the battalion's band and which actively recruited new students.

The battalion's band took over the musical activities of the city by performing in soirées, at the celebrations of prominent figures in the city, charity concerts for bourgeois families of limited means and others in need, as well as at church services, balls and many other private and public events that needed a musical programme. At this point, after a devastating fire in the city in 1852, the development of the orchestral activities was greatly affected by the restaurant keepers returning to the city and providing the necessary facilities for organizing events, especially dance events. Itinerant theatre groups were important employers for local orchestras as well, as they were needed to play music during the intermission and to accompany songs during the performance (see BT 7 Jul. 1877; BT 2 Nov. 1878; Hirn 1998, p. 102; Korhonen 2015, p. 151).

As in Vaasa, Pori battalion's signalists also set up a band. August Nordeman (1819–86) was invited to be the leader of the group. He was born in Eskilstuna, Sweden, and had completed an organ and a chant singing degree as well as a conducting degree at the Stockholm Royal Academy of Music. In addition to his position as a conductor, he worked in Pori as a singing teacher and organist (BT 14 Jun. 1882). Already in the summer of 1861, the band played regularly at the recreational places of the city for remuneration. The main clientele of the band was the wealthy bourgeoisie of the city, although servants and other working-class citizens also attended the entertainment venues. As in Vaasa, the Pori battalion's band assisted in free charity events, which was considered a kind of obligation.

At the end of the decade, however, the promising beginning of musical activities in Vaasa and Pori experienced a setback. The army was remodelled again and, except for the Finnish guard located in Helsinki, all sharpshooter battalions were scrapped. This also meant the end of the battalion's band activity. The 'farewell concert' of the Vaasa battalion's band was held in January 1868. There were more than 200 people in the audience (Vb 11 Jan. 1868). A local newspaper in Pori highlighted the gratitude of the citizens for the musicians who for years had worked 'satisfactorily fulfilling all the efforts and needs of the community when it comes to all kinds of musical performances'. They were particularly grateful that this had been done for free (Bj 1 Feb. 1868). In reality, the band had only played for free at formal festivals and charity events. For other performances, it had been recompensed. In Vaasa as well, the orchestra usually charged a fee for their performances.

Private and amateur bands

The significance of the sharpshooter battalions in the social life of the bourgeoisie was obviously high, because both cities began to raise funds to continue the band activities. This stage is particularly interesting from the point of view of the domestication of the orchestral institution, as the battalion's influence in Pori and Vaasa was more dramatic than in Turku, Helsinki and Vyborg, whose musical life was not dependent on military bands. The continuation of orchestral activities in Pori and Vaasa demanded particular attention from the bourgeoisie of the cities, as they played an increasingly important role in the design and financing of musical life. With regard to orchestral issues, the coordinating discourse took place, above all, in the musical associations established according to European models (see Broyles 2000, p. 102) particularly for these purposes throughout Finland, including Pori and Vaasa. The discourse of these associations was reported in local newspapers. The role of the local musical association in orchestral endeavours was particularly pronounced in Vaasa, where plans did not proceed in the desired way.

In Pori, the fundraising apparently yielded results, because in the fall of 1868 the new band was already marketing its services in the newspaper. The issues of the orchestra were handled by the city's trustee, and the Swedish conductor Johan August Jansson (1839–81) was hired as the leader of the band. New sheet music was purchased from Stockholm (Bj 5 Dec. 1868, 18 Sep. 1869). The band continued its activities as the battalion's band before. It performed at evening socials, dances, private and public festivals, and charity concerts – in other words, at all events organized by the local bourgeoisie where music was deemed necessary. Musicians earned extra income, for example, by giving singing lessons and copying sheet music. Jansson himself set up a photography studio. Nevertheless, financial arrangements and fees did not match the musicians' wishes and, in the spring of 1873, they threatened to stop the band activities if the city did not support the band financially. The city's bourgeoisie held a meeting and decided to give the band 2,000 marks per year for five years. In return, the band had to perform for the amusement of the ordinary people in a public place six times a year without any remuneration.

In Vaasa, also, the citizens began to plan for a new orchestra. A special committee was set up for the project, consisting of members of the drama and music club founded in 1864. The members of the committee belonged to the city's bourgeoisie. In order to exploit the existing resources, the committee planned to gather the members of the new band from the battalion musicians who, after the abolition of the battalion, had stayed in the city and assisted, for example, in the musical programmes of the soirées (Vb 14 Mar. 1868, 4 Apr. 1868).

In addition to acquiring the musicians, the committee benefited from the battalion's band by purchasing the instruments that the band had used and that the battalion's lieutenant was now advertising in the newspaper at discount prices. Woodwinds as well as brass and string instruments were on sale (Vb 18 Apr. 1868, Vb 9 May 1868, Vb 23 May 1868). According to the instrument purchases, the new band might have been a blended orchestra, that is, able to play both brass music and string music, but this cannot be fully verified based solely on the data. Palin, who had demonstrated his ability to lead the choir and organize the city's musical activities, was again nominated as the leader of the new orchestra, this time called the *city band* ('stadskapell', see Vb 23 May 1868). In addition, he had excellent networks that the orchestral committee wanted to exploit (Vb 18 Jan. 1868).

In order to promote the orchestral issue, the committee invited music and dance lovers to meet in the town hall to discuss the details of assembling the orchestra (Vb 23 May 1868). The committee members wanted music-consuming citizens to be involved in the coordinative discourse concerning orchestral matters. A separate invitation was also sent to those who would have the opportunity to support the project financially, since, after the poor harvests and famine at the end of the decade (1867–68), the city's cash resources were low (Vb 20 Jun. 1868). After that, things proceeded quickly. In early July 1868, the orchestral committee announced in the newspaper that a new orchestra had been established in the city (Vb 4 Jul. 1868). The orchestra, comprised partly of the battalion musicians, held its first concert with Palin at the local hotel on the first day after Christmas. The programme included 'new and modern dance music' (Vb 5 Dec. 1868, Vb 24 Dec. 1868).

According to the newspapers, the band performed actively in early 1869. It was employed mostly by the commissioned soirées and balls organized in the city's restaurants, where the citizens were allowed to buy advance tickets covering the whole season. In addition to dance performances, the orchestra played brass music in the Ernst Pavilion, at the anniversary celebration of the town's children's homes, at the celebrations of the emperor's name day and birthday, and on the nearby Sandö island, which had become the city's most important venue for outdoor events. In addition, the orchestra featured in many religious and secular concerts held in the city. However, putting the musical life of the whole city at the mercy of one person only was risky. In Vaasa, this became apparent at the end of 1869, when the orchestral committee dismissed Palin due to issues of distrust. The reasons for the lack of trust were not specified, but apparently the orchestra had missed the agreed performances.

After that, the commission tried to form an orchestra with Arnold Lohse. Born in 1829, he was from the town of Geyer in Saxony, Germany, and had arrived in Finland in the 1850s for work (FAT 10 Dec. 1859; Vb 29 Nov. 1862). At the time of recruitment, Lohse worked as the orchestra director of the nearby Kristinestad. Like Palin, Lohse was both an organist and a violinist. He was also a piano instructor and, like Palin and Nordeman, had studied at the Stockholm Royal Academy of Music (Brummert n.d., p. 4). Lohse also worked as a travelling musician and piano tuner. He began his work by recruiting talented, 'well brought up' young musicians with musical skills through newspapers in Vaasa and elsewhere (Vb 18 Dec. 1869). The goal was also to employ musicians from Germany exploiting Lohse's relations to his home country. His attempts, however, failed (Vb 16 Jul. 1870). Soon after this, Lohse left Vaasa and moved to Vyborg to work as a violinist in the orchestra led by Ernst Schnéevoigt.

The orchestra committee was not discouraged and, after the departure of Lohse, they tried to cooperate with Albert Fliege and his orchestra. Fliege came from Königsberg, East Prussia, and toured in Finland with his four-member band, which later expanded to six musicians. In addition to Albert Fliege, his sons Bernhard, Hubert and Emil played in the orchestra (Svenska teaterns arkiv [SLSA 1270], Personalkontrakt). The group was familiar with the committee since it had appeared in Ernst's restaurant during the previous winter season. In 1870, the committee commissioned Fliege to enter into a year-long agreement that committed his ensemble to playing 'horn and dance music' in the city. The composition of the ensemble was a blended orchestra. The agreement included a certain number of free concerts and other prearranged performances in the province (Vb 16 Jul. 1870).

Fliege's orchestra had a flying start, but a year later *Vasabladet* reported that the band had suffered serious financial problems (Vb 9 Dec. 1871). In addition, the performances of the orchestra began to receive increasingly critical reviews in the newspapers (e.g. Vb 17 Feb. 1872). The situation eventually led to the discharge of Fliege and his group. The orchestra left behind a debt of about 1,000 marks, followed by a four-year silence in the city's orchestral life. This dramatically affected the musical life of the city, as many travelling artist groups were used to using city orchestras as assistants in their performances. The blame for the poor state of the city's musical situation was put on Fliege and his band. In newspapers, however, the debate on the setting up of an orchestra continued.

The 'blended orchestra' in Pori

In the nineteenth century, there was a constant need for outdoor brass music in European cities and spa resorts. Brass music was needed to heighten the spirit at public festivities, to provide entertainment in parks and promenades and to accompany 'taking waters' at spas. Most of the time this need was satisfied by military bands (see Brucher and Reily 2013, pp. 7–14; Nilsson 2017). However, in smaller premises in smaller towns, brass bands were often considered too loud. For this reason, at Pori town hall, which often served as a venue for public celebrations and lotteries, a separate gallery for the band was constructed. Thus, the sound was more evenly distributed around the room, and conversations could be had without a cornet playing next to one's ear. In 1872, two violins and a flute were added to the instrument arsenal of August Jansson's band, which was greeted with gratitude in a newspaper (Bj 30 Nov. 1872).

However, the practice and use of the new instruments were apparently minor, since in summer 1877 discussion on the string instruments began again. A particular complaint was that the brass band was able to perform between the acts at the theatre performances, but it could not accompany the song numbers. The performances of itinerant theatre companies were the most significant form of public entertainment in winter time. There had apparently already been some coordinating discourse, because, according to the press article, a calculation of the cost of a string orchestra was requested from Ernst Schnéevoigt, the conductor in Vyborg. However, the 20,000 marks a year calculated by Schnéevoigt could not be afforded. As an alternative, the newspaper suggested that the current brass band should train apprentices to play string instruments (BT 7 Jul. 1877).

A Danish-born church organist Theodor Sörensen (1846–1914) had a central role in reorganizing the band. He proposed that the orchestra should have a string quartet, a flute, a clarinet, two horns, a trumpet and timpani. In the newspaper, this was justified by the fact that the proposed orchestra would be able to play both string and horn music. In addition, it was considered a more useful line-up in winter time, especially for the needs of the theatre, for the reason already discussed.

For the management of the orchestra, Sörensen suggested that a society should be founded, based on the model of Turku's musical society (BT 11 Aug. 1877, 22 Sep. 1877, 6 Oct. 1877). The first meeting of the society was held on 4 October. One reason for the swift action was the concerts held in Pori at the same time by the 25-member orchestra of *Musikaliska Sällskapet i Åbo*, led by the German conductor Louis Fichtelberger. The orchestra's programme included classical 'gems', such as Beethoven and Haydn, as well as two pieces of a symphony composed by Sörensen himself in 1873, dedicated to the orchestra. The critic was very hopeful that with Sörensen's talent it would also be possible to set up a 'decent' orchestra of the same kind in Pori. In any case, he tried to persuade the newspaper-reading public to accept the idea that old brass music should not return: as long as the city had such a 'surrogate', there was no hope for the better and people should rather be without music altogether (BT 26 Sep. 1877, 3 Oct. 1877, 6 Oct. 1877).

The society was named *Musikaliska Sällskapet i Björneborg*, and its rules were copied almost word for word from the rules of the Turku Society. The conductor would receive the profit from the orchestra's performances. A board of five members was elected from among the city bourgeoisie and Sörensen was appointed conductor (BT 6 Oct. 1877, 10 Oct. 1877, 13 Oct. 1877, 17 Oct. 1877, 20 Oct. 1877).

Carl Theodor Sörensen was born in Copenhagen and studied, according to his own statement, composition, the organ and the piano under Niels Gade's guidance. However, his letter of recommendation was written by another well-known Danish organist, Gottfred Matthison-Hansen. Sörensen arrived in Finland in 1867 and initially settled in Turku, where he began teaching music and organizing concerts. Later, he served as an organist in Kristinestad and Norrmark, until in 1874 he was appointed as organist in Pori. As was customary for organists at that time, he began to organize the musical life in the city – just as Palin had done in Vaasa. Sörensen put together a temporary orchestra and choir for a concert, organized musical evenings and taught the piano, singing and harmony. If not before, the performances of his first symphony in autumn 1877 must have finally convinced the city dwellers of the skills he had acquired in his native country of Denmark.[3]

If the society was set up quickly, organizing the orchestra did not take much longer. In order to find competent musicians, Sörensen placed an announcement in the newspapers in Turku, Helsinki and Vyborg, even before his formal election as conductor. The first concert of the orchestra was on 15 December and, according to the newspaper, it included string and especially horn music, although the main emphasis of the programme seems to have been on the former. At the same time, the society announced that ten dance evenings were planned for the spring. In accordance with the *Turmmusik* tradition dating back to the Middle Ages, on New Year's Eve in 1878 the orchestra played hymns from the church tower for the citizens' pleasure.[4] Pori had been given a 'decent orchestra' (ÅU 16 Oct. 1877; BT 28 Nov. 1877, 12 Dec. 1877, 15 Dec. 1877; Sk 5 Jan. 1878).

The activities of the orchestra hardly deviated from the activities of the previous brass band (BT 12 Jan. 1878, 4 May 1878). During the first year, the orchestra had 141 performances. There was a total of 79 musical evenings, picnics and balls. The orchestra accompanied theatrical performances 29 times. There were 5 public festivities, and the orchestra played brass music in the park for free 6 times. In addition, the orchestra performed at 5 weddings, 3 funerals, and 10 other private events. The orchestra accompanied visiting artists in a concert 4 times (BT 2 Nov. 1878).

As Sörensen had to resign after a year due to an illness, the board published an announcement for a new conductor in the newspapers in (at least) Pori, Turku, Helsinki, Vyborg, Stockholm and Copenhagen. The announcement emphasized that the band consisted of an 11-member string orchestra and a 7-member brass band (BT 8 Jan. 1879). Carl Gottschalksen (1854–1939) was chosen for the post (BT 22 Mar. 1879; Gottschalksen 1920, pp. 57–58). He was born in Copenhagen where he received private lessons in violin, piano and theory. At the age of 18, he was recruited to the army as an alto horn player. After that, he worked as a conductor in itinerant theatre companies for a few years, until he moved to Pori (Gottschalksen 1920).

The activities of the orchestra continued essentially unchanged. Gottschalksen had brought with him 4 Danish musicians, and there were now 12 musicians in the orchestra, including the conductor. With the assistance of a few amateurs, the orchestra was able to perform Beethoven's first and Mozart's fortieth symphonies.

At the same time, the orchestra began to hold concerts for ordinary people at a reduced ticket price. At the annual meeting in November 1879, the society's economy was found to be on solid ground, one of the reasons being the activity of the orchestra: during the 150 days of Gottschalksen's leadership, it had performed 120 times, at public and private occasions. Over 100 new shares were marked for 1880–82, and when the city further budgeted a subsidy of 3,000 marks for the following year, the future of the orchestra was secured for a long time. The year changed, and as had become customary, the orchestra once again climbed up to the church tower to play an anthem to the happy townspeople (BT 31 Dec. 1879).

The influence of versatile professional musicians such as Sörensen and Gottschalksen on the development of local orchestral activities was decisive. Both had received their musical education in Copenhagen, with its centuries-old music traditions and close ties to European music centres. For example, Niels Gade, under whose tutelage Sörensen studied, was a teacher at the Leipzig Conservatory and later founded a conservatory in Copenhagen. In addition to string orchestras, Gottschalksen also had experience in brass bands and, in fact, during the latter part of his career he led the Copenhagen Tivoli brass band (Gottschalksen 1920, pp. 183–88). Sörensen later moved to Vyborg, where he led a military brass band (Heikkinen 2013). In cooperation with the local actors, they domesticated the skills they had acquired in Copenhagen to the more modest resources of Pori, which led to the creation of a 'blended orchestra'.

From the fire brigade's band to the city orchestra

In Pori, the orchestral endeavours progressed seamlessly. The discussions between the city bourgeoisie and the foreign professional musicians responsible for the musical activities had gone smoothly. Most importantly, the city council of Pori was willing to invest financially in the orchestra's maintenance, which assured its stability. After the failed attempts in Vaasa, too, efforts to set up an orchestra began to bear fruit in 1876, when the orchestral committee started planning for a brass band that would function in connection with the city's fire brigade. Fire brigades were a part of wider organizational activities increasing in Finland at the time and had a fundamental impact on the formation of a public musical life. Due to the development of the so-called 'national public sphere', the lower classes also began to have access to public activities (Nieminen 2009). More broadly, these changes were connected to the rise of the nationalistic movement in Finland, which aimed at educating the working class and preparing them to participate in the construction of the Finnish nation-state. Music had a central role in the process. In Vaasa, the pioneer in organizing musical activities open to all classes of society was the fire brigade, which from the beginning (1868) organized choir and brass band activities that aimed at involving the working class (Jalkanen 2003, pp. 137–39). At the same time, the city's musical activities gained the boost for which the orchestral commission had hoped.

Early in 1876, the fire brigade began recruiting musicians via newspaper announcements. The project was again under the orchestral committee, which was committed to cooperating with the brigade. The main goal was to finally establish an orchestra in Vaasa, even if it was 'merely' a brass band. In addition to the musicians, students interested in playing brass instruments were sought. In the advertisement, they were also offered an opportunity to receive training under the instruction of the conductor (Vb 15 Jan. 1876). Thus, the committee sought to ensure the continuity of the musical activities.

The newspaper announcements seem to have produced no results, as the fire brigade's brass band was eventually made up of the members of the brigade. The band was a sextet, and Palin, who still had influence in the city, was again chosen as the leader (Vb 15 Sep. 1877). According to the newspapers, the citizens were pleased with the band, but in the end, from the viewpoint of the orchestral committee, the amateur brass band was unable to satisfy the musical needs of the city. The orchestral advocates wanted a 'professional orchestra' alongside the brass band that would be able to perform at events that required more versatile repertoire and followed European trends (Vb 28 Mar. 1877). In the newspapers, the committee argued that 'in spite of the depressing experiences of the past, any city the size of Vaasa should by now be further along when it comes to performing instrumental music at major public events'. They also emphasized the civilizing importance of music: 'We hope that no one will deny the cultivating and educational influence that good music and the practice of it has' (Vb 11 Jan. 1879).

The decisive factor for the establishment of a professional orchestra in Vaasa was finally the decision of the city council to join the financing of the operation (Vb 15 Jan. 1879). Immediately after the decision, the town's restaurateurs and associations began to organize concerts and other events to raise funds for the orchestra. Arnold Lohse was re-elected as the leader of the group, and this time he succeeded in assembling the band and recruiting musicians to Vaasa. Musicians were employed from Germany utilizing Lohse's relations, although the newspaper was ready to point out how 'experience has taught that foreigners cannot always be trusted'. Even when discussing the selection of the director, the committee emphasized that the person should be a Finn or someone who had spent longer periods in Finland (Vb 11 Jan. 1879). Albert Fliege's orchestra had left a permanent mark on the orchestral activities in the city.

On 21 June 1879, *Vasabladet* reported that the musicians of the orchestra had arrived. The group was a blended orchestra. In its first performance at the annual event of the fire brigade, the programme consisted of horn music and, in October, the orchestra organized its first concert with string instruments (Vb 6 Oct. 1879, Vb 11 Oct. 1879, Vb 25 Oct. 1879). In summer, the orchestra played many free concerts in the city parks. In the autumn, the 'city orchestra', which is what the orchestra with seven musicians was called immediately after its establishment, organized concerts, performances and children's balls and took care of the musical programme during the intermissions of theatre performances. The new promenade concerts became a popular form of recreation among the city bourgeoisie. This was the beginning of the development after which citizens no longer had to worry about not hearing enough music in the city.

Conclusions

Our cases make it clear that orchestras formed a key part of the musical and cultural life in Finnish cities in the nineteenth century – even in smaller ones. The orchestral activities in Vaasa and Pori in the 1860s and 1870s were very similar. In exchange for support from the city and the bourgeoisie, the orchestras played at public festivities and other events in the city as well as at the open-air promenade concerts during summertime. Moreover, the regular public balls organized by restaurant owners formed one of the most prominent sources of income. Further income was provided by organizing musical evenings and concerts. In addition, orchestras were ordered to accompany theatrical performances, assist guest artists and perform music at private balls and get-togethers.

The orchestras developed from brass bands towards orchestras with both string and wind instruments. In the 1860s, battalion bands were able to take care of the musical needs of the townspeople, especially outdoors in summer, but playing indoors required string instruments due to both the volume level and diversity of the programme. A brass band was able to perform a variety of music – from dance pieces to opera overtures – but it could not perform a symphonic repertoire. In addition to entertainment, there was a need for civilizing efforts, which were constantly being compared with those of other cities in newspapers. In Vaasa, one of the benchmarks was Pori, which in turn modelled itself on Turku. The goal was to develop and maintain musical life and keep up-to-date on new European trends.

The 'blended orchestra' was a strategic concept in the domestication of two central contemporary orchestral institutions: the brass band and the symphony orchestra. Help for the process was sought from abroad, especially from versatile musicians educated in Germany, Copenhagen and Stockholm. These cosmopolitan musicians brought global ideas and models with them and applied them to local conditions. In Pori, Sörensen and Gottschalksen assumed great responsibility for organizing orchestral activities in the city. They participated in discourse on the subject with the city bourgeoisie, making concrete suggestions that were presented to other townsfolk in the newspapers. In Vaasa, on the other hand, the orchestral committee of the city bourgeoisie served as the main promoter. Employing reliable and sufficiently qualified professional musicians in Vaasa proved to be difficult, partly because of bad luck, partly due to lack of permanent funding. In all likelihood, the situation in Vaasa was also hampered by its more peripheral geographical location compared to Pori, which was further south with good connections to Turku.

The modern conception of the orchestra whose main function is to hold symphony concerts, and which can be called a 'symphony orchestra', was formed quite late in Finland. The Helsinki Philharmonic Orchestra, which travelled to the Paris World's Fair in 1900 and held concerts in several European cities, was at the forefront of the development. German-language journals, widely referenced in Finland, were especially fond of calling an orchestra a 'symphony orchestra'. In the grant given by the Finnish Senate in 1904, the maintenance of a 'symphony orchestra' was explicitly stated (PL 12 Feb. 1904). In 1919, the Helsinki

Philharmonic Orchestra played its last promenade concert and thereafter focused on symphony concerts (Heikkinen, 2018, p. 27). Today, holding symphony concerts is still the core activity of the Pori Sinfonietta and the Vaasa City Orchestra.

Notes

1 Until the beginning of the twentieth century in both the Finnish and the Swedish language brass bands (*soittokunta, kapell*) were also called orchestras (*orkesteri, orkester*). This is due to the similar functions that brass bands and orchestras with string instruments fulfilled in the cities. This becomes evident later in the article.
2 Robert Kajanus (1853–1933) was a Finnish conductor and composer and a central figure in the musical life of Helsinki.
3 On Sörensen's career in Finland, see Heikkinen 2013.
4 Since the Medieval period, town musicians had been obligated to play a harmonized hymn or some shorter secular piece from the church tower at certain times of the day (Andersson 2003, p. 252).

Bibliography

Alasuutari, Pertti, 2015. The discursive side of new institutionalism. *Cultural Sociology* 9, 162–184.
Andersson, G., 2003. I stadens tjänst. In: J. Kreslins, S.A. Mansbach and R. Schweitzer, eds. *Gränsländer. Östersjön i ny gestalt*. Stockholm, Sweden: Atlantis, pp. 237–256.
Andersson, O., 1952. *Turun soitannollinen seura 1790–1808*. Turku, Finland: Silta.
Borris, S., 1969. *Die grossen Orchester. Eine Kulturgeschichte*. Hamburg, Germany: Claassen.
Broyles, M., 2000. Ensemble music moves out of the private house: Haydn to Beethoven. In: Joan Peyser, ed. *The Orchestra. Origins and Transformations*. New York: Billboard Books, pp. 101–26.
Brucher, K. and Reily, S.A., 2013. Introduction: The world of brass bands. In: S.A. Reily and K. Brucher, eds. *Brass Bands of the World: Militarism, Colonial Legacies, and Local Music Making*. Farnham, UK: Ashgate, pp. 1–31.
Brummert, J.L., n.d. *Vaasan kaupungin musiikkielämää ennen vanhaan*. Unpublished manuscript.
Dahlström, F. and Salmenhaara, E., 1995. *Suomen musiikin historia 1. Ruotsin vallan ajasta romantiikkaan*. Porvoo, Finland: WSOY.
DiMaggio, P., 1982a. Cultural entrepreneurship in nineteenth-century Boston, I: The creation of an organizational base for high culture in America. *Media, Culture and Society* 4(1), pp. 33–50.
DiMaggio, P., 1982b. Cultural entrepreneurship in nineteenth-century Boston, II: The classification and framing of American art. *Media, Culture and Society* 4(4), pp. 303–22.
Flodin, K. and Ehrström, O., 1934. *Richard Faltin och hans samtid*. Helsinki, Finland: Holger Schildt.
Gottschalksen, C., 1920. *En glad musikantens dagbok*. Copenhagen, Denmark: Kunstforlaget Danmark.
Habermas, J., 2004 [1962]. *Julkisuuden rakennemuutos. Tutkimus yhdestä kansalaisyhteiskunnan kategoriasta*. Suom. Veikko Pietilä. Tampere, Finland: Vastapaino.
Heikkinen, O., 2013. 'Urkuri Sörensenin rikos'. *Musiikki* 43(2), pp. 5–23.

Heikkinen, O., 2018. Sinfoniaorkesteri-instituution kotoistaminen Suomessa. *Etnomusikologian vuosikirja* 30, pp. 6–34.

Heikkinen, O. and Rantanen S., 2018. Itämeren kaupunkien muusikot kaupunginmuusikkoinstituution jälkeen. Vaasan ja Porin orkesteritoiminta 1860– ja 1870–luvuilla. *Trio* 7 (2), pp. 77–97.

Hirn, S., 1998. *Alati kiertueella. Teatterimme varhaisvaiheita vuoteen 1870.* Helsinki, Finland: Yliopistopaino.

Jalkanen, P., 2003. Autonomian ajan Suomi: Biedermeier ja tingeltangel. In: P. Jalkanen and V. Kurkela, eds. *Suomen musiikin historia. Populaarimusiikki.* Helsinki, Finland: WSOY, pp. 112–251.

Korhonen, K., 2015. *Sävelten aika. Turun Soitannollinen Seura ja Turun filharmoninen orkesteri 1790–2015.* Helsinki, Finland: Siltala.

Kuula, P., 2006. *Viipurin Musiikin Ystävien orkesteri suomalaisen musiikin ja kansallisen identiteetin edistäjänä 1894–1918.* Helsinki, Finland: Sibelius-Akatemia.

Marvia, E. and Vainio, M., 1993. *Helsingin kaupunginorkesteri 1882–1982.* Porvoo, Finland: WSOY.

Nieminen, H., 2009. *Kansa seisoi loitompana. Kansallisen julkisuuden rakentuminen Suomessa 1809–1917.* Tampere, Finland: Vastapaino.

Nilsson, A., 2017. *Musik till vatten och punsch: kring svenska blåsoktetter vid brunnar, bad och beväringsmöten.* Möklinta, Sweden: Gidlund.

Ringbom, M. ed., 1965. *Turun soitannollinen seura 1790–1965. 175-vuotisjuhlajulkaisu.* Turku, Finland: Turun Soitannollinen Seura, pp. 30–78.

Schmidt, V.A., 2008. Discursive institutionalism: The explanatory power of ideas and discourse. *Annual Review of Political Science* 11, pp. 303–26.

Tolvas, I. ed., 1990. *Turun soitannollinen seura 200 vuotta: 1790–1990: juhlajulkaisu.* Turku, Finland: Turun Soitannollinen Seura.

Vuolio, J., 1985. Piirteitä suomalaisesta sotilasmusiikista autonomian aikana. In: T. Leisiö ed. *Muutoksia musiikissa, musiikkia muutoksissa.* Suomen Harmonikkainstituutin julkaisuja 11. Ikaalinen, Finland: Suomen Harmonikkainstituutti, pp. 56–71.

Weber, W., 1975. *Music and the Middle Class. The Social Structure of Concert Life in London, Paris, and Vienna.* London: Croom Helm.

Archives

Svenska teaterns arkiv

Newspapers

ÅU, *Åbo Underrättelser*
Bj, *Björneborg*
BT, *Björneborgs Tidning*
FAT, *Finlands Allmänna Tidning*
Hb, *Hufvudstadsbladet*
Ilm, *Ilmarinen*
LS, *Länsi-Suomi*
PKS, *Porin Kaupungin Sanomia*
Pl, *Päivälehti*
Sk, *Satakunta*

TS, *Tampereen Sanomat*
Vb, *Vasabladet*
WT, *Wiborgs Tidning*

11 'A foreign cosmopolitanism'
Treaty port Shanghai, ad hoc municipal ensembles, and an epistemic modality

Yvonne Liao

> If cosmopolitanism means an abiding curiosity in 'looking out', then Shanghai in the 1930s was the cosmopolitan city par excellence.
>
> (Lee 1999, p. 315)

Cosmopolitan and colonial: the treaty port

Shanghai studies in recent decades, for example Leo Lee's *Shanghai Modern*, has not only substantiated but also brought the idea of a cosmopolitan Shanghai into sharp focus.[1] In centring his discussion on Shanghai's writers and translators, Lee highlights a Chinese cosmopolitanism in the early decades of the twentieth century, and a distinctly cosmopolitan city shaped by 'the western hegemonic presence [of] bank and office buildings, hotels, churches, clubs, cinemas, coffeehouses, restaurants, deluxe apartments and a racecourse' (Lee 1999, p. 6). In attending, for example, to Zhang Ruogu (張若谷) and other Francophile writers in Shanghai's cafés, Lee observes a 'bohemian self-image' in and through which they are said to 'embrace western modernity openly, without fear of colonisation' (Lee 1999, p. 312). A Westernized Shanghai provides fertile ground, then, for a Chinese cosmopolitanism to take root. Further the very cosmopolitanism of Shanghai can be noted in its myriad communities; as Jeffrey Wasserstrom points out, 'by the 1930s, no other Chinese city had large blocks of new immigrants, sojourners and second-generation settlers with ties to such a wide array of different places [and in addition] most of China's other regions were represented within the local demographic kaleidoscope as well' (Wasserstrom 2000, p. 193).

Yet, the backstory here – a cosmopolitan city with a deep-seated colonial influence – is found wanting. For the emergence of a 'global Shanghai' was inextricably tied to its status as a treaty port (1842–1943), a multi-colonial setting rather than a colony with no fewer than a dozen signatory foreign powers, many an imperial power too, with Britain, France, Japan, Russia and the United States as notable examples. Indeed, the presence over time of these powers and their settler, expatriate and/or émigré communities was part and parcel of the globality of the treaty port and its appearance on the (then-imperial) world map.

The establishment along China's coast, waterways and railways of treaty ports such as Shanghai, Tianjin and Hankou, which numbered no fewer than 80 at the start of the twentieth century, had an earlier history in the southern port of Canton, and in the precarious trade relations there between Qing Empire officials and foreign merchants since the mid-eighteenth century. The East India Company's attempted import of opium became a catalyst for Sino-British conflict from the late 1830s through to the early 1840s, a series of clashes known generally as the First Opium War. Following the Qing Empire's defeat in 1842 and exploitative agreements now commonly referred to as the 'Unequal Treaties', signatory foreign powers, first Britain, with others following suit, were guaranteed a host of economic privileges and jurisdictional immunities aimed at serving their (respective) interests in China – a cumulative act of legal imperialism. Its pervasiveness meant, too, that multiple groups of signatory subjects were able to reside and lease land at favourable rates, and to do trade in ports deemed strategic locations, enabling them to expand further beyond Canton throughout the later decades of the nineteenth century. Shanghai of the 1930s, arguably the most prominent treaty port at the time, can be described as an administrative 'city of cities' comprising Greater Shanghai, a municipality run by the Chinese Nationalists; the French Concession, which was presided over by the French Consul-General; and the so-called International Settlement – a merger of the English and American Settlements with other signatory powers in it. The Settlement was overseen by the British-influenced Shanghai Municipal Council, which was answerable to the Settlement's various foreign as well as Chinese ratepayers, namely its taxpayers.

To be sure, *Shanghai Modern* is less concerned with the city's status as a treaty port than with the writings in the 1930s of Zhang and his contemporaries. Zhang's encounter with an imperial anthem casts doubt, however, on whether he was always able to maintain his 'abiding curiosity' and cosmopolitan outlook as Lee sees it. In a *Shenbao* (申報) review, Zhang, penning as the paper's music critic, recounts a concert with the Shanghai Municipal Orchestra, an ensemble administered chiefly by the British. The concert, which was presented by the Shanghai Municipal Council (SMC), concluded with Weber's *Jubel Overture*, with the tune 'God Save the King' appearing towards the end of the piece.[2] As employees of the British-influenced SMC, whose executive councillors and senior employees were mostly British/-affiliated subjects, the Orchestra's musicians, none of whom were British, had no choice but to oblige and play it. Zhang, in contrast to the other (foreign) patrons, saw no reason to rise for the anthem; the coercive message of empire disconcerted him, a self-made cosmopolitan and an apparent epitome of modern Shanghai.

Zhang's account exposes, moreover, an ambiguity of self-positioning within the treaty port, whose 'cosmopolitanism' and image as a cosmopolis are in many ways a strange yet striking outcome of the legal imperialism of the Unequal Treaties. By extension, this lived experience of self-positioning is not unique to Shanghai's Chinese writers or for that matter Chinese historical actors. In the cosmopolitan and colonial setting that is the treaty port, its foreign locals – unlikely subjects at first glance – face a similar predicament over time. Especially noteworthy are Shanghai's British administrators, specifically the senior employees in charge of the SMC Secretariat. Amid and despite the prevailing institutional worldviews, their agency and handling of musical matters reveal a self-positioning more complex than meets the eye. Ad hoc municipal ensembles in the 1930s, catering for (well-heeled) individuals, clubs, hotels and societies, provide a fascinating case for that reason, if not for the fact that they have hitherto been neglected in Chinese- and English-language scholarship, which has tended to focus on their parent ensemble, the Shanghai Municipal Orchestra. The provision of private services by 'subsidiary' ensembles of the Orchestra came about earlier in the century; however, while their surviving records date back to the 1910s, the Municipal Dance Band, originally termed the Jazz Band, was only set up in the 1930s.[3] Related documents tell, for example, of the Shanghai Country Club's brief engagement of the newly available Dance Band, exposing not only the musical criticisms of the Club, an establishment in which the SMC had a stake, but also the curtness with which it replaced the Dance Band with a British military band for its balls.[4] The Dance Band's termination saw, shortly after, a memo to SMC Secretary John Robert Jones from Deputy Secretary George Godfrey Phillips, in which the latter expressed some frustration and sympathy for the fired musicians.[5] Such concern was offset at the same time by Phillips's 'neutrality' as an administrator who opted not to question the Club's decision. But, precisely because of their teetering between duty and empathy, senior employees like Phillips and Jones were also caught between their personal sentiments and the exclusionary worldviews of treaty port institutions such as the SMC and the Country Club. Phillips's education at Harrow and Cambridge, coupled with Jones's background as a barrister, might suggest that these men continued to enjoy privileged status as they switched from their legal professions in the empire to senior administrative posts in the treaty port.[6] Yet there was more to that trajectory, and their actual circumstances merit closer attention.

The SMC in the 1930s employed nearly 10,000 people of multiple nationalities. Yet despite its size, the SMC cannot be deemed a monolith, and Isabella Jackson (2017) has extensively explored that aspect, noting both a transnational colonialism and an increasing Chinese participation from the late 1920s. The SMC's multinational workforce should not, however, detract from the British administrative presence in treaty port Shanghai since its establishment in 1842. Of the SMC's executive council and senior employees in the Secretariat, Jackson observes:

> The most important trading companies in Shanghai, representing the interests of big businesses, dominated [the executive council], and most of these companies were British […] The SMC usually preferred to recruit foreign staff directly from Britain as far as possible, though it also recruited locally and from the British empire […] [The] secretaries were typical employees in many ways, in terms of their background (British or Anglophile and middle class) and also, significantly, in the force of their personalities […] Heads of SMC departments were almost all British [with Mario Paci, the Orchestra's Italian Music Director as the key exception], as were their deputies for the most of the existence of the SMC.
>
> (Jackson 2017, pp. 81, 97–98, 100)

The facts point, then, to a symbolically British, colonial institution whose senior employees were unelected officers often hired directly from the empire, and to an institutional worldview reflective of the British presence in the treaty port. Yet the same facts can also be limiting, inasmuch as they shed little light on how such individuals as the officers operated within a parochial sphere of influence, and how they handled and responded to situations similar to that involving the Municipal Dance Band and the Country Club. On that basis it makes sense to bring these individuals into the picture, and to locate Shanghai of the 1930s as a setting *at once* cosmopolitan and colonial.

'A foreign cosmopolitanism'

It is important to understand how, at one level, historical actors such as Phillips and Jones position themselves, and at the other, the ambivalence they encounter. This finds resonance, too, with Sarah Collins and Dana Gooley's idea of a critical cosmopolitanism. In essence, Collins and Gooley caution against conflating cosmopolitanism with the transnational, the international and the global, and argue instead for a tighter focus on questions of stance-taking:

> [In] emphasising its philosophical and attitudinal aspects, [our idea of cosmopolitanism] disjoins it from the stereotype of the rootless or effete cosmopolitan, which took place in the late nineteenth century and effectively reduced 'cosmopolitan' to an identity marked by a lifestyle of luxury and travel […] The risk [with the co-application of concepts] is that as the term [cosmopolitanism] expands to all kinds of global phenomena and circulations its critical and ethical dimensions will get lost in the wash and it will become a generalised synonym for globally interrelated phenomena.
> (Collins and Gooley 2017, pp. 141, 150)

Their discussion of a critical cosmopolitanism as an attitudinal cosmopolitanism – one that is not predefined by such markers as 'identity' – extends, moreover, to an increased reflexivity around the writing of music history:

> What new cosmopolitan discourse can offer our own work is a heightened alertness to the ways in which our own standpoints – the places where we stand geographically, socially, politically, and aesthetically – inform our understanding of the standpoints of musicians and musical listeners of the past.
> (Collins and Gooley 2017, p. 160)

The cosmopolitan subject is thus a dual subject *co*-defined by the historical actor and the historian. Collins and Gooley's idea can be pushed further too, for the agents in and of music history do not just comprise musicians and listeners, and stance-taking is not merely concerned with analysing what the available source documents can reveal about them and their sentiments. It is also concerned with interpretation as an (inevitably) adjudicative act, through which registers past and present, for example colonial documents and their postcolonial readings, are brought into play. In other words, stance-taking suggests not only an examination of individuals and their circumstances, but also, an epistemic modality through which the historian (re)calibrates knowledge while mediating between past and present. The need to traverse that ever-widening gap echoes what John Lewis Gaddis has observed: 'The past is something we can never have [in the present]. For by the time we've become aware of what has happened it's already inaccessible to us: we cannot relive, retrieve, or rerun it as we might some laboratory experiment or computer simulation. We can only *represent* it [author's italics]' (Gaddis 2002, p. 3). Sanjay Seth (2007) goes further: with reference to Western education in colonial India and the historiography of 'non-Western pasts', he theorizes history as a code in and through which representation of the past writes itself (back) into historical knowledge.[7] In other words, such knowledge and its 'foundational assumptions' cannot be assumed (Seth 2007, p. 9).

Yet, the very (in)stability of historical knowledge is also a salient point insofar as colonial settings and stance-taking are concerned. While Collins and Gooley are careful not to overplay global circuits of power, notably circuits of empire in the nineteenth and twentieth centuries, it is worth applying their idea of cosmopolitanism to such settings as treaty port Shanghai of the 1930s, and to the port's symbolically colonial institutions and key employees. So appears the variant idea of a foreign cosmopolitanism, which can be explored through the surviving documents of the SMC. Given their provenance in a treaty port institution, these documents suggest the possibility of fusing Collins and Gooley's idea of an attitudinal cosmopolitanism with postcolonial readings of colonial documents as exemplified by the work of Ann Laura Stoler and of Ricardo Roque and Kim Wagner. Stoler advocates reading along rather than against the colonial 'archival grain'; with reference to the Netherlands Indies she speaks (metaphorically) of the granular textures of archival material (Stoler 2010, pp. 49, 53). And in emphasizing archival granularity, she notes disparate affective registers within Dutch colonial documents, thereby cautioning against a Foucauldian reification of colonial authority (Stoler 2010, p. 43). Similarly, Roque and Wagner call for a reading of colonial documents that distinguishes between 'different accounts and [focuses] on the documents' distinct histories and itineraries, which confer to each individual account its peculiar historical specificity and biographical identity' (Roque and Wagner 2012, p. 14). In other words, Stoler, Roque and Wagner all warn against taking colonial documents for granted, highlighting instead the importance of troubling interpretatively such documents from within. In that sense, their readings throw into relief both the agency of the historical actor and that of the historian challenging existing metanarratives about colonial authority.

In bringing cosmopolitanism, colonial documents and postcolonial readings together, the dual agency of the actor and historian is rendered even more explicit. That is to say, the idea of a foreign cosmopolitanism helps not only to bring to light the stance-taking of the treaty port's senior administrators, but also to calibrate an alternative knowledge around historical stance-taking. Here, the historical actor is a foreign municipal employee who may not always be an unquestioning bureaucrat, but is examined instead as an individual negotiating institutional worldviews. And in investigating the foreign municipal employee within a symbolically colonial institution, the historian intervenes by probing beyond the idea of Shanghai as, simply, the 'cosmopolitan city par excellence', and exploring how this more complex, alternative knowledge can be brought to bear on the writing of twentieth-century colonial music history.

Ad hoc municipal ensembles

The Dance Band and other 'subsidiaries' provide some useful insights into institutional worldviews within the treaty port, and to understand what those worldviews were about, it makes sense to begin with the SMC's citywide publicity in September 1934 for ad hoc municipal ensembles, namely its promotion of the Orchestra's semi-public and private services: 'Any number of musicians from the complete Orchestra down to a single soloist may be engaged and a small concert band and a jazz band have recently been introduced to meet the needs of the smaller type of public functions.'[8] Targeted recipients extended from consulates, the French municipality and the (Nationalist) Shanghai City Government to chambers of commerce, national societies, and clubs, hotels and associations such as the Chinese and foreign YMCAs. Accompanying the announcement was a table of particulars regarding 'the nature of performance, whether concert, dance or otherwise'; the number of musicians; and requirements for 'any special music or national anthem'.[9] The ensembles were listed as follows:

Half Orchestra
Full Brass Band
Special Small Concert Band (for Dinner Music, Private Entertainment, Receptions, Ceremonies, Weddings, etc., consisting of five first-class musicians (Europeans), i.e., Piano, First Violin, Second Violin, Cello and Double Bass)
New Jazz Band (To consist of seven musicians, i.e., Piano, Violin-Saxophone, Saxophone-Clarinet, Trumpet, Trombone, Double Bass and Drummer)
Individual Musicians
Pianist
Soloists[10]

The scope of the publicity reveals the importance attached to these ensembles – potential streams of revenue for a parent ensemble confronted throughout the 1930s with the threat of abolition, and with complaints from disgruntled funders, the International Settlement's ratepayers, about the Orchestra's programming and the expenses entailed.[11] The SMC's publicity speaks also of an 'inclusive' worldview in which ad hoc municipal ensembles were promoted as citywide services in and across the treaty port, covering the gamut of classical, light and dance entertainment. Yet at a deeper level, this worldview is also symptomatic of British self-regard, which can be observed in a local British report from the 1930s. Given that the report dates from around the same time as the said publicity, it makes sense to read the two together. Looking back at the history of the International Settlement, the report lauds the Settlement as 'an unprecedented chapter in the history of the world's municipalities'; comparing it with the French Concession, it notes, furthermore, that the 'difference of spirit characterising the authorities of the Settlement and the French Consul-General [resulted] in the liberal administration of the Settlement on the one hand and the autocratic manner in which the French Concession was governed by the French Consul on the other'.[12] Viewed in the light of the report, the ad hoc ensembles were not only (envisaged as) citywide services, but were also bound up with British civic pride in the treaty port.

Despite the Chinese and foreign establishments for which the publicity was intended, and the SMC's attempted promotion across the treaty port of its musical services, the ad hoc ensembles smack of an exclusionary worldview centred around race, class and genre. 'First-class musicians' in the Special Small Concert Band were deemed synonymous with Europeans – a blatant exclusion of the Orchestra's Chinese, Filipino and Japanese players. The New Jazz Band, arguably a bold venture for a municipal classical ensemble, was renamed a month later as the Dance Orchestra, though it continued to be referred to by some as the Jazz Band and by others as the Dance Band. Regardless of the name change, whether classical musicians could pass muster as jazz musicians was a key concern for members of the SMC's Orchestra and Band Committee such as L. R. Hossenlopp.[13] They were sceptical from the outset about jazz as a 'class of music', with Hossenlopp cautioning: 'whether this Band [should] be maintained [must] be considered after a fair trial, in say six months' time'.[14]

In contrast to the Jazz Band, the ad hoc classical ensembles had a more positive reception. The reply from B. James, manager of the New Asia Hotel is telling in that regard:

> We are glad to receive your letter of September 26 saying that the services of the Shanghai Municipal Orchestra are available for concert engagements. Our hotel does not permit any sing-song girls, mahjong [a Chinese tile-based game], or any other things that would debase the morals of our guests, so we need to have wholesome entertainment for them. In fact we have often been asked by our guests where to get the services of a high-class Orchestra. We were not able to inform them before. Now that we have received your letter, we believe that it comes to us very timely. We propose to give the concerts in our auditorium on the seventh floor for our guests free of charge. We are not making it a business by charging our guests for admission fees. We have several hundreds [of] guests in our hotel every day and no doubt when they hear the performance of your Orchestra they will remember it. This is also an indirect way for you to find customers for your Orchestra. Now we would like to engage the service of your Half Orchestra once each month during the whole year.[15]

Judging from his response, James wanted to instigate good morals at the hotel and associated the Orchestra with 'wholesome' and 'high-class' entertainment. With the Half Orchestra, he saw an opportunity to counter such vices as prostitution (sing-song girls) and gambling (mahjong) with monthly auditorium concerts. James's enthusiasm for the Half Orchestra, coupled with Hossenlopp's reservations about the Jazz Band, casts doubt, too, on whether the ad hoc ensembles could provide classical, light and jazz entertainment on equal terms. James's aversion to mahjong and sing-song girls, a courtesan tradition originating from the nineteenth century, suggests, moreover, his disdain for Chinese popular entertainment at the New Asia. The (enforced) differentiation here between high- and low-status, Western and non-Western entertainment reaffirms, even if only inadvertently, the exclusionary worldview of the SMC.

To be sure, the ad hoc ensembles announced in 1934 cannot and do not entirely reflect musical values in a treaty port that was municipally divided. Yet the publicity for these ensembles, coupled with its various recipients across the treaty port, also attests to the SMC's ongoing influence in musical matters, and to the expansion of that influence beyond the International Settlement. Their different perspectives notwithstanding, Hossenlopp and James both equated the Orchestra with European classical music presented by the SMC, a symbolically British institution of which the Orchestra, an emblem of that tradition, functioned as a department. These individuals adopted a stance distinct from that of Collins and Gooley's (shifting) cosmopolitan subject, remaining attached to an institutional worldview shaped by race, class and genre.

Against that status quo, the SMC's British senior administrators may seem unlikely cosmopolitan subjects due to their close connections with empire and their privileged status as officers-in-charge. But, precisely because of that status and their visible involvement in treaty port administration, they were frequently called upon to set forth their views, and not surprisingly, their individual voices find expression in the paperwork concerning the Country Club's engagement of the Municipal Dance Band, which also echoes what Stoler, Roque and Wagner have emphasized about the textured nature of colonial documents.

Having specially recruited Henry Nathan, a celebrated bandleader, to train the musicians, the Band appears to have made a successful début at the Country Club, reported as a 'favourably judged' trial.[16] Nathan was in charge of the All-American Dance Orchestra at the (upscale) Cathay Hotel in the International Settlement; with the Municipal Band he was tasked with rehearsing a large dance repertoire for the Club's balls. Yet despite its initially positive reception the Band's subsequent performance was met with much criticism, with the Club's General Secretary issuing a complaint to the SMC Secretariat: 'The music is laboured and although the Band usually starts the evening by playing in a fairly brisk manner, it gradually becomes lifeless and too slow, also the time [tempo] varies during a number. It is considered that too many new tunes are attempted.'[17] Three weeks later the Band was fired: '[T]he small improvement in [its] playing is not sufficient to warrant continuing with their services any longer.'[18] Mario Paci, Music Director of the Municipal Orchestra sent this protest to the Secretariat:

[The musicians] report to me that their success was continually marred by the fact that when the dancers were enthusiastically calling for encores, which they would have given with pleasure to keep alive the merry mood of the ball, the [Club] Secretary was always there to emphatically order not to give [too] many encores, saying that the Club would not make any business in drinks, if people keep on dancing. It is conceivable that the dancers, all members of the Club, were disappointed and dissatisfied. Further the musicians report to me that the Club [has] engaged a band of fourteen players [from] one of the British military bands present in Shanghai, at a much lower charge, [and] they are convinced that the reasons for [cancelling] the service of the Municipal Jazz Band should be found not in the standard of playing but in the Club's wish to reduce the expenses, while making a larger show with fourteen players instead of seven, and help[ing] and support[ing] the British soldiers.[19]

Whether or not the said issues constitute cause for termination is beside the point; worth noting, rather, is the Country Club's replacement of the Municipal Dance Band with a British military band, and the Club's assistance to British troops stationed in Shanghai. The British 'disposition' of the Country Club should not come as a surprise though, considering that its members included such figures as Allan George Mossop, chief judge for the British Supreme Court in China. Whereas the SMC's worldview is defined by race, class and genre, the Country Club's worldview centres conspicuously around local British interests.

Paci's letter to the SMC Secretariat did not go unheeded, prompting shortly after a memo in which Deputy Secretary G. G. Phillips indicated to Secretary J. R. Jones his frustration: 'I suppose we can do nothing? I pass this on to you because there seems to be a good deal in what Paci says.'[20] Phillips's sentiments were echoed to an extent by Jones: 'I think there is a good deal in what Paci says. It is no use taking any action but I suggest reporting the facts to the [Council's] Band Committee and pointing out to the Club that it is not a satisfactory position.'[21] There followed a letter of protest to the Country Club, a copy of which was circulated to the Orchestra and Band Committee, with a member commenting, 'much too mild! Very unsatisfactory in fact', while another disagreed: 'I don't think it wise to pursue the matter further; it will not do the Orchestra any good. The actual mistake was to hold out the Orchestra as ready to take jazz contracts, knowing it is not specially trained in this class of music.'[22] Differences among the members did not deter a second letter of protest from Phillips: 'I would point out that much time was given in an expensive preparation to meet your Club's requirements; that other engagements have been refused; and that the cancellation adversely affects the reputation of the musicians.'[23] A brief reply from the Club's Secretary concludes the (surviving) correspondence: '[T]he decision which involved finding another dance band was come to with the greatest regret.'[24]

Stoler's idea of the colonial archival grain is pertinent here, with the Secretariat responding not unanimously but ambiguously to the termination by a local British establishment of a new municipal ensemble. Phillips's position can be described as one of allegiance and ambivalence, inasmuch as he was not forthcoming about the course of action the Secretariat should adopt. However, his empathy for Paci and the musicians was made clear all the same, albeit in private. The 'historical itinerary' to which Roque and Wagner draw attention is relevant too, for in reading Phillips's memo and letter of protest, there is a sense that he vacillated between the worldviews of the institutions he served, and personal sentiments arising from his role as a municipal officer. The worldviews of the SMC and the Country Club doubtless reflect the British influence in the treaty port, yet Phillips's memo also suggests he was en rapport with Paci and the musicians and was fairly sympathetic to the ill fate of the Municipal Dance Band. In comparison with Phillips, Jones seemed to play by the book but was not averse to pursuing the matter further in writing. He did not object to a second letter of protest to the Club, whose emphasis was on the tarnished reputation of the musicians, though contrary to suggestions from the Orchestra and Band Committee, Phillips did not raise the question of compensation with an institution whose ethos he would likely have had an affinity with, given his apparently elite background.

On the surface this amounts to nothing more than Secretariat paperwork, but, precisely because it involved senior municipal officers, the paperwork exposes an ambiguous self-positioning within seemingly dominant institutions of power in the treaty port, and stance-taking by actors like Phillips who mediated between the prevailing worldviews and their personal sentiments. In that sense their behaviour is not dissimilar to what Collins and Gooley have observed about 'cosmopolitan stance': '[It] does not negate modes of belonging and cannot be their substitute. Rather, it takes distance from existing attachments, in a manner that limits the beholder's ability to invest in them exclusively or unilaterally' (Collins and Gooley 2017, pp. 156–57). As officers in charge of the SMC Secretariat, Phillips and even Jones disengaged briefly from the institutional worldviews with which they were familiar, shifting to a position from which they acted (to a certain degree) for the musicians affected by the Country Club's decision. Their repositioning, however temporary, meant, too, that these actors were not always duty-bound to the institutions they served and liaised with. Their world-belonging in the treaty port was less a set belief than a contradictory state of mind, meaning that their cosmopolitan stance developed alongside as well as in (some) conflict with treaty port institutions. And in fusing Collins and Gooley's idea of an attitudinal cosmopolitanism with Stoler, Roque and Wagner's readings of colonial documents, it also becomes apparent, through the surviving paperwork, that while the Deputy Secretary and Secretary felt compelled to respond to the Club's (mis)treatment of the Municipal Dance Band, they did not record similar sentiments. Far from being a uniform body of documents, this paperwork sheds light not only on the administrators as (unwitting) cosmopolitan subjects, but also on their agency as individuals, notwithstanding their shared affiliation as senior employees.

An epistemic modality

The foregoing analysis reveals an element of stance-taking within a symbolically colonial institution, complementing as well as complicating such narratives as

Shanghai Modern, which have tended to engage with questions of cultural identity rather than with the actual circumstances encountered by individuals and their shifting outlooks. Such analysis is significant, moreover, in terms of its epistemic modality: an alternative knowledge (re)shaped around the dual agency of the actor and historian, given that historical knowledge is continually (re)written, and that the so-called past is a product of its historical representation in the present.

To elaborate it is worth returning once more to Collins and Gooley, who, having discussed the parameters of a critical cosmopolitanism, conclude their article with the following remarks:

> Cosmopolitanism, then, does not have fixed social coordinates and does not determine a specific politics, but emerges in consciousness relationally, as a reaction to the appearance of narrow or limited interests, and normally in some sort of critique or disapproval of the exclusivity of those interests.
> (Collins and Gooley 2017, p. 160)

In a similar vein, historical actors such as Phillips respond to 'narrow or limited interests' precisely because of their position as insiders, which allows them some purchase to query, albeit to a limited degree, the values and practices of the institutions they worked for and corresponded with. It may seem counterintuitive to cast these insiders as cosmopolitan subjects, but by the same token, the keywords with which they are easily associated – status and privilege – can lead to a priori assumptions about the ways they conduct themselves, not least an indifference to 'the exclusivity of [institutional] interests'. The agency of the historian proves an especially important intervention here, with the effect of recalibrating knowledge as a matter of historical representation. That is to say, the idea of a foreign cosmopolitanism urges the historian to dislodge from (which is not to reject) such narratives as *Shanghai Modern*, and to mediate anew between past and present by poring more closely over colonial documents such as those archived within and by the SMC. In that regard, the historian acts too as a cosmopolitan subject who, having detached from the existing knowledge, takes another stance with a view to exploring other cosmopolitan expressions in addition to an emergent Chinese modernity. Accordingly, cosmopolitanism in the context of the treaty port is understood to reflect not only native cultural discourse, but also foreign individuals and their stance-taking within symbolically colonial institutions, as the case of the ill-fated Municipal Dance Band has come to show.

This alternative knowledge also suggests a different conception of twentieth-century colonial music history, especially in the light of the trend in recent decades to trace and assess colonial influence in so-called global terms. Notable examples include Andrew Jones's *Yellow Music* (2001) and Michael Denning's *Noise Uprising* (2015); both give insight into the transnational movement around the globe of musicians, recorded music and related paraphernalia in the early decades of the twentieth century. In orienting his discussion around the 'Chinese Jazz Age', Jones situates Chinese cultural production and, by extension, the writing of Chinese cultural history amidst such processes as the transmission of new sound technologies. Denning, who is interested in the phenomenon in the late 1920s of recording sessions with vernacular musicians, locates this phenomenon in what he describes, in his 2015 book, as 'an archipelago of colonial ports'. Although they pose different research questions, the resultant knowledge nonetheless centres around the global technological circulation of musical culture. Denning, for example, refers to a 'world musical revolution' in the title of his book. Yet, this 'worldness' of culture is neither synonymous nor entirely reflective of musical activity on the ground. Granted, Jones's and Denning's narratives of transnational musical culture do not preclude them from examining the localities in which everyday activity shapes and reshapes musical culture, but, ultimately, their observations are part and parcel of an overarching narrative concerned with meta-global processes. The idea of a foreign cosmopolitanism, which emphasizes simultaneously the actor's and the historian's agency, suggests by contrast a different leverage: an applying of (more) interpretative pressure to musical activity and its attendant sentiments, whilst keeping in mind the peculiar, global condition of a twentieth-century cosmopolitan city that was inextricably bound up with the legal imperialism of the nineteenth century. The epistemic modality of a foreign cosmopolitanism facilitates, then, not only another conception but also another epistemology of colonial music history – one that brings to the fore the very slippage over time between cosmopolitan and colonial values, not least the subjects for whom that constitutes a lived experience.

Notes

1 The author wishes to acknowledge the Leverhulme Trust for funding this work through an Early Career Fellowship.
2 *Shenbao*, 28 May 1927.
3 Regarding the Orchestra's private services, see, for example, U1-3-1105 and U1-5-117 at the Shanghai Municipal Archives (hereafter SMA).
4 SMC dossier titled 'Orchestra and Band: Outside Services'; SMA, U1-4-935.
5 SMA, U1-4-935-2444, January 1935.
6 Jones, a native of Llanuwchllyn in Wales, later moved to Hong Kong and became a legal adviser to the Hong Kong and Shanghai Banking Corporation; he passed away in 1976.
7 Sanjay Seth, 'Does History Travel? Historiography and Non-Western Pasts', a Critical Theory Seminar at All Souls College, University of Oxford, 15 February 2018.
8 SMA, U1-4-935-2491, 26 September 1934.
9 SMA, U1-4-935-2389-90; see also U1-4-939-0132-0134.
10 SMA, U1-4-935-2389-90.
11 See SMA, U1-4-939 for a 'summary of attempts' to abolish the Orchestra (1927; 1928; 1931; 1934; 1935; 1936).
12 The report appears in the reprint of *Land Regulations and Bye-Laws for the Foreign Settlement of Shanghai* (Shanghai: ABC Press, 1937); held now at the Xujiahui Library in Shanghai.
13 Hossenlopp was manager of Marcel, a French restaurant and confectionary; *A Guide to Catholic Shanghai* (Shanghai: T'Ou-Wè-Sè Press, 1937).
14 SMA, U1-4-935-2460, 16 and 24 October 1934.
15 SMA, U1-4-935-2432, 28 September 1934.
16 SMA, U1-4-935-2468, début in October 1934.

17 SMA, U1-4-935-2452, 3 December 1934. Thanks to Derek Scott for pointing out what might have been a symptom of a common problem – musicians negotiating between their performances and maintaining a strict tempo for dancing.
18 SMA, U1-4-935-2450, 27 December 1934.
19 SMA, U1-4-935-2446-2449, 5 January 1935.
20 SMA, U1-4-935-2444, 7 January 1935.
21 SMA, U1-4-935-2444, 7 January 1935.
22 SMA, U1-4-935-2443, 10 January 1935.
23 SMA, U1-4-935-2440, 11 January 1935.
24 SMA, U1-4-935-2438, 18 January 1935.

Bibliography

Collins, S. and Gooley, D., 2017. 'Music and the New Cosmopolitanism: Problems and Possibilities'. *The Musical Quarterly* 99(2): pp. 139–65.

Denning, M., 2015. *Noise Uprising: The Audiopolitics of a World Musical Revolution.* London: Verso.

Gaddis, J.L., 2002. *The Landscape of History: How Historians Map the Past.* New York: Oxford University Press.

Jackson, I., 2017. *Shaping Modern Shanghai: Colonialism in China's Global City.* Cambridge: Cambridge University Press.

Jones, A.F., 2001. *Yellow Music: Media Culture and Colonial Modernity in the Chinese Jazz Age.* Durham, NC: Duke University Press.

Lee Ou-fan, L., 1999. *Shanghai Modern: The Flowering of a New Urban Culture in China, 1930–1945.* Cambridge, MA: Harvard University Press.

Roque, R. and Wagner, K.A. eds., 2012. *Engaging Colonial Knowledge: Reading European Archives in World History.* Basingstoke, UK: Palgrave Macmillan.

Seth, S., 2007. *Subject Lessons: The Western Education of Colonial India.* Durham, NC: Duke University Press.

Stoler, A.L., 2010. *Along the Archival Grain: Epistemic Anxieties and Colonial Common Sense.* Princeton, NJ and Oxford: Princeton University Press.

Wasserstrom, J.N., 2000. Locating Old Shanghai: Having Fits about Where It Fits. In: J. Esherick ed., *Remaking the Chinese City: Modernity and National Identity, 1900–1950.* Honolulu, HI: University of Hawai'i Press, pp. 192–210.

Index

(Cities are listed under countries.)

Adorno, Theodor W. 14
Africa 90, 91, 97
Alary, Giulio
   Le tre nozze 38
alcohol 137, 170
Aldana, José Miguel 60
All-American Dance Orchestra, The 169
Alzedo, Bernardo
   La Araucana 68
Anderson, Benedict 13
Andolija *see* Stanković, Vaso
Andrino, José Escolástico 64–5
Animierung 137, 139–40
Appiah, Kwame A. 3, 7, 47, 55
Arditi, Luigi 43
Argentina 61, 66, 90, 98, 101
aria 135
Asia 90, 98
Askenaze, Stefan 106
atonality 86, 94, 99
Auber, Daniel
   Fra diavolo 24
   La muette de Portici 17, 19, 24, 26
   La part du diable 19
   Le dieu et la bayadère 19
   Le domino noir 19
   Les diamants de la couronne 19
   Les mousquetaires de la reine 19
   Zanetta 19
Australia 98, 108–9
   Sydney 14
Austria
   Austrian Littoral (Österreichisches Küstenland) 137
   Bregenz 115
   Franz Joseph I 47–8
   Gmunden 49
   Habsburg Monarchy 7, 47–50, 55, 137
   Salzburg 134
   Salzkammergut 49
   Vienna 19, 23, 27, 37, 43, 47–55, 64, 90, 102, 134
      Court Opera [later, State Opera] 24, 26, 49; Viennese Ladies' Orchestra
   Portugal 133–7, 143
autonomy 120–2, 124, 128–9

Bach, Johann Sebastian 86
Balfe, Michael William
   Les quatre fils Aymon 39
Baltic Sea 8
Bañón, Manuel 66–7
   La Americana 68
Barbaja, Domenico 37
Barbieri, Antonio 79, 81–2
   'Mbraccia a me' 82
   'Nanninella' 79–82, 88
   'Questa non si tocca?' 82
Barbieri-Nini, Marianna 38
Barnum, P.T. 40
Bartók, Béla 86, 90–1, 118
Bayard, Jean-François 41
Beatles, The 4
Beck, Ulrich 1, 3, 16
Beer, August 52
Beethoven, Ludwig van 8, 59–60, 86, 117, 121, 128, 154–5
   Fidelio 24
Belgium 99, 106
   Brussels 17
   Flanders 99
   Queen Elizabeth Competition 106
   Wallonia 99
Belina, Anastasia 8
Bellini, Vincenzo 18, 60
   I Capuleti e i Montecchi 19, 27, 34

Norma 19
I puritani 36
Bello, Andrés 63, 69
Beloachaga, Felix Falcó de 60
Benelli, Giovanni Battista 35
Berg, Alban 118
Berger, Johann Nepomuk 49
Bethell, Leslie 66
Bhabha, Homi 3
Billroth, Theodor 49
Biro, Gustav 137
Biro, Milan 137–40
Bizet, Georges
   Carmen 135
Blair, Tony 5
Boieldieu, François-Adrien 14, 19
Bolívar, Simón 62
Bolivia
   Sucre 67
Bosnia and Herzegovina
   Ilidža 141
   Mostar 134, 137–9
   Sarajevo 8, 133–4, 137–42
      Imperial-Orpheum variety theatre 133
   Trebinje 138
Boulanger, Lily 90
Boulanger, Nadia 106
Boulez, Pierre 86, 100
Bournonville, August 19
Bozen/Bolzano 134–5
Brahms, Johannes 47, 49, 86
brass band 147, 149, 154–8
Brassens, Georges 82, 84
brass music 153–4
Brazil 66, 100
   Rio de Janeiro 101, 111
Brecht, Bertolt 84
Brexit 1–2
Briggs, Ronald 62
Britten, Benjamin 86, 90
Brodbeck, David 7
Brown, Bruce A. 64
Bulgaria
   Plovdiv 141
   Sofia 141
Bulwer-Lytton, Edward
   Lady of Lyons, The 19
Burke, Edmund 126
Busoni, Ferruccio 118, 121

Cage, John 86
Canada 98
capitalism 6

Capurro, Giovanni
   'O sole mio' 80
Castile-Blaze 17
Cebrián, Rósa 53
Central Europe 7, 15, 47, 50, 55, 98, 133, 137, 140
character piece 135
Charle, Christophe 13
Chávez, Carlos 66
Chiara, Vincenzo Di 79–82
   'Mbraccia a me' 82
   'Nanninella' 79–82, 88
   'Questa non si tocca?' 82
   'Tticchete ttì tticchete ttà' 80
Chile 63
Chin, Unsuk 91
China 15–16, 97–9
   Beijing 99
      Beijing Opera 15
   Chengdu 99
   Guangzhou (formerly Canton) 163
   Hankou 162
   Hong Kong 16, 18, 99, 111
   Macao [Macau] 16, 18
   Nanning 99
   Shanghai 8–9, 14, 16, 18, 162–8, 170, 172
      Shanghai Municipal Orchestra 163–4, 167–8
   Tianjin 162
Clash, The 4
class 117, 128, 151, 156, 164, 168–70
Coleridge-Taylor, Samuel 90, 126
Collins, Sarah 8, 165–7, 169, 171–2
Colombia 61, 98, 102
colonialism 7–8, 14, 55, 60–3, 66, 70, 119, 162–7, 171–3
community 2, 7, 22, 78, 81–6, 109, 113, 117–21, 128, 151
conductor 8, 43, 50, 127, 148–50, 154–5, 157
conservatoires 59, 94–5, 101–2
copyright 38, 41–2, 82
Cordero, Roque 100
Crawford, Ruth 90
Croatia
   Dubrovnik 139–40
   Zagreb 141
Croatia-Slavonia 8
Cruvelli, Sofia 38–9
Cuba 59, 98
   Cuban habanera 84
cultural transfer 7, 9, 14, 16, 19, 27, 33, 42–3, 61–2, 102, 118, 173

Czechoslovakia 97–8
Czech Republic
   Hradec Králové/Königgrätz 134
   Lochenice/Lochnitz 134
   Prague 19

de André, Fabrizio 82
Debussy, Claude 78
de Iturbide, Agustin 59
de la Rue, Pierre 60
de Lassus, Orlande 60
Delgado, Manuel 60
Denmark
   Copenhagen 26–7, 155–6, 158
   Kongelige Teater 18–23
d'Ennery, Adolphe &Dumanoir [Philippe François Pinel]
   Don César de Bazan 19
Denning, Michael 172–3
Dent, Edward J. 8, 117–29
   A Theatre for Everybody 117
Derrida, Jacques 119
de Saint-Georges, Jules-Henri Vernoy 41
de Salinas, Francisco 60
Dessoff, Otto *50*
Deutschtum (Germanness) 50
Diamantídhis, Andónis (aka Dalgás)
   'Mánghas' 82–3
Diogenes of Sinope 2
dodecaphony 86, 91, 97, 99–102
domestication 8, 148, 151, 156, 158
Donizetti, Gaetano 14
   La fille du régiment 41
   L'elisir d'amore 24
   Lucia di Lammermoor 17–18
   Lucrezia Borgia 42
   Marino Faliero 34, 36
Donnarumma, Elvira 79
Dual Monarchy (Austria-Hungary) 47, 54–5
Dun, Tan 91
Duprez, Caroline 38
Dutch East Indies *see* Indonesia
Dylan, Bob 84
   Chronicles 84
   'A Hard Rain's A-Gonna Fall' 84
   'It's Alright, Ma (I'm Only Bleeding)' 84
   'Mr. Tambourine Man' 84

East India Company, The 18, 163
Edison, Thomas Alva 77, 78, 88
Egypt
   Cairo 23, 27

Azbakeyah 23–4; Circus 23; *Comédie* 23–4; Khedival Opera House 23–5
electronic dance music 5
Elízaga, Mariano 7, 59–65, 70
Ellinikí Estoudiantína 79, 81
El Salvador 64
Erić, Jovan 143
Estoudiantina Néas Ionías 80–1
Estoudiantina Tchanakas Smyrne 80
Estudiantina Española 78
Everist, Mark 7
Exposition Universelle 78
expressionism 86

Fabbri, Franco 8
Falla, de, Manuel 90–1, 118
fascism 86
Ferré, Léo 84
Fichtelberger, Louis 154
Finland 5, 8, 98, 101
   Helsinki 147, 149, 151, 155
      Helsinki Philharmonic Orchestra 147, 158–9
   Kristinestad 153, 155
   Noormarkku/Norrmark 155
   Pori 147–52, 154–6, 158
      Pori Sinfonietta 159
   Turku 147, 149, 151, 155, 158
   Vaasa 147–53, 155–8
      fire brigade 156–7; Vaasa City Orchestra 159
   Viipuri (*see* Russia, Vyborg)
Fliege, Albert 153, 157
Fliege, Bernhard 153
Fliege, Emil 153
Fliege, Hubert 153
Flotow, Friedrich von
   Martha 17, 24
folk music 51, 78, 133, 137–40, 144
Foster, Stephen 77
Foucault, Michel 166
France 60
   Du Fay, Guillaume 60
   Paris 7, 19, 33–43, 64, 84, 88, 90, 92–3, 98, 100–1, 106, 158, 160, 171
      conservatoire 101; Eiffel Tower 78; Exposition Universelle 78; Mardi Gras 78; Opéra 17, 37; Opéra Comique 15, 26; Théâtre de la Renaissance 15, 17; Théâtre Italien 33–8, 40–2; Théâtre Lyrique 26; World's Fair 158
   Thionville/Diedenhofen 137

Frankl, Peter 109
Franzel 138
Frappert, Louis
    Saltarello 26

Gaddis, John Lewis 166
Gade, Niels 155–6
Gallilei, Vincenzo 60
gambling 168–9
Gandarias, Igor de 64
Ganszauge, Carl 149
Genet, Jean 84
genre 18–19, 23–4, 27, 67, 69, 77–8, 83–5, 99, 168–70
Gerhard, Roberto 101
Germany 60–1
    Berlin 148
    Düsseldorf 133
    German Democratic Republic 97
    Geyer 153
    Hamburg 14, 137
    Hanover 14
    Leipzig 101, 148, 156
        Leipzig Conservatory 156
    Magdeburg 140
    Saxony 49
    Thüringer Grottenhalle 135
    Völklingen 137, 140
    Zwickau 140
Gilbert, Jeremy 5–6
Gilbert, Susie
    Opera for Everybody 117
Ginastera, Alberto 90–1
globalization 2, 4–6, 14–16, 27, 70, 162
Gluck, Christoph W. 15
Goethe, Johann Wolfgang von 50
Goldmark, Carl 7, 47–50
    Das Heimchen am Herd 51
    Die Königin von Saba 49–50, 52
    Merlin 50
    Violin Concerto 53
Goldmark, Rubin 48
Gooley, Dana 165–6, 169, 171–2
Gottschalksen, Carl 155–6, 158
Gounod, Charles 26
    Faust 16
    Roméo et Juliette 27
gramophone 77–80, 118, 142
Grande, Edgar 1
Graničar 8, 133, 137–40, 143–4
Greece 80, 98
    Athens 2
    Rhodes 81–2
    Smyrna 79–82
        Smyrnaikí Estoudiantína
            Kostantinoúpoli 79
    Tilos 81–2
Grisi, Giulia 35–6, 40
Grossmith, George
    Diary of a Nobody 110–11
Gruneisen, Charles 36
Guatemala 64, 68
Gye, Frederick 36, 42
Gyrowetz, Adalbert 67

Habermas, Jürgen 4
Halévy, Fromental
    Les mousquetaires de la reine 17
Handel, George F. 60
Hanslick, Eduard 49
Hauer, Josef Matthias 99
Hausen, Anton Rudolf 149
Haydn, Joseph 8, 59–60, 63–4, 66–7, 154
Heartz, Daniel 64
Heikkinen, Olli 8
Heile, Björn *8*
Heimat 54
Herschkowitz, Philip 100
Hertel, Peter Ludwig & Peter Taglioni
    Flick und Flock 26
    Sardanapal 26
Hesmondhalgh, David 4–5
historiography 13, 91, 93, 147, 149, 165–7, 172
Holstein, Franz von 50
homosexuality 107–10, 113, 119
Honegger, Arthur 118
Horváth, Lajos 142
Hosokawa, Toshio 91
Hossenlopp, L.R. 168–9
Hubay, Jenő 53
Hugo, Victor 41–2
Hungary 7, 47, 49, 51–2, 90–1
    Budapest 49, 141
    Deutschkreuz (formerly Sopronkeresztúr) 54
    Keszthely 53–4
    Lake Balaton (Plattensee) 53
    Magyars 47, 51–3
hybridity 4–5, 83

Ibert, Jacques 118
identity 1–2, 4, 6, 22, 49–51, 54–5, 61, 66, 69, 91, 107–12, 117, 119, 165–6, 172
imperialism 6, 16, 51, 59, 62, 84, 135, 141, 162–3, 173

India 98, 166
  Kolkata (formerly Calcutta) 15
Indonesia
  Jakarta (formerly Batavia) 16–18, 23, 27
institutionalism 37, 50, 148
interculturalism 5–6
International Society for
  Contemporary Music (ISCM) 94–8,
  101–2, 118, 123
Ireland 98–9
Italy 60
  Merano/Meran 134
  Milan 37, 134
  Naples 37, 43, 79–80, 82
    Eldorado Theatre 79; Piedigrotta
    Festival 82
  Rome 19, 111
Ives, Charles 86, 90
Izquierdo König, José Manuel 7–8

Jackson, Isabella 164
James, B. 168–9
Jansson, Johan August 151, 154
Japan 90–1, 98
  Tokyo 101
jazz 86, 164, 167–70, 172
Jews 2, 7, 47–51, 55, 106–15, 123
Jones, Andrew 172–3
Jones, John Robert 164–5, 170–1
Judson, Pieter M. 49

Kahn, Erich Itor 100
Kajanus, Robert 147
Kamposch, Anton 135
Kant, Immanuel 3–4
Katić, Marko 142
Kaufmann, Dorothea 135
Keynes, John Maynard 118, 122
  *General Theory of Employment, Interest
  and Money* 126
King Alexander 142
Kodály, Zoltán 91
Koellreutter, Hans Joachim 100
Komisarjevsky, Theodore 107
Korhonen, Kimmo 149
Krenek, Ernst 118

Lablache, Luigi 35–6, 38
Lakatos, Miklós 142
Laporte, Pierre François 33–6, 40, 42
Latin America 7, 16, 18, 59–71, 90–1, 98, 100–1
Lee, Leo 162–3

Leibowitz, René 100
Leoncavallo, Ruggero
  Pagliacci 135
Lessing, Gotthold Ephraim 50
Levy, Lazar 106
Liao, Yvonne 8–9
liberty 6, 108, 124, 129
Lind, Jenny 36–7, 39–40
Lipiner, Siegfried 50
Liszt, Franz 15, 52
Lithuania 97
Livonia (now split between Estonia and
  Latvia) 149
Lohse, Arnold 153, 157
Lortzing, Albert
  Zar und Zimmermann 19
Lowe, Louis 149
Lumley, Benjamin 7, 33, 36–43
Lutyens, Elizabeth 90

macro-regions 7, 14–16, 18, 27–8
Mádlo, Vojta 135
Magaldi, Cristina 66
Mahler, Gustav 50
Malaysia 16
Mann, Michael 15–16
Mapleson, James Henry 43
mapping 92–4, 97, 102
march 135
Marchetti, Filippo
  Ruy Blas 24
Maretzek, Max 39, 43
Mario (Giovanni Matteo de Candia), 40
Mascagni, Pietro
  Cavalleria Rusticana 135
Mason, Thomas Monck 34–5
Massol, Jean-Etienne-August 38
Matthison-Hansen, Gottfred 155
Maxner, Rosa 134
May, Theresa 2
Méhul, Étienne 19
melee 19, 22–23, 27
Mercadante, Saverio 36
Merelli, Bartolomeo 37
Mertahaus, Emma 134
Meserón, Juan 64–5, 68
metropolitan 3, 15, 133
Mexico 8, 59–62, 111
  Mexico City 101
  Morelia (formerly Valladolid) 59–60
Meyerbeer, Giacomo 15, 18
  Les Huguenots 17
  Robert le diable 17, 27

Index 179

military band 135, 149–51, 154, 156, 164, 170
Mimić, Stanko 141
Mingotti, Pietro & Angelo 33
Minkus, Ludwig & Artur de St-Léon
  Fiamma d'amore 26
mobility 9, 33, 63, 102
modernism 7–8, 70, 90–103, 118, 124, 129
modernity 50, 101, 122, 124, 162, 172
Molière, Jean-Baptiste 19, 23
Montemerli, Lorenzo 42
Moore, George 120
Mossop, Allan George 170
Mozart, Wolfgang A. 8, 15, 59–60, 63, 66, 118, 121, 127, 129, 155
  Die Zauberflöte 24, 117, 127–9
  Don Giovanni 19, 24
  Le nozze di Figaro 19, 24
multiculturalism 6
Municipal Dance Band, The 164–5, 167, 169–72
Munkácsy, Mihály 52

Nancy, Jean-Louis 19
Nathan, Henry 169
nationalist populism 2
national narratives 1–2, 9, 13, 147
neoclassicism 99
Nešić, Marko 139
Netherlands 18
New Zealand 108–9
Nordeman, August 150, 153
North America 40, 43, 90–1, 98, 100–2
Nussbaum, Martha C. 3

Offenbach, Jacques
  Orpheus in the Underworld 135
opera 7–8, 13–28, 33–43, 49–51, 55, 63, 83–4, 86, 115, 117–29, 135, 137, 140, 158
operetta 135, 137, 139–40
opium 163
Orientalism 5, 9
Osterhammel, Jürgen 15, 33

Paci, Mario 164, 169–71
Pakistan
  Karachi 3
Palestrina, Giovanni Pierluigi da 60
Palin, Bror Wilhelm 150, 152–3, 155, 157
Panama 91
Parodi, Teresa 39
Paz, Juan Carlos 90, 100

Pennanen, Risto Pekka 8
Pericles 2
Peru 59–60, 98
  Arequipa 66–7
  Lima 65, 67–8
Pessoa, Fernando 110, 115
Phillips, George Godfrey 164–5, 170–2
phonograph 77–8
Piazzolla, Astor 66
Pilňáček, Jaroslav 134–5
Planchart, Alejandro 100
Pleyel, Ignaz 63, 67
Poland 7–8, 47, 49, 108, 137
  Warsaw 106, 111–12
    Warsaw ghetto 109, 111, 113–14
  Wrocław/Breslau 137, 140
polka 38, 135, 138
Portugal 98
Portugal, Maria 134–6
Portugal, Marie 134
postcards 133–7, 139–40, 143
postcolonialism 8
potpourri 135
Poultier, Placide 38
propaganda 3, 49, 142
prostitution 168–9
Püringer, August 51, 55

race 9, 50, 168–70
Radosavljević, Miloš 141
Radosavljević, Mito 141
Radosavljević, Pajo 141
Radosavljević, Paun 141
Radosavljević, Pavle 141
Radosavljević, Vaso 141
Ramos, Bartolomeo 60
Rantanen, Saijaleena 8
Rea, William *100*
Rebel of the Keys 114
rebetiko 82–3
Red Crescent 138
Reeves, Sims 38
Regev, Motti 4
Robert, Bartolomé 62
Robert, Edouard 34–6, 40, 42
Rodríguez, Simón 62
Rojas, Lorenzo 67
Roma 8, 133, 138–44
Romania
  Bucharest 141
Ronconi, Giorgio 37
rootless cosmopolitan 2
Roque, Ricardo 166, 169, 171

Rossi, Count 37
Rossini, Gioachino 13, 18, 28, 60, 86
　Guillaume Tell 19, 27
　Il Barbieri di Siviglia 17–19, 24
Rubini, Giovanni Battista 36
Rubinstein, Arthur 109
Russia 2, 90–1, 94, 100, 107–8, 162
　Kaliningrad (formerly Königsberg) 153
　Soviet Union 94, 97–8, 101
　Vyborg/Viipuri 147, 149, 151, 153–6

Salmenhaara, Erkki 147
salon 8, 67, 134, 137–8, 143
Samayoa, José Eulalio 68
Šašić, Branko 141
Schenker, Heinrich 14
Schiller, Friedrich 50
Schnéevoigt, Ernst 149, 153–4
Schoenberg, Arnold 99, 102, 118
Schrammelgitarre 135
Schrammelharmonika 135
Schubert, Franz 86
Scriabin, Alexander 90
Serbia 8
　Belgrade 141
　Drenovac 141
　Novi Sad 139
　Šabac 141–2
　Serbian Orthodox Church Choir Society Sloga 141
　Subotica/Szabadka 141
serialism 86, 99–100
Seth, Sanjay 166
sevdalinka 139, 142
Severini, Carlo 34–6, 42
Shakespeare, William 19, 23, 112, 114, 116
　The Merchant of Venice 106
　The Tempest 107
Shenbao 163
Shostakovich, Dmitri 86
Sibelius, Jean 86, 118
Siber, Wilhelm Friedrich 149
Singapore 16, 18, 101
Slavs 50
social media 7, 94
Sontag, Henriette 37–8, 40–2
Sörensen, Carl Theodor 154–6, 158
South Korea 102
Spain 59–61, 90–1, 93, 101–2
　Salamanca, University of 78
Spillan, Harry 37
Spohr, Carl 149

Stanković, Dimitrije 141
Stanković, Ilija 141
Stanković, Jefto 141
Stanković, Jovan 141
Stanković, Jovo 141
Stanković, Marinko 141
Stanković, Milan 141
Stanković, Milorad 141
Stanković, Nikola 141
Stanković, Paun 141
Stanković, Simo 141
Stanković, Vaso 133, 140–3
Steinberg, Michael 49
Stephens, Angharad Closs 19, 22
Stockhorst, Stefanie 61
Stojković, Stanko 141
Stokes, Martin 6–7
Stoler, Ann Laura 166, 169–70
Stravinsky, Igor 121
　Le Sacre du printemps 102
Supičić, Ivo 64
Sweden
　Eskilstuna 150
　Gotland 99
　Stockholm 64, 155, 158
　　Stockholm Royal Academy of Music 150, 153
symphony 67–70, 128–9, 147, 149–50, 154–5, 158–9
syncretism 4–5

Tábory, Josef 138
Taiwan
　Taipei 99
Takemitsu, Toru *91*
tambura 138–9
Tamburašen-Damen-Kapelle Biró 140
tamburica 133, 137, 139, 142, 144
Tamburini, Antonio 34–6
Tapia, Mariano 67
Tchaikovsky, Pyotr 108
Tchaikowsky, André 8, 106–15
　The Merchant of Venice 106, 115
　Seven Sonnets of Shakespeare 107
Teutonic Universalism 13–14, 23
Thalberg, Sigismond
　Florinda 39
Ther, Philippe 13
Thillon, Anna 15
Third Reich 97, 111, 115
Thomas, Ambroise
　Mignon 27
Trachtenkapelle 133, 137–8

transculturalism 3, 6, 9
transnationalism 6–7, 14–16, 33, 36, 42–3, 51, 108, 120, 123–5, 143, 164–5, 172–3
Trump, Donald 2
Truppel, Béla 139
Ts'ong, Fou 114
*tuna*78
Turkey
  Istanbul 5, 79–80, 83
  Izmir (*see* Greece, Smyrna)
Turmmusik 155

Ukraine 94, 97
United Kingdom 3, 90, 99–101, 118, 124, 162–4
  Birmingham 2–3
  Cambridge 108, 117–20, 122, 126–8, 164
  England 60–1
  London 7, 19, 33–43, 64
    Drury Lane Theatre 15; English National Opera 117, 119, 123; Fulham 37; Her Majesty's Theatre (formerly King's) 33–7, 39–40; Old Vic 117, 120, 125; Sadler's Wells 117, 120, 125; Theatre Royal Covent Garden 34, 36, 123
  Manchester 3
  Northern Ireland 1, 99
  Scotland 1, 99
  Wales 1, 99
United States of America 5, 39–40, 42–3, 61, 77, 90–1, 99–100, 110–11, 163, 169
  Boston 148
  Louisiana Purchase 15
  New Orleans 16
  New York 2
  Philadelphia 64
  San Francisco 15
  Washington 77–8

Vamvakáris, Markos 80–1
vaudeville 19, 23
Venezuela 63–4, 100
  Caracas 63, 68
Verdi, Giuseppe 28, 36
  Aida 24
  Don Carlo 27
  Ernani 24, 38, 42
  Il trovatore 17–18, 24
  Rigoletto 24
  Un ballo in Maschera 24
Vertovec, Steven 3, 6
Vian, Boris 84
Vietnam
  Saigon (now Ho Chi Minh City) 16, 18
Villa-Lobos, Heitor 66, 90
Volkmann, Robert 49
Volkonsky, Andrei 100

Wagner, Johanna 42
Wagner, Kim 166, 169, 171
Wagner, Richard 50–1
waltz 135
Wasserstrom, Jeffrey 162
Weber, Carl Maria von
  Der Freischütz 24
  Jubel Overture 163
Weber, William 13, 62
Webern, Anton 100, 118
Weill, Kurt
  Threepenny Opera, The 84
White Cross Society 141
Wieland, Martin 3
world music 6
World War I 3

Ximénez Abrill, Pedro 66–7

Yugoslavia 94, 97–8

Zaslaw, Neal 64
Zavala, Pedro
  La Limeña 68
Zdanov, Andrei 87
Zechner, Ingeborg 7
Zhang Ruogu 162–3
Žižek, Slavoj 3